KU-798-481

SWITZERLAND

TOP SIGHTS, AUTHENTIC EXPERIENCES

Gregor Clark, Kerry Christiani,
Craig McLachlan, Benedict Walker

Contents

Plan Your Trip

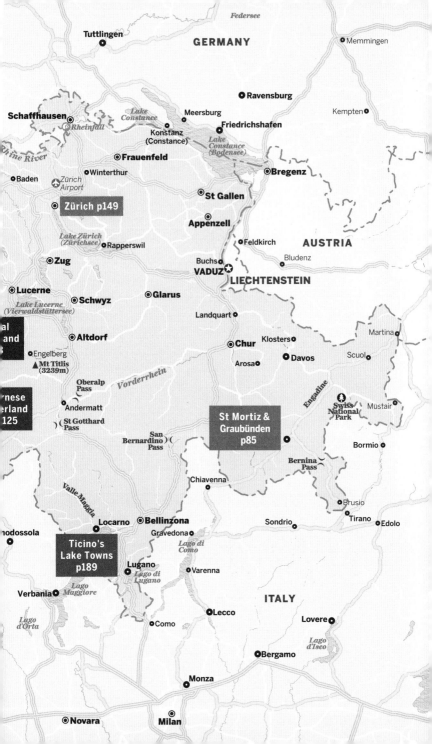

Welcome to Switzerland

Look beyond the chocolate, cuckoo clocks and yodelling – contemporary Switzerland, land of four languages, is all about once-in-a-lifetime journeys, heart-racing alpine pursuits, spectacular natural beauty and vibrant urban culture.

Switzerland's ravishing landscapes demand immediate action – grab boots, leap on board, ring bike bell and let spirits rip. In summer, hiking and biking trails invite exploration of Switzerland's glacier-encrusted mountains and deep green valleys, glittering lakeshores and terraced vineyards. View the grandeur from a hot-air balloon, parachute, or white-water raft, or seek out close-up encounters with Eiger's chiselled north face and Jungfraujoch's crevassed icy expanses (extraordinarily, you don't need to be a mountaineer to do it). Come winter, skiing and snowboarding in Graubünden, Valais, Bernese Oberland and Central Switzerland take centre stage.

The perfect counterpoint to Switzerland's rural beauty is its urban edge. A host of great cities awaits you here: Bern with its medieval old town and world-class modern art; chic Geneva astride Europe's largest lake; and ubercool Zürich with its riverside bars and reborn industrial districts.

Ever innovative, the Swiss have always embraced the new and the experimental. Capturing the zeitgeist throughout the country – even in back-of-beyond corners of the Alps – are cutting-edge cultural venues, avant-garde galleries, attention-grabbing architecture and fresh-faced design.

And then there's Swiss cuisine: a hearty and flavoursome celebration of gooey cheese desperate to be dipped in, comfort food favourites such as rösti and *Spätzli* (egg noodles), air-dried meats and autumnal game and, of course, velvety Swiss chocolate.

The perfect counterpoint to Switzerland's rural beauty is its urban edge.

View towards the Fraumünster (p165), from Limmat riverbank
MARINADA/SHUTTERSTOCK ©

In Focus

Survival Guide

Cow in the Bernese Oberland (p125)
STEVEN VAN AERSCHOT/SHUTTERSTOCK ©

Switzerland's Top Nine

ANGYALOSI BEATA/SHUTTERSTOCK ©

Geneva

Switzerland's international city by the lake

More than 150 nationalities jostle for a stool at the bar in this French-speaking cosmopolitan city (p32), where luxury watchmakers, chocolate gods, diplomats and artists come together around lovely Lake Geneva. Canary-yellow *mouettes* ('seagulls') ferry locals across the water and Mont Blanc looks over the action. Strolling Old Town streets, savouring the vibrant cafe and museum scene, paddleboarding on the lake and dashing beneath the iconic Jet d'Eau fountain is what life's about here.

Lake Geneva

Terraced vineyards, dazzling lake, mountain backdrop

The largest lake in Western Europe (p52) forms the setting for one of Switzerland's prime wine-growing regions. The emerald vines of the Lavaux (pictured at top), framed by the glittering lake and spellbinding views of the snow-capped Alps, are complemented by some stand-out cultural attractions, from Lausanne's student-fuelled urban buzz to the age-old Château de Chillon to the brand-new Chaplin's World museum near Vevey. Above top: Lavaux vineyards (p60); Bottom: Château de Chillon (p56)

SHOTAROBKK/SHUTTERSTOCK ©

Zermatt

The allure of Europe's most charismatic peak

The Matterhorn (pictured) exudes a magnetic attraction like no other mountain. Stunningly dramatic and shapely beyond belief, it demands to be admired, ogled and repeatedly photographed at sunset, sunrise, in different seasons and from every angle. There is no finer place to obsess over the mountain's beauty than Zermatt (p68), one of Europe's most desirable Alpine resorts, in fashion with the skiing, climbing, hiking and hip social set since the 19th century.

3

Central Switzerland

Lakeside living at its finest

Start with flower-bedecked medieval bridges; throw in sparkling lake vistas, alfresco cafe life, candy-coloured architecture and Victorian curiosities; and, yes, lakeside Lucerne (p106) could well be the start of a very beautiful love affair. With the town under your belt, step back to savour the ensemble from a wider perspective: cruising the spectacular lakeshore and climbing Mt Pilatus, Mt Rigi or Stanserhorn for views across the water to green meadows and hidden lake resorts. Kapellbrücke (p106), Lausanne

St Moritz

Venerable resort in pristine Engadine wilderness

Switzerland's original winter wonderland, St Moritz (p84) has been luring royals, celebrities and moneyed wannabes since 1864. The real riches, however, lie outdoors in the mountains, with superb carving on Corviglia, hairy black runs on Diavolezza (pictured) and magnificent hiking in Switzerland's century-old, high-altitude national park. Trails here thread through flower-strewn meadows to piercing blue lakes, knife-edge ravines, rocky outcrops and Alpine shepherds' huts, offering a rare glimpse of the Swiss Alps before the dawn of tourism.

GEVISION/SHUTTERSTOCK ©

Bernese Oberland
Mountain majesty in Switzerland's Alpine heartland

No trio is more immortalised in mountaineering legend than Switzerland's 'big three' – Eiger (Ogre), Mönch (Monk) and Jungfrau (Virgin) – peaks that soar above the gorgeous 19th-century resort of Grindelwald (p124). Whether you choose to schuss around on skis, shoot down Europe's longest toboggan run on an old-fashioned sledge, bungee jump in the Gletscherschlucht or ride the rails to Europe's highest station at 3454m, your pulse will race. James Bond, eat your heart out.

6

Zürich

Nightlife, fine dining and infectious urban edge

One of Europe's most liveable cities, German-speaking Zürich (p149) is an ode to urban renovation. Hip and trend-setting (yes, this is where Google employees shoot down a slide to lunch), with enough of a rough edge for it to resemble Berlin at times, Zürich means drinking in waterfront bars, dancing until dawn in Züri-West, shopping for recycled fashion accessories in Kreis 5 and boogying with the best of them at Europe's largest street party in August.

Ticino's Lake Towns

Palm trees, Italian culture: Switzerland's sunny south

An intrinsic part of Switzerland's appeal is its mixed bag of languages and cultures, and no spot exalts the country's Italianate soul with more gusto than Ticino's Lago di Lugano (p188). This shimmering Alpine lake is fringed with palm-tree promenades and pretty villages of delicate pastel hues. Lugano, the biggest town on the lake and the country's third-largest banking centre, is especially vivacious, with porticoed alleys, cafe-packed piazzas and boats yo-yoing between lakeside destinations.

Lago di Lugano, Gandria (p204)

LIANEM/SHUTTERSTOCK ©

MARKUS BOLLIGER/SHUTTERSTOCK ©

9

Bern
*Medieval meets modern in this
unconventional capital*

No capital city in the world charms visitors quite
like Bern (p173). Stroll through its medieval streets,
past arcaded boutiques, folk figures frolicking in
fountains and the city's charismatic 13th-century
clock tower, and it's hard not to feel smitten. A wealth
of museums, including Renzo Piano's cutting-edge
Zentrum Paul Klee, invite you to linger, as does the
surrounding region of Mittelland, where pastoral
landscapes dotted with pretty brown-and-white
cows are home to Switzerland's quintessential
Emmental cheese.

Plan Your Trip

Need to Know

When to Go

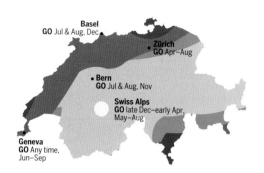

Basel
GO Jul & Aug, Dec

Zürich
GO Apr–Aug

Bern
GO Jul & Aug, Nov

Swiss Alps
GO late Dec–early Apr,
May–Aug

Geneva
GO Any time,
Jun–Sep

Warm to hot summers, mild winters
Warm to hot summers, cold winters
Mild summers, cold winters
Cold climate
Polar climate, below zero year round

High Season (Jul, Aug & Dec–Apr)

o In July and August walkers and cyclists hit high-altitude trails.

o Christmas and New Year see serious snow-sports action.

o Late December to early April is high season for skiing.

Shoulder (Apr–Jun & Sep)

o Get accommodation deals in ski resorts and hot spots.

o Spring is warm and idyllic, with flowers and local produce.

o Watch the grape harvest in autumn.

Low Season (Oct–Mar)

o Mountain resorts hibernate until early December.

o Prices are up to 50% lower than in high season.

o Sights and restaurants open for fewer days and shorter hours.

Currency
Swiss franc (officially CHF, also Sfr)

Language
German, French, Italian, Romansch

Visas
Generally not required for stays of up to 90 days. Some non-European citizens require a Schengen Visa.

Money
ATMs are at every airport, most train stations and on every second street corner in towns and cities; Visa, MasterCard and Amex widely accepted.

Mobile Phones
Most mobile (cell) phones brought from overseas will function in Switzerland; check with your provider about costs. Prepaid local SIM cards are widely available.

Time
GMT/UTC plus one hour. Daylight-saving time starts on the last Saturday in March; clocks go back again on the last Saturday in October.

Note that, in German, *halb* is used to indicate the half-hour before the hour, hence *halb acht* (half eight) means 7.30, not 8.30.

Daily Costs

Budget: Less than Sfr200

- Dorm bed: Sfr30–60

- Double room in budget hotel: from Sfr100

- Lunch out and self-catering after dark: from Sfr25

Midrange: Sfr200–300

- Double room in two- or three-star hotel: from Sfr200 (Sfr150 at weekends)

- Dish of the day (*tagesteller*, *plat du jour*, *piatto del giorno*) or fixed two-course menu: Sfr40–70

Top End: More than Sfr300

- Double room in four- or five-star hotel: from Sfr350 (Sfr250 at weekends)

- Three-course dinner in upmarket restaurant: from Sfr100

Useful Websites

ch.ch (www.ch.ch) Swiss authorities online.

Lonely Planet (www.lonelyplanet.com/switzerland) Destination information, hotel bookings, traveller forum and more.

My Switzerland (www.myswitzerland.com) Swiss tourism.

SBB (www.sbb.ch) Swiss Federal Railways.

Swiss Info (www.swissinfo.ch) Swiss news and current affairs.

Opening Hours

Each Swiss canton currently decides how long shops and businesses can stay open. With the exception of convenience stores at 24-hour service stations and shops at airports and train stations, businesses shut completely on Sunday. High-season opening hours appear in listings for sights and attractions; hours are almost always shorter during low season.

Banks 8.30am–4.30pm Monday to Friday

Restaurants noon–2.30pm and 6pm–9.30pm; most close one or two days per week

Shops 10am–6pm Monday to Friday, to 4pm Saturday

Museums 10am–5pm, many close on Monday and stay open late on Thursday

Arriving in Switzerland

Zürich Airport Up to nine SBB (www.sbb.ch) trains run hourly to Hauptbahnhof from 5am to midnight; taxis cost around Sfr60 to the centre; during the winter ski season, coaches run to Davos and other key resorts.

Geneva Airport SBB trains run at least every 10 minutes to Gare de Cornavin; taxis charge Sfr35 to Sfr50 to the centre; in winter coaches run to Verbier, Saas Fee, Crans-Montana and ski resorts in neighbouring France.

Getting Around

Public transport in Switzerland is among the world's most efficient. However, travel is expensive and visitors planning to use intercity routes should consider investing in a Swiss Travel Pass. For timetables and tickets, see www.sbb.ch.

Bicycle Switzerland is well equipped for cyclists. Many cities have free-bike-hire schemes. Bicycle and e-bike rental is usually available at stations.

Bus Filling the gaps in more remote areas, Switzerland's PostBus service is synchronised with train arrivals.

Car Handy for hard-to-reach regions where public transport is minimal.

Train Swiss trains run like a dream. Numerous discount-giving travel cards and tickets are available.

For more on **getting around**, see p247

Plan Your Trip

Hotspots for...

BORIS-B/SHUTTERSTOCK ©

Hiking

Impeccably signposted and maintained, Switzerland's network of walking trails invites you to get out and explore the psychedelic beauty of its lakes and mountains.

Bernese Oberland
This region's Alpine meadows and glacier-carved valleys are a hiker's dream.

Kleine Scheidegg
Walk from beneath Eiger's north face. (p134)

Ticino
The Alps' sunny southern slopes and balmy lakeshores offer a different Swiss walking experience.

Sentiero di Gandria
Pass terraced villages on sparkling Lago di Lugano. (p195)

Swiss National Park
Switzerland's showpiece for wildlife and pristine grandeur, protected from development for over a century.

Lakes of Macun
Blue-green tarns and sweeping vistas abound. (p89)

SKIING, ZERMATT/EAKWIPHAN SMITABHINDHU/SHUTTERSTOCK ©

Skiing

Switzerland and skiing are virtually synonymous. From Davos to Diavolezza, Klein Matterhorn to Kleine Scheidegg, you'll find a slope to suit your skill and style.

Zermatt
The Matterhorn and Monte Rosa form a stunning backdrop for 360km-worth of snow-sports terrain.

Summer Skiing
Zermatt's summer runs are Europe's best. (p72)

St Moritz
St Moritz boasts 350km of downhill runs and 220km of groomed cross-country trails.

Engadine Ski Marathon
A gruelling 42km March event. (p93)

Engelberg
With world-class slopes tucked into a secluded valley, Engelberg is a well-kept secret worth discovering.

Mt Titlis
Glacier skiing and 2000m vertical drops. (p112)

History & Culture

Tiny Switzerland surprises with its wealth of cultural offerings, from national art and history museums to private collections to internationally renowned music festivals.

ZYTGLOGGE, BERN/HENRYK SADURA/GETTY IMAGES ©

Zürich
No city in Switzerland is more culturally vibrant. There's live music, museums and an active arts scene.

Street Parade
Epic techno party that draws 1 million people. (p22)

Bern
From its medieval core to its audacious Paul Klee museum, Bern embodies centuries of Swiss heritage.

Zytglogge
Watch Bern's 13th-century clock strike the hour. (p176)

Lucerne
Alongside picture-postcard looks, Lucerne boasts thriving museums and music festivals.

Sammlung Rosengart
Typifies exceptional private art museums. (p107)

Food

When it comes to comfort food, nothing compares with Switzerland's trinity of fondue, raclette and rösti, supplemented by abundant local produce, fish and game.

FONDUE/LAURENTLESAX/SHUTTERSTOCK ©

Café Tivoli, Châtel-St-Denis
This family-run restaurant specialises in fondue *moitié-moitié*, made with local cheeses. (p66)

Fondue by Firelight
Grab a friend, grab a fork, let the cheese-twirling begin.

Le Petit Lac, Corsier
This waterfront restaurant is renowned as a prime place to sample Geneva's favourite fish. (p49)

Lakeside Perch
Lake Geneva's fresh-caught perch is legendary.

Hotel Parc Naziunal Il Fuorn
In the heart of the Swiss National Park, this country inn cooks up locally sourced Swiss feasts. (p89)

Autumnal Feasts
Wild game, trout and *Spätzli* (egg noodles) rule the menu.

Local Life

Activities

Switzerland offers a mind-boggling array of outdoor pursuits for travellers of all ages and fitness levels. Whether you're looking for a leisurely stroll in the mountains with your tots in tow or an adrenaline-fuelled free fall off the sheer face of Eiger, you'll find it here.

With 60,000km of marked walking paths, 9000km of cycling trails and 4500km of mountain-biking routes, Switzerland has enough variety to keep any hiker or cyclist happy for a lifetime. Come winter, the country's legendary ski slopes cater to daredevils and novices alike, with everything from bunny slopes to death-defying drop-offs.

For mountaineers, Switzerland has long been the fabled land, ever since Edward Whymper made the first successful ascent of the Matterhorn in 1865. Other classic climbs within reach for hard-core Alpinists are Monte Rosa (4634m), Mont Blanc (4807m) and Eiger (3970m).

A host of other pursuits awaits here, from paddling the shores of Lake Lucerne to scrambling across a Bernese Oberland cliff face on one of Switzerland's dramatic *vie ferrate* (hiking routes with grab cables). Rafting, skydiving, bobsledding, bungee jumping... the list goes on, and there are operators across the country offering pretty much any adventure you can dream up.

Shopping

Decent shopping isn't restricted to the cities, though there you'll find everything from edgy urban fashion to one-of-a-kind design buys. All over the country there are markets and gift shops where you can stock up on local treats to take home, including the edible/drinkable kind (Swiss chocolate, mountain cheese, air-cured sausage, Alpine herb–infused liqueurs) and the traditional kind (Victorinox knives, watches, kitsch-cute cows, fondue pots, cuckoo clocks).

STEFAN EMBER/SHUTTERSTOCK ©

Entertainment

Most of Switzerland's big, dynamic entertainment venues – from alternative arts to theatre and opera – are concentrated in major cities like Zürich, Bern, Basel, Geneva and Lucerne. Gigs happen all over the country. In summer, jaunty *Volksmusik* (folk music) enlivens many a rustic shindig in the Alps. Tourist offices often have up-to-date event listings, making it easy for anyone to plug into the local scene.

Eating

There's more to Swiss cuisine than cheese and chocolate. The food in this largely rural country is driven by season and setting: air-dried meats on a farm, fondue in a forest – you name it. If Alpine tradition gives Swiss food its soul, geography gives it an unexpected edge. Cooks in French-speaking cantons take cues from France, Ticino kitchens turn to Italy and a fair chunk of the country looks to Germany and Austria for culinary clues.

★ Best Drinking & Nightlife

Frau Gerolds Garten, Zürich (p170)

Hüsi Bierhaus, Interlaken (p142)

Village du Soir, Geneva (p50)

Rathaus Bräuerei, Lucerne (p119)

Das Viertel, Basel (p181)

Drinking & Nightlife

Switzerland's nightlife swings from a low-key *apéro* (aperitif) at a lakeside cafe with knockout views of the Alps to wine bars with urban attitude, casual craft-beer bars, chic lounges, and pumping après-ski in resorts when the flakes fall. Most cities ramp things up with clubs open until dawn. In summer, informal open-air bars pop up like wildflowers.

From left: Cycling in the Valais Alps; Zürich (p149)

Plan Your Trip
Month by Month

January

The winter cold empties towns of tourists, but in the Alps the ski season is in full swing. Glitzy celebrity station, lost Alpine village – Switzerland has a resort for every mood.

🎿 World Snow Festival

Grindelwald glitters with astonishing ice sculptures during this six-day festival in late January (www.worldsnowfestival.com). Sculptors from across the globe gather to flaunt their ice-carving skills, with everything from giant animals to abstract creations.

🎿 Snow Polo World Cup

Upper-crust St Moritz is the chic venue for this four-day event (p92) that sees world-class polo players saddle up and battle it out on a frozen lake. Buy tickets online, dress up and don't forget your shades.

🎿 Harder Potschete

What a devilish day it is on 2 January in Interlaken when warty, ogre-like *Potschen* run around town causing folkloric mischief. The party ends on a high with cockle-warming drinks, upbeat folk music and fiendish merrymaking (www.harderpotschete.ch).

February

Crisp, cold weather in the mountains – there are lots of blue skies now – translates to ski season in top gear. Families mob resorts during the February school holidays and accommodation is at its priciest.

🎿 Fasnacht

Never dare call the Swiss 'goody two-shoes' again: pre-Lenten parades, costumes, music and all the fun of the fair sweep through Catholic cantons during Fasnacht (Carnival; p120). Catch the party – stark raving bonkers – in Lucerne or Basel.

March

The tail end of the ski season stays busy thanks to temperatures that no longer turn lips blue and, depending on the year, Easter holidays.

CORNFIELD/SHUTTERSTOCK ©

🎿 Engadine Ski Marathon

The gruelling Engadine Ski Marathon (www.
engadin-skimarathon.ch) is hosted by St
Moritz. The event sees cross-country skiers
race from Maloja to S-chanf, a distance of
42km.

April

Spring, with its pretty, flower-strewn meadows, suddenly pops into that magnificent
Alpine vista and the first fair-weather walkers arrive. By the end of the month, most
ski resorts have gone into hibernation.

🎭 Sechseläuten

Winter's end is celebrated in Zürich on the
third Monday of the month with costumed
street parades and the burning of a
firework-filled 'snowman', aka the terrifying
Böögg, during Sechseläuten (www.sechse
laeuten.ch). Be prepared to be scared.

☆ Lucerne Festival

Easter ushers in this world-class music
festival (p109), with chamber orchestras,

★ Best Festivals

Lucerne Festival, April
Montreux Jazz, July
Swiss National Day, 1 August
Zürich's Street Parade, August
L'Escalade, December

pianists and other musicians from all
corners of the globe performing in Lucerne.
True devotees of the festival can return in
summer and November.

June

As the weather heats up, so Switzerland's
events calendar increases the pace
with a bevy of fabulous arts festivals.
In the mountains, chalet hotels start to
emerge from hibernation to welcome
early-summer hikers.

From left: Snow Polo World Cup; Fasnacht parade

☆ St Galler Festspiele

It's apt that Switzerland's 'writing room of Europe', aka St Gallen, should play host to this wonderful two-week opera season (www.stgaller-festspiele.ch). The curtain rises in late June and performances spill into July.

✿ Pride

Zürich sings a rainbow at this huge LGBT street festival (www.zurichpridefestival. ch). Expect a high-spirited roster of parties, parades, concerts, shows and events.

July

The month of music: days are hot and sun-filled, and lakeshores and Alpine meadows double as perfect summer stages for Swiss yodellers, alpenhorn players and flag throwers.

☆ Montreux Jazz

A fortnight of jazz, pop and rock in early July is reason enough to slot Montreux Jazz (p57) into your itinerary. Some concerts are free, some ticketed, and dozens are staged alfresco with heavenly lake views.

☆ Paléo

Another Lake Geneva goodie, this six-day open-air world-music extravaganza – a 1970s child – is billed as the king of summer music fests (www.paleo.ch). Nyon in late July are the details to put in the diary.

August

It's hot and cloudless, and the sun-baked Alps buzz with hikers, bikers and families on holiday – a pedalo on Lake Geneva is a cool spot to watch fireworks on 1 August, Switzerland's national day.

✿ Swiss National Day

Fireworks light up lakes, mountains, towns and cities countrywide on this national holiday (🕙1 Aug) celebrating Switzerland's

very creation. Some of the most impressive illuminations light up the Rheinfall.

⚔ Schwingen

This high-entertainment festival (p94) in Davos sees thickset men with invariably large tummies battle it out in sawdust for the title of *Schwingen* (Swiss Alpine wrestling) champion.

✿ Zürich's Street Parade

Mid-August brings with it Europe's largest street party in the form of Zürich's famous Street Parade (www.streetparade.com), around since 1992.

☆ Fêtes de Genève

Geneva hosts one of summer's hottest festivals (www.fetesdegeneve.ch), with pop-ups, parties and concerts aplenty over 10 days in August.

September

Golden autumn days and grape harvests make this a great month for backcountry rambles. In the Alps, the cows come home in spectacular style.

✗ Food Zürich

Zürich wings its way into autumn with this foodie festival (www.foodzurich.com), featuring pop-ups, cookery workshops, market brunches, starlit dinners and more.

December

Days are short and it's cold everywhere. But there are Christmas markets and festive celebrations around the corner, not to mention the first winter Alpine skiing from mid-December on.

✿ L'Escalade

Torchlit processions in the Old Town, fires, a run around town for kids and adults alike, and some serious chocolate-cauldron smashing and scoffing make Geneva's biggest festival on 11 December a riot of fun.

Plan Your Trip
Get Inspired

Read

Heidi (Johanna Spyri, 1881) Classic tale of an orphaned girl in the Alps.

The Magic Mountain (Thomas Mann, 1924) By a German literary great, this novel immerses you in Davos.

Eiger Dreams: Ventures Among Men and Mountains (Jon Krakauer, 1990) An evocative account of mountaineering.

Swiss Watching (Diccon Bewes, 2012) Amusing, astute insight into the land of 'milk and money'.

Frankenstein (Mary Shelley, 1818) Gothic-horror inspired by Shelley's time in Switzerland.

A Tramp Abroad (Mark Twain, 1880) Twain's entertaining take on his 1878 hike through the Alps.

Watch

Puppylove (2013) Coming-of-age story starring Lausanne-born Vincent Perez.

Sister (2012) Ursula Meier's award-winning film about the complicated dynamics between poor siblings at a ski resort.

Home (2008) A family unravels in this Ursula Meier drama.

Journey of Hope (1991) Oscar-winning tale of a Kurdish family seeking a better life in Switzerland.

Breathless (1960) New-wave classic by Swiss avant-garde film-maker Jean-Luc Godard.

The Divine Order (2017) The story of a housewife-turned-activist in small-town Switzerland in the 1970s.

Listen

Change de Crémerie (Sonalp, 2006) Vibrant ethno-folk mix of yodelling, cow bells, musical saw, classical violin and didgeridoo.

Supermoon (Sophie Hunger, 2015) This Bern-born singer mixes jazz, folk and pop while flipping between English, German and Swiss German.

Joolerei (Nadja Räss, 2012) In her 'yodelling tour of Switzerland,' yodeller Räss collaborates with a host of other Swiss musicians.

Above: The Swiss Alps

DAVID MCMILLAN/SHUTTERSTOCK ©

Plan Your Trip
Five-Day Itineraries

The Glacier Express

This 290km train ride has been a must-do since its inception in 1930. Take the journey any time of year – breaking it into several short segments interspersed with overnight stays in some of Switzerland's most glamorous Alpine resorts.

Fiesch/Aletsch Glacier (p76) Climb by cable car to Fiescheralp for close-up views of Switzerland's most magnificent glacier.
🚃 1 hr to Andermatt

Chur (p75) Explore Chur's quaint old town, with its historic hotels and vibrant street life.

Andermatt (p75) Pause overnight to hike, bike or ski, exploring lofty Alpine passes from this mountain outpost.
🚃 2¼ hrs to Chur

Zermatt (p69) Spend two days basking in the Matterhorn's glow in this low-key resort.
🚃 2 hrs to Fiesch

Graubünden and Ticino

Swinging through the rugged mountain landscapes of Graubünden and the sunnier climes and lakeside towns of Italian-speaking Ticino, this circular route in the southeast reveals two different, but equally spectacular, sides of the Swiss Alps.

Zernez (p88) Discover the Alps' oldest national park from this village at the wilderness's edge.
🚌 45 mins to St Moritz

❶

❷ **St Moritz** (p85) Hit the slopes during your two-night stay at this venerable mountain resort.
🚌(Bernina Express) 6¾ hrs to Lugano

llinzona (p192)
ish with a day in
no's enchanting
alianate capital.

❹

Lugano (p194) Enjoy a day of Swiss-style *dolce vita* among the vineyards and villages.
🚌 3hrs to Bellinzona

❸

Plan Your Trip
10-Day Itinerary

City to City

This Geneva-to-Lugano 385km trip is for urbanites keen to experience the metropolitan energy of Switzerland's biggest cities while still enjoying some quintessential Swiss scenery on the train rides in between. Join and leave the route wherever you like, or visit all seven!

Basel (p178) World-class art and architecture make this city by the Rhine a worthwhile one-day stop.
🚊 55 mins to Zürich

Zürich (p149) Spend two days embracing the creative buzz and vibrant nightlife of Switzerland's largest metropolis.
🚊 45 mins to Lucerne

Bern (p173) Wander the halls of Switzerland's Federal Assembly and the enchanting streets of Bern's medieval centre.
🚊 1 hr to Basel

Lausanne (p58) Lausanne's draws include its Olympic Museum, its hillside setting and its student-fuelled, forward-looking energy.
🚊 65 mins to Bern

Lucerne (p106) Indulge in a two-day love affair with Switzerland's most picturesque and romantic lakeside city.
🚊 2 hrs to Lugano

Geneva (p33) Start with two days in Switzerland's most international city, on the shores of gorgeous Lake Geneva.
🚊 50 mins to Lausanne

Lugano (p194) Stroll among Italianate campaniles, sunny lakeside gardens and Vespa-filled piazzas in Ticino's largest city.

FROM LEFT: /GETTY IMAGES ©

Two-Week Itinerary

Switzerland's Greatest Hits

This tour brings you the best of Alpine Switzerland in an epic two-week tour – from lakes to vineyards, mountains to museums, châteaux to cowbells. Linger wherever you like; another train will arrive to whisk you away whenever you're ready.

Interlaken (p136) Go climb a mountain, or paraglide off one, in Switzerland's belle époque adventure sports capital.
35 mins to Grindelwald

Grindelwald (p132) Bliss out for three days among high Alpine meadows framed by the Jungfraujoch.
3½ hrs to Zermatt

Montreux (p56) Spend two days absorbing Château de Chillon's iconic lakeside beauty and exploring the Lavaux wine country.
2½ hrs to Interlaken

Zermatt (p69) Give yourself four days to contemplate the magnificent Matterhorn from every possible angle.
(Glacier Express) 7 hrs to St Moritz

ALEX TOR/SHUTTERSTOCK ©

Zürich (p149) Embrace Zürich's full array of urban attractions: dining, shopping, nightlife, great museums and more.
🚃 1 hr to Brunnen

Brunnen (p110) Visit the land of William Tell and the Swiss Army Knife on Lake Lucerne's gorgeous eastern shore.
🚃 2 hrs to Engelberg

St Moritz (p85) Make this venerable resort your home for three days of exploring Graubünden's wild backcountry.
🚃 3¼ hrs to Zürich

Engelberg (p112) Lose yourself in the beauty of this off-the-beaten track valley below glaciated Titlis.

FROM LEFT: LEONARD ZHUKOVSKY/SHUTTERSTOCK ©, DENIS LININE/SHUTTERSTOCK ©

Plan Your Trip
Family Travel

Orderly, clean and not overly commercial, Switzerland is a dream for family travel.

Tips

○ The Swiss tourist board's meaty *Families* brochure is packed with ideas; its website, www.myswitzerland.com, lists kid-friendly accommodation, family offers and so on.

○ In mountain resorts, tourist offices have information on pushchair-accessible walking trails and dozens of other activities for children of every age, toddler to teen.

○ Staying in a B&B is family fabulous: little kids can slumber sweetly upstairs while weary parents wine and dine in peace downstairs (don't forget your baby monitor!). Pick a B&B on a farm or sleep on straw in the hay barn for adventurous kids to have the time of their life.

○ Those with kids aged six to 12 years should buy Dianne Dicks' *Ticking Along with Swiss Kids*, part children's book about

Switzerland, part guide for parents on what to see, where to eat and what to do. Also check out Lonely Planet's *Travel with Children*.

Transport

Family train travel with **Swiss Railways** (www.sbb.ch) is staggering value. Kids under six years travel for free and those aged six to 16 years get free unlimited rail travel with an annual **Junior Card** (Sfr30) or – should it be grandparents travelling with the kids – the **Grandchild Travelcard** (Sfr30). Otherwise, buy a one-day **child's travelpass** (Sfr16), which allows unlimited rail travel. Cards include travel on many cable cars in mountain resorts. Switzerland's mountain of scenic journeys by train and boat enchants children of all ages. Upon arrival at point B, dozens of segments of the perfectly signposted hiking, biking, in-line skating and canoeing trails designed strictly for non-motorised

GEVISION/SHUTTERSTOCK ©

traffic by **Switzerland Mobility** are flagged as suitable for younger children.

Most of the major car-hire companies rent out child, baby and booster seats equipped to the latest safety standards for an extra fee of around Sfr45 to Sfr65.

Practicalities

The Swiss are mostly very accommodating when it comes to families.

o Many large hotels have dedicated family or interconnecting rooms, and even some smaller places will often squeeze in a cot or an extra bed at a moment's notice.

o Nappy-changing facilities are widespread and disposable nappies (diapers) can be readily purchased in pharmacies and supermarkets.

o The Swiss are generally tolerant when it comes to breastfeeding in public provided it is done discreetly.

★ Best Kid-Friendly Attractions

Verkehrshaus, Lucerne (p107)

Matterhorn Glacier Paradise, Zermatt (p72)

Swiss Knife Valley Museum, Brunnen (p121)

Kindermuseum Creaviva, Bern (p183)

Baby Plage, Geneva (p41)

o Many hotels and tourist offices can point you in the direction of local childcare agencies and babysitting services.

o Some – but by no means all – restaurants provide high chairs and special children's menus. If in doubt, check ahead.

From left: Bern (p173); Diavolezza (p91)

Lake Geneva (p53)

Geneva Old Town (p36)

Arriving in Geneva

Gare de Cornavin More-or-less-hourly connections run to Geneva's central train station from most Swiss cities.

Geneva Airport Trains run at least every 10 minutes from the airport to Gare de Cornavin (Sfr3, six minutes). Grab a free public transport ticket from the machine in the arrivals baggage hall. A metered taxi into town costs Sfr35 to Sfr50 and takes about 15 minutes.

Sleeping

Geneva's predominantly business, midrange and top-end hotels are scattered throughout the town centre. Rates are substantially higher Monday to Thursday. When checking in, be sure to get your free Public Transport Card, which offers unlimited local bus and tram travel for the duration of your stay. Plug into the complete list of hotels at www.geneva-hotel.ch.

Geneva Old Town

Dominated by its Gothic cathedral, and filled with cobble-stoned streets that invite aimless strolling, Geneva's picturesque Old Town commands a prime hilltop location above the lake.

Great For...

☑ **Don't Miss**

Picnicking, giving the kids a play break, or enjoying the views from Terrasse Agrippa d'Abigné.

Cathédrale St-Pierre

Geneva's **cathedral** (www.cathedrale-geneve. ch; Cour de St-Pierre; towers adult/child Sfr5/2; ☺9.30am-6.30pm Mon-Sat, noon-6.30pm Sun Jun-Sep, reduced Oct-May) is predominantly Gothic with an 18th-century neoclassical facade. Inside, 96 steps spiral up to the northern tower offering a fascinating glimpse of the cathedral's architectural construction. From here, another 60 steps climb into the southern tower, revealing close-up views of the bells and panoramic city vistas. From June to September, daily free carillon (5pm) and organ (6pm) concerts are a bonus.

Site Archéologique de la Cathédrale St-Pierre

The highlights of this small **archaeological site** (Map p44; ☑022 310 29 29; www. site-archeologique.ch; Cour de St-Pierre; adult/

Cathédrale St-Pierre

IN GREEN/SHUTTERSTOCK ©

❶ Need to Know

Walking is the best way to explore Geneva's Old Town. Trams stop downhill at Molard.

✕ Take a Break

Pause to people-watch over coffee or the reasonably priced *plat du jour* (dish of the day) at Café du Bourg-de-Four.

★ Top Tip

Many local museums are closed on Mondays.

child Sfr8/4; ⊘10am-5pm) in the basement of Geneva's cathedral are its 4th-century floor mosaics and the rather eerie tomb of an Allobrogian (Gallic tribe) chieftain.

Musée International de la Réforme

This modern **museum** (Museum of the Reformation; Map p44; ☏022 310 24 31; www.mir. ch; Rue du Cloître 4; adult/child Sfr13/6; ⊘10am-5pm Tue-Sun) in an 18th-century mansion zooms in on the Reformation. State-of-the-art exhibits and audiovisuals bring to life everything from the earliest printed bibles to the emergence of Geneva as 'Protestant Rome' in the 16th century, and from John Calvin all the way to Protestantism in the 21st century.

A combined ticket covering the museum, Cathédrale St-Pierre and Site Archéologique de la Cathédrale St-Pierre is Sfr18/10 per adult/child.

Café du Bourg-de-Four

There's a great pedestrian vibe to this classic **cafe-bar** (Map p44; ☏022 311 90 76; www.cafedubourgdefour.ch; Pl du Bourg-de-Four 13; mains Sfr22-34; ⊘7am-midnight Mon-Fri, noon-midnight Sat, noon-6pm Sun; 🖉) on the fringe of the Old Town, with a *plat du jour* offering excellent value. In summer, the action spills out onto a terrace where locals and tourists dine casually, side-by-side, on stodgy French and Swiss delights such as steak tartare and unspeakably good rösti.

Terrasse Agrippa d'Abigné

This lovely tree-shaded **park** (Map p44; Rue de l'Evêché 7) has benches, a sandpit and a seesaw for kids, and a fine rooftop and cathedral view.

Maison de Rousseau et de la Literature

Geneva's greatest thinker, Jean-Jacques Rousseau, was born in this **house** (Map p44; ☏022 310 10 28; www.m-r-l.ch; Grand-Rue 40; adult/child Sfr5/3; ⊘11am-5.30pm Tue-Sun) in 1712. A 25-minute audiovisual display traces his troubled life.

Geneva Alfresco

When the sun comes out, the Genevois love diving into the clear waters of Lac Léman, strolling the magnificent lakeshore, and gathering at the city's open-air markets, bars and parks.

Great For...

☑ **Don't Miss**

The Pleinpalais flea market (p41), filled with local colour and unexpected finds.

Jet d'Eau

If you arrive by plane, this **lakeside fountain** (Quai Gustave-Ador) is the first dramatic glimpse you get of Geneva. The 140m-tall structure shoots up water with incredible force – 200km/h, 1360HP – to create the sky-high plume, kissed by a rainbow on sunny days. At any one time, 7 tonnes of water is in the air, much of which sprays spectators on the pier beneath. Two or three times a year it is illuminated pink, blue or another colour to mark a humanitarian occasion.

The Jet d'Eau is Geneva's third pencil fountain. The first shot water into the sky for 15 minutes each Sunday between 1886 and 1890, to release pressure at the city's water station, and the second spurted 90m high from the Jetée des Eaux-Vives

Horloge Fleurie, Jardin Anglais

ℹ **Need to Know**

Mouettes (p51), Geneva's popular yellow shuttle boats, offer a fun, inexpensive way to cross the lake.

✕ **Take a Break**

Nosh lakeside on everything from wine and oysters to evening fondue at Pâquis' beloved Buvette des Bains (p48).

> ★ **Top Tip**
> As of 2017 (first time since 1929), women can freely bathe topless in the lake.

on Sundays and public holidays from 1891 onward. The current one was born in 1951.

Jardin Anglais

On the lakeshore just below the Vieille Ville, this **flowery waterfront garden** (The English Garden; Map p44; Quai du Général-Guisan) was landscaped in 1854 on the site of an old lumber-handling port and merchant yard. Join the crowds taking selfies in front of the Horloge Fleurie, the park's *pièce de résistance*; crafted from 6500 living flowers, this enormous waterside clock has been ticking since 1955 and boasts the world's longest second hand (2.5m).

Quai du Mont-Blanc

Flowers, statues, outdoor art exhibitions and views of Mont Blanc (on clear days

only) abound on this picturesque northern lakeshore promenade, which leads past the Bains des Pâquis, where the Genevois have frolicked in the sun since 1872, to Parc de la Perle du Lac, a city park where Romans built ornate thermal baths. Further north, the peacock-studded lawns of Parc de l'Ariana ensnare the UN and Geneva's pretty Conservatoire et Jardin Botaniques (Conservatory and Botanic Garden).

Bains des Pâquis

This hip and trendy **pool** (Map p44; ☎022 732 29 74; www.bains-des-paquis.ch; Quai du Mont-Blanc 30; pools adult/child Sfr2/1, sauna, hammam & Turkish bath Sfr20; ☺9am-9.30pm Mon-Sat, from 8pm Sun) in Pâquis, with its waterfront bar and restaurant, is a Real McCoy vintage child – it dates to 1872. From May to September it's abuzz with swimmers enjoying a refreshing dip in Lake Geneva. The rest of the year, the focus shifts to the on-site sauna, hammam and Turkish baths – open to the general public from Wednesday to Monday, women only on Tuesday.

Conservatoire et Jardin Botaniques

Celebrating its bicentenary in 2017, Geneva's premier **botanical park** (Conservatory & Botanical Gardens; ☎022 418 51 00; www.ville-ge.ch/cjb/index_en.php; Chemin de l'Impératrice 1; ◷8am-5pm Nov-Apr, to 7.30pm Apr-Nov) **FREE** – renowned for its Botanical Conservatory – boasts over 12,000 species of plant from around the world, meticulously arranged in a series of beautiful themed gardens. Highlights include a spectacular collection of roses and the loved-by-everyone Animal Park protecting ancient species of indigenous and often endangered animals as well as everyday chickens, goats and sheep and the more exotic peacocks, flamingos and deer.

Waterfront Drinking & Dining

In summer, often-perfect weather and the backdrop of the Alps draw constant throngs to pop-up lakeshore bars, like **La Terrasse** (Map p44; ☎078 691 13 78; www.laterrasse.ch; Quai Wilson 31a; ◷8am-midnight Apr-Sep). Further afield from Quai du Mont-Blanc you'll find some special summertime shacks on the water for alfresco dining and drinking, and living the good life.

For casual Right Bank eats, pop into Rhône-side **Terrasse Le Paradis** (Map p44; ☎076 715 83 70; www.terrasse-paradis.ch; Quai Turrettini; ◷9am-9pm Jun-Sep) where you can recline on a deckchair and while away civil hours in the sunshine eating sandwiches and sipping beakers of homemade lemonade or pots of mint tea.

Conservetoire et Jardin Botaniques

Le Bateau Lavoir (Map p44; ☎022 321 38 78; www.bateaulavoir.ch; Passerelle des Lavandières; ☺11am-midnight Mon-Thu, 11am-2am Fri, 5pm-2am Sat May-Sep) is an eye-catching boat with rooftop terrace moored between the old market hall and Pont de la Coulouvrenière. Its cabin-size dining area cooks fondue and other basic local dishes, the crowd is hip, and there are 360-degree lake views. Its very design and name evokes the washhouse boats – yes, where undies et al were washed – that floated here in the 17th century.

☂ Don't Miss
Travelling with kids? Baby Plage (Quai Gustave-Ador; ⚑) is a quirky Tarzan-inspired tree park with plenty of play-things and a lovely swimming area, on Lake Geneva's southern shore.

La Barje des Lavandières (Map p44; ☎022 344 83 56; www.labarje.ch; Promenade des Lavandières; ☺11am-midnight Mon-Fri, noon-midnight Sat, noon-11pm Sun May-Sep) is not a barge but a vintage caravan parked on the banks of the Rhône near the Bâti-ment des Forces Motrices. Part proceeds from the sale of food, booze (which, in summer, flows) and the variety of concerts and performances hosted here, go towards providing training programs for disadvan-taged young people.

CinéTransat
On a warm summer's evening, nothing beats this free **summer movie series** (www.cinetransat.ch; Parc de La Perle du Lac, Rue de Lausanne; ☺lounge-chair rental from 7pm, films start at sunset) **FREE**, held under the stars in Parc de la Perle du Lac. For more comfort-able viewing, arrive early and hire a transat (lounge chair, Sfr5).

Télépherique du Salève
Across the border into France, 9km south-east of Geneva, this **cable car** (☎+33 04 50 39 86 86; www.telepherique-du-saleve.com; Rte du Téléphérique, Étrembières; round trip adult/student/child €11.80/8.60/6.50; ☺9.30am-7pm Sun-Wed, to 11pm Thu-Sat; ⚑), in operation since 1932, will whisk you to an altitude of 1100m at the summit of Mont Salève, for breathtaking views of Geneva, Lake Gene-va, the Jura mountains and the Alps, with (if you're lucky) a clear view of the majestic Mont Blanc massif.

Pleinpalais Flea Market
You'll find a plethora of quirky treasures at Geneva's twice-weekly **flea market** (Map p44; Plaine de Plainpalais; ☺Wed & Sat), which completely takes over Plainpalais' enor-mous main square.

★ Top Tip
For a fun day on the lake, join a themed tour aboard one of the belle époque steamers operated by CGN (p50).

⊙ SIGHTS

Geneva's major sights are split by the Rhône, which flows westwards from Lake Geneva through the city centre. On the *rive gauche* (left bank), mainstream shopping districts Rive and Eaux-Vives climb from the water to Pleinpalais and **Old Town** (Map p44) – Vieille Ville in French – while the *rive droite* (right bank) holds grungy bar-and-club-hot Pâquis, the train-station area and the international quarter with most world organisations.

Musée d'Ethnographie de Genève
Museum

(Geneva Museum of Ethnography; Map p44; 022 418 45 50; www.ville-ge.ch/meg; Bd de Carl-Vogt 65-67; ⊙11am-6pm Tue-Sun) **FREE** Admission is free to the permanent collection of this excellent hands-on museum, 'The Archives of Human Diversity', which examines the similarities and differences between our planet's myriad cultures. It showcases around 1000 artefacts from the museum's 80,000-strong collection. In 2017 the 'MEG' was awarded the prestig-

ious title of European Museum of the Year. Admission fees (adult/child Sfr 9/6) apply to visiting temporary exhibitions.

CERN
Research Centre

(022 767 84 84; www.cern.ch; Meyrin; ⊙guided tours in English 11am & 1pm Mon-Sat) **FREE** Founded in 1954, the European Organization for Nuclear Research, 8km west of Geneva, is a laboratory for research into particle physics. It accelerates protons down a 27km circular tube (the Large Hadron Collider, the world's biggest machine) and the resulting collisions create new matter. Come anytime to see the permanent exhibitions shedding light on its work, but for two-hour guided tours in English reserve online up to 15 days ahead and bring photo ID.

Switzerland's second-largest city is packed with luxury hotels, boutiques, jewellers, restaurants, chocolatiers...

Favarger (p46)

MARTIN GOOD/SHUTTERSTOCK ©

Musée International de la Croix-Rouge et du Croissant-Rouge Museum

(International Red Cross & Red Crescent Museum; ☏022 748 95 11; www.redcrossmuseum.ch; Av de la Paix 17; adult/child Sfr15/7; ⊙10am-6pm Tue-Sun Apr-Oct, to 5pm Nov-Mar) Compelling multimedia exhibits at Geneva's fascinating International Red Cross and Red Crescent Museum trawl through atrocities perpetuated by humanity. The litany of war and nastiness, documented in films, photos, sculptures and soundtracks, is set against the noble aims of the organisation founded by Geneva businessman Henry Dunant in 1863. Excellent temporary exhibitions command an additional entrance fee.

Palais des Nations Historic Building

(Palace of Nations; ☏022 917 48 96; www.unog.ch; Av de la Paix 14; adult/child Sfr12/7; ⊙10am-noon & 2-4pm Mon-Sat Apr-Aug, Mon-Fri Sep-Mar; guided tours 10.30am, noon, 2.30pm & 4pm) Home to the UN since 1966, the Palais des Nations was built between 1929 and 1936 to house the now-defunct League of Nations. Visits are by guided tour (bring photo ID; no reservation required for groups with fewer than 15 people) and include a one-hour tour of the building and entry to the surrounding 46-hectare park, generously peppered with century-old trees and peacocks.

Musée d'Art et d'Histoire Gallery

(Museum of Art and History; Map p44; ☏022 418 26 00; www.mah-geneve.ch; Rue Charles-Galland 2; ⊙11am-6pm Tue-Sun) FREE Built between 1903 and 1910, this elegant museum holds masterpieces in its treasure chest. There are excellent temporary exhibitions (per adult/child Sfr15/free). In an interesting twist, plans for a Sfr127-million renovation of the museum by world-class architect Jean Nouvel were shelved after Geneva's citizens voted against the project in a mid-2016 referendum.

⌐▷ᴲ Detour into Bohemia

Bohemia strikes in Carouge, where the lack of any real sights – bar fashionable 18th-century houses overlooking courtyard gardens and the tiny **Musée de Carouge** (www.carouge.ch/musee; Pl de la Sardaigne 2; ⊙2-6pm Tue-Sun) FREE displaying 19th-century ceramics – is part of the charm.

Carouge, today a neighbourhood 3.5km south of Gare CFF de Cornavin (p50), was refashioned by Vittorio Amedeo III, King of Sardinia and Duke of Savoy, in the 18th century in a bid to rival Geneva as a centre of commerce. In 1816 the Treaty of Turin handed it to Geneva and today its narrow streets are filled with bars, boutiques and artists' workshops.

Trams 12 and 18 link central Geneva with Carouge's plane-tree-studded central square, **Place du Marché**, abuzz with market stalls on Wednesday and Saturday mornings. Horses trot along the streets during April's Fête du Cheval, and horse-drawn carriages line up on Place de l'Octroi in December to take Christmas shoppers for a ride.

In summer there are dozens of scenic spots all around Geneva where you can lounge in the sun over a mint tea or mojito – Carouge is strewn with seasonal cafe terraces.

Umbrellas hanging over a Carouge street
ANNETTE DUCASSE/SHUTTERSTOCK ©

Central Geneva

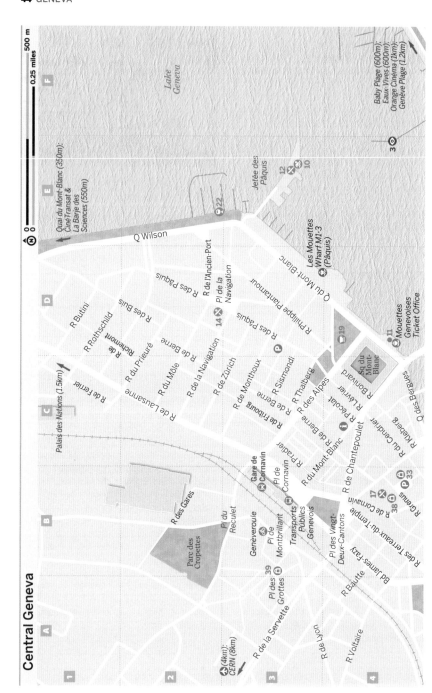

0.25 miles
500 m

Lake Geneva

Baby Plage (600m);
Eaux-Vives (600m);
Orange Cinema (1km);
Genève Plage (1.2km)

Quai du Mont-Blanc (350m);
CinéTransat &
La Barje des
Sciences (550m)

Q Wilson

Jetée des Pâquis

12
10

22

R de l'Ancien-Port

Pl de la Navigation

R des Pâquis
R des Buis
R Butini
R Rothschild
R de Richemont
R du Prieuré
R de Berne
R du Môle
R de Lausanne
R de la Navigation

R Philippe Plantamour

14
R des Pâquis

R de Zürich

Les Mouettes
Wharf M1-3
(Pâquis)

Q du Mont-Blanc

R de Montthoux

R de Fribourg
R de Berne
R Sismondi
R Thalberg
R des Alpes

19

Mouettes
Genevoises
Ticket Office

11

Sq du Mont-Blanc

R de Berne
R Pécolat
R Lévrier
R Bonivard

Q des Bergues

R du Chantier
R Kléber

Palais des Nations (1.5km)

R de Ferrier

R des Gares

Parc des Cropettes

Pl du Reculet

Gare de Cornavin
Pl de Cornavin

R Pradier

Transports Publics Genevois

Pl de Montbrillant

Geneveroule

R du Mont-Blanc

R de Chantepoulet

17
38
R de Cornavin

33

R Gevray

Pl des Vingt-Deux-Cantons

R des Terreaux-du-Temple

Bd James-Fazy

Pl des Grottes

39

R de la Servette

R de Lyon

R Baulite

R Voltaire

CERN (8km);
(4km)

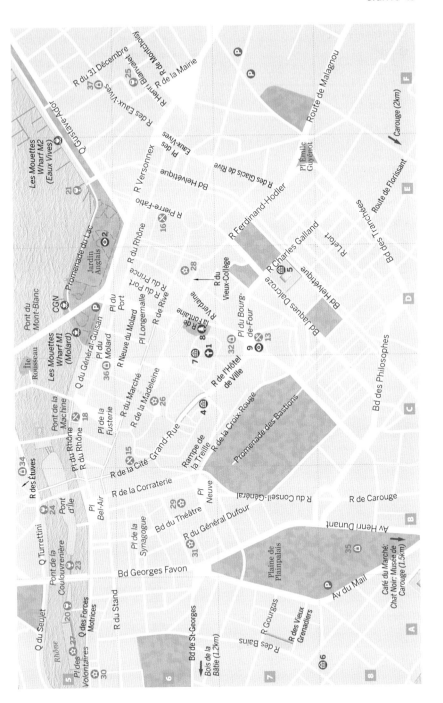

Central Geneva

🛈 SHOPPING

Designer shopping is wedged between Rue du Rhône and Rue de Rive. **Globus** (Map p44; www.globus.ch/fr/store/116/globus-geneve; Rue du Rhône 48; ⊙9am-7pm Mon-Wed, to 9pm Thu, to 7.30pm Fri, to 6pm Sat; food hall 7.30am-10pm Mon-Fri, 8.30am-10pm Sat) and **Manor** (Map p44; ☏022 909 46 99; www.manor.ch; Rue de Cornavin 6; ⊙9am-7pm Mon-Wed, to 9pm Thu, to 7.30pm Fri, 8.30am-6pm Sat) are the main department stores. The Carouge district and Grand-Rue in the Vieille Ville are peppered with art and antique galleries; try the Thursday-evening **Marché des Grottes** (Map p44; www.ville-geneve.ch/plan-ville/marches/marche-grottes; Place des Grottes 1; ⊙Thu 4-8.30pm) for food, wine and cheese.

Collection Privée   Homewares
(Map p44; ☏076 323 71 94; Pl De-Grenus 8; ⊙2-6pm Tue-Fri, to 5pm Sat) Art deco lamps, furniture and other 19th- and 20th-century objets d'art and curiosities.

Caran d'Ache – Maison de Haute Écriture   Arts & Crafts
(Map p44; ☏022 310 90 00; www.carandache.com; Pl du Bourg-de-Four 8; ⊙10am-6pm Mon-Sat) Beautifully designed boutique packed with a rainbow of pencils, pastels, paints and crayons crafted by Swiss colour maker Caran d'Ache in Geneva since 1915.

Favarger   Chocolate
(Map p44; ☏022 738 18 26; www.favarger.com; Quai des Bergues 19; ⊙10am-6pm Mon-Fri, 9am-5pm Sat) A veteran on the Swiss chocolate scene, this respected chocolatier has a stylish lake-facing boutique near the spot where its first factory opened in 1826. A favourite for its vintage and contemporary design packaging, its speciality is Avelines, a supersmooth cocktail of milk chocolate, almonds and hazelnuts bundled into glorious melt-in-the-mouth bites.

Le Verre en Cave
Wine

(Map p44; ☏022 736 51 00; www.verreencave.ch; Rue des Eaux-Vives 27; ⏱10am-7pm Mon-Wed & Fri, to 8pm Thu, to 6pm Sat) A great resource for wine lovers, with dozens of vintages from Switzerland and 10 other countries, and a 'try-before-you-buy' selection of 32 wines available for free tasting.

🔆 ENTERTAINMENT

Geneva offers an amazing variety of cultural events for a city of its size. Buy theatre, concert and gig tickets at **FNAC Billetterie Spectacles** (Map p44; ☏022 816 12 56; www.ch.fnacspectacles.com; Rue de Rive 16), or at box offices inside the tourist office. See www.leprogramme.ch (in French) for what's playing.

L'Usine
Performing Arts

(Map p44; www.usine.ch; Pl des Volontaires 4) At the gritty heart of Geneva's alternative culture scene, this nonprofit collection of 18 arts-related initiatives is housed beside the Rhône in a former gold-processing factory. On any given night, expect to see cutting-edge theatre at **TU** (www.theatredelusine.ch), live music at **Le Zoo** (www.lezoo.ch) or up-and-coming VJ artists at **Kalvingrad** (www.kalvingrad.com).

Alhambra
Live Music

(Map p44; ☏078 966 07 97; www.alhambra-geneve.ch; Rue de la Rôtisserie 10) Reopened in 2015 after extensive renovations, this gorgeous historic theatre with its cut-glass chandeliers, embossed silver ceilings and scarlet chairs makes a classy venue for live concerts ranging from Brazilian 'electro-tropical' to African drumming, disco to salsa, and Afro-Caribbean to R&B.

Bâtiment des Forces Motrices
Performing Arts

(Map p44; ☏022 322 12 20; www.bfm.ch; Pl Volontaires 2) Geneva's one-time riverside pumping station (1886) is now a striking space for classical-music concerts, dance and other performing arts.

 What's the Scoop?

Ice cream! On a warm day, nothing beats a lakeside stroll and a sweet treat from one of these Geneva staples.

Gelatomania (Map p44; Rue des Pâquis 25; ⏱11.30am-11pm Sun-Thu, to midnight Fri & Sat May-Sep, noon-7pm Oct-Apr; 🖉) There's a reason why this gelateria has a constant queue: quirky flavours including organic carrot, and combinations such as orange and lemon, cucumber and mint, lime and basil as well as caramel, pistachio and all your old-school faves. It is also a local favourite for its prime position en route to the Bains des Pâquis (p39).

Mövenpick (Map p44; ☏022 311 14 00; Rue du Rhône 19; 1/2/3 scoops in cornet Sfr5/9/12; ⏱noon-11pm daily Apr-Oct, to 8pm Wed-Sun Nov-Mar; 🚼) The luxe address to sit down riverside and drool over the creamiest of Swiss ice cream topped with whipped cream, hot chocolate sauce and other decadent treats.

Mövenpick
MARTIN GOOD/SHUTTERSTOCK ©

Grand Théâtre de Genève
Opera

(Map p44; ☏022 322 50 50; www.geneveopera.ch; Bd du Théâtre 11) While Geneva's stunning Grand Théâtre is undergoing a major transformation, concerts will be held in a temporary venue, **Opéra des Nations** (Ave de France 40), which will be deconstructed in 2018.

Top Five Places to Eat

Buvette des Bains

Le Petit Lac

Le Relais d'Entrecôte

La Finestra

Manora

From left: Dining alfresco; Cafes on Place du Bourg-de-Four; Boat moored on Lake Geneva

Victoria Hall
Live Music

(Map p44; ☑022 418 35 00; www.ville-ge.ch/culture/victoria_hall; Rue du Général Dufour 14) Concert hall for the Orchestre de la Suisse Romande and Orchestre de Chambre de Genève.

✕ EATING

Geneva flaunts ethnic cuisines galore. If it's local and traditional you're after, dip into a cheese fondue or platter of pan-fried *filets de perche* (perch fillets), a simple Lake Geneva speciality.

Buvette des Bains
Cafeteria $

(Map p44; 022 738 16 16; www.bains-des-paquis.ch; Quai du Mont-Blanc 30, Bains des Pâquis; mains Sfr14-23; ☺7am-10.30pm; P ☑) Meet Genevans at this earthy beach bar – rough and hip around the edges – at the Bains des Pâquis lakeside pool and sauna complex. Grab breakfast, a salad or the *plat du jour,* or dip into a *fondue au crémant* (sparkling-wine fondue). Dining is self-service on trays and alfresco in summer.

Manora
Cafeteria $

(Map p44; ☑022 909 44 80; www.manor.ch/fr/u/manora; Centre Commercial Manor, Rue de Cornavin 6; small plates Sfr4-14; ❄ ♠) ✎ The cafeteria in the Manor (p46) shopping centre by Gare CFF de Cornavin is one of the best spots in town to get a reasonably priced lunch and everybody knows it – you won't be dining alone. The food is fresh and keeps on coming. There's a veritable smorgasbord of choice from salads to sandwiches, seafood, soups, meats, pasta and pastries. Meals are created using products sourced from within a 30km radius of the restaurant.

Le Relais d'Entrecôte
Steak $$

(Map p44; ☑022 310 60 04; www.relais entrecote.fr; Rue Pierre-Fatio 6; steak, salad & chips Sfr42, desserts SFr 9-14; ☺noon-2.30pm & 7-11pm) Key vocabulary at this timeless classic where everyone eats the same dish is *à point* (medium), *bien cuit* (well done) and *saignant* (rare). It doesn't even bother with menus, just sit down, say how you like your steak cooked and wait for it to arrive – two handsome servings pre-empted by a

green salad and accompanied by perfectly crisp skinny fries.

La Finestra
Italian $$$

(Map p44; ☑022 312 23 22; www.restaurant-lafinestra.ch/fr; Rue de la Cité 11; mains Sfr29-52, set menu Sfr85; ☻noon-2.30 & 7-10.30pm Mon-Fri, 7-10.30pm Sat) Since 2006 this handsome little restaurant nestled in the heart of the Old Town has been serving authentic Italian haute cuisine in a casual yet refined setting. The low ceilings and tiny tables wedged into the basement level of this historic building make for an intimate, if not slightly claustrophobic atmosphere, but the presentation, flavour and service make up for it.

Le Petit Lac
Seafood $$$

(☑022 751 11 44; www.lepetitlac.ch; Quai de Corsier 14, Corsier; 3-course set menu Sfr 52, mains Sfr27-43; ☻noon-2pm & 7-10pm; 🅿) Take an afternoon boat with CGN (p50) from Jardin-Anglais or Genève-Pâquis to Corsier for an early dinner at this superb lakefront seafood restaurant, which serves a mean rendition of the local speciality *filets de*

perche. As it's near the French border, those with their own wheels could combine a meal here with a visit to Yvoire or a ride on the Téléphérique du Salève (p41).

Café du Marché
French $$$

(☑022 301 26 47; www.cafedumarchecarouge. ch; Pl du Marché 4, Carouge; mains Sfr25-54; ☻6.30am-11.30pm Mon-Sat, 11.30am-11.30pm Sun) Location and ambience alone might tempt you through the door, but the food is what you'll really remember from this re-fined restaurant on Carouge's picturesque central square. Everything from salmon baked en papillote to slow-roasted lamb with Moroccan spices is well prepared and served with effortless courtesy. Save room for desserts such as pear tarte Tatin or Grand Marnier soufflé.

🍸 DRINKING & NIGHTLIFE

La Buvette du Bateau
Bar

(Map p44; ☑022 508 56 89; www.bateau geneve.ch; Quai Gustave-Ador 1; ☻noon-mid-night Tue-Thu, noon-2am Fri, 5pm-2am Sat,

11am-10pm Sun mid-May–mid-Sep) Few terraces are as dreamy as this. Moored permanently by the quay near Jet d'Eau, this fabulous belle époque paddle steamer sailed Lake Geneva's waters from 1896 until its retirement in 1974, and is now one of the busiest lounge bars in town in summer. Flower boxes festoon its decks and the cabin kitchen cooks tapas, bruschetta and other drink-friendly snacks.

Cottage Café — Cafe

(Map p44; ☑022 731 60 16; www.cottagecafe.ch; Rue Adhémar-Fabri 7; ☺7am-midnight Mon-Fri, from 9am Sat; ☝) This charming little cafe in the **Square des Alpes** near the waterfront is a great spot for a chat over coffee and cake or a glass of wine any time of the day, with tapas served from 6pm and light breakfasts daily. On clear days, views of Mont Blanc from its garden are swoonworthy, and lunching or lounging inside is akin to hanging out in your grandma's book-lined living room.

Yvette de Marseille — Bar

(Map p44; ☑022 735 15 55; www.yvettede marseille.ch; Rue Henri Blanvalet 13; ☺3.30pm-midnight Mon & Tue, to 1am Wed & Thu, to 2am Fri & Sat) No bar begs the question 'what's in the name?' more than this buzzy drinking hole. Urban and edgy, it occupies a mechanic's workshop once owned by Yvette. Note the garage door, the trap door in the floor where cars were repaired and the street number 13 (aka the departmental number of the Bouches-du-Rhône department, home to Marseille).

Village du Soir — Club

(☑022 301 12 69; www.villagedusoir.com; Rte des Jeunes 24, Carouge; ☺8pm-5am Fri-Sun) Get in quick to enjoy the 'Village of the Night', which has a five-year lease (from 2017) to repurpose an industrial site by Geneva Stadium. Until they're turfed out, it's *the* place to be for a regularly packed calendar of events including DJ nights and gigs by local and visiting bands, exhibitions, pop-up restaurants, food-trucks, fun and general mayhem...okay, frivolity at the very least.

Chat Noir — Bar

(☑022 307 10 40; www.chatnoir.ch; Rue Vauthier 13; ☺6pm-4am Tue-Thu, to 5am Fri & Sat) One of the busiest night spots in Carouge, the Black Cat is packed most nights thanks to its all-rounder vibe: arrive after work for an aperitif with selection of tapas to nibble on, and stay until dawn for dancing, live music and DJ sets.

❶ INFORMATION

Geneva Tourist Information Office (Map p44; ☑022 909 70 00; www.geneve.com; Rue du Mont-Blanc 18; ☺10am-6pm Mon, 9am-6pm Tue-Sat, 10am-4pm Sun) Just downhill from the train station, this bright office has excellent helpful staff who speak a multitude of languages. The office produces a variety of local maps and guides including a variety of themed walking maps in several languages with selected itineraries chosen to suit the tastes and sensibilities of the cultures linked to that language. Cool!

❶ GETTING THERE & AWAY

Air Geneva (Cointrin) Airport (GVA; Aéroport International de Genève; www.gva.ch), 4km northwest of the town centre, is served by a wide variety of Swiss and international airlines.

Boat CGN (Compagnie Générale de Navigation; Map p44; ☑0900 929 929; www.cgn.ch; Quai du Mont-Blanc; ☝) runs up to four steamers per day from Jardin Anglais and Pâquis to other Lake Geneva villages, including Lausanne (Sfr66, 3½ hours).

Train Trains run regularly from Geneva's central train station, **Gare CFF de Cornavin** (www.sbb. ch; Pl de Cornavin), to most Swiss towns and cities, including **Lausanne** (Sfr22.40, 35 to 50 minutes), **Bern** (Sfr50, 1¾ hours) and **Zürich** (Sfr87, 2¾ hours)

❶ GETTING AROUND

Bicycle From May to October, free bikes are available for up to four hours at **Genèveroule** (Map p44; ☑022 740 13 43; www.geneveroule.

Cottage Café

ch; Pl de Montbrillant 17; 4hr free, then per hour
Sfr2; ⊙8am-9pm May-Oct, to 6pm Nov-Apr), just
outside the train station; simply show your photo
ID and leave a Sfr20 cash deposit.

Boat Yellow shuttle boats called **Les Mouettes** (Map p44; ☑022 732 29 44; www.
mouettesgenevoises.ch; Quai du Mont-Blanc 8;
single/60min ticket Sfr2/3; ⊙7:30am-7:30pm
Mon-Fri, 10am-2pm Sat, 3-6pm Sun Sep-
May, until 9pm May-Sep) – the name means
'seagulls' – cross the lake every 10 minutes
between 7.30am and 6pm. Buy single-ride
tickets from machines on the dock, or use any
valid TPG bus ticket.

*On clear days, views of Mont
Blanc...are swoon-worthy*

Bus Tickets for buses, trolley buses and trams
run by **TPG** (TPG; Map p44; www.tpg.ch; Rue de
Montbrillant; ⊙7am-7pm Mon-Fri, 9am-6pm Sat)
are sold from dispensers at stops and inside
Geneva's train station. A one-hour ticket costs
Sfr3; a *saut-de-puce* ticket valid for three stops
in 30 minutes is Sfr2. A day pass costs Sfr10, or
Sfr8 if purchased after 9am.

Taxi Hop in one at the train station, book online
(www.taxi-phone.ch) or call 022 331 41 33.

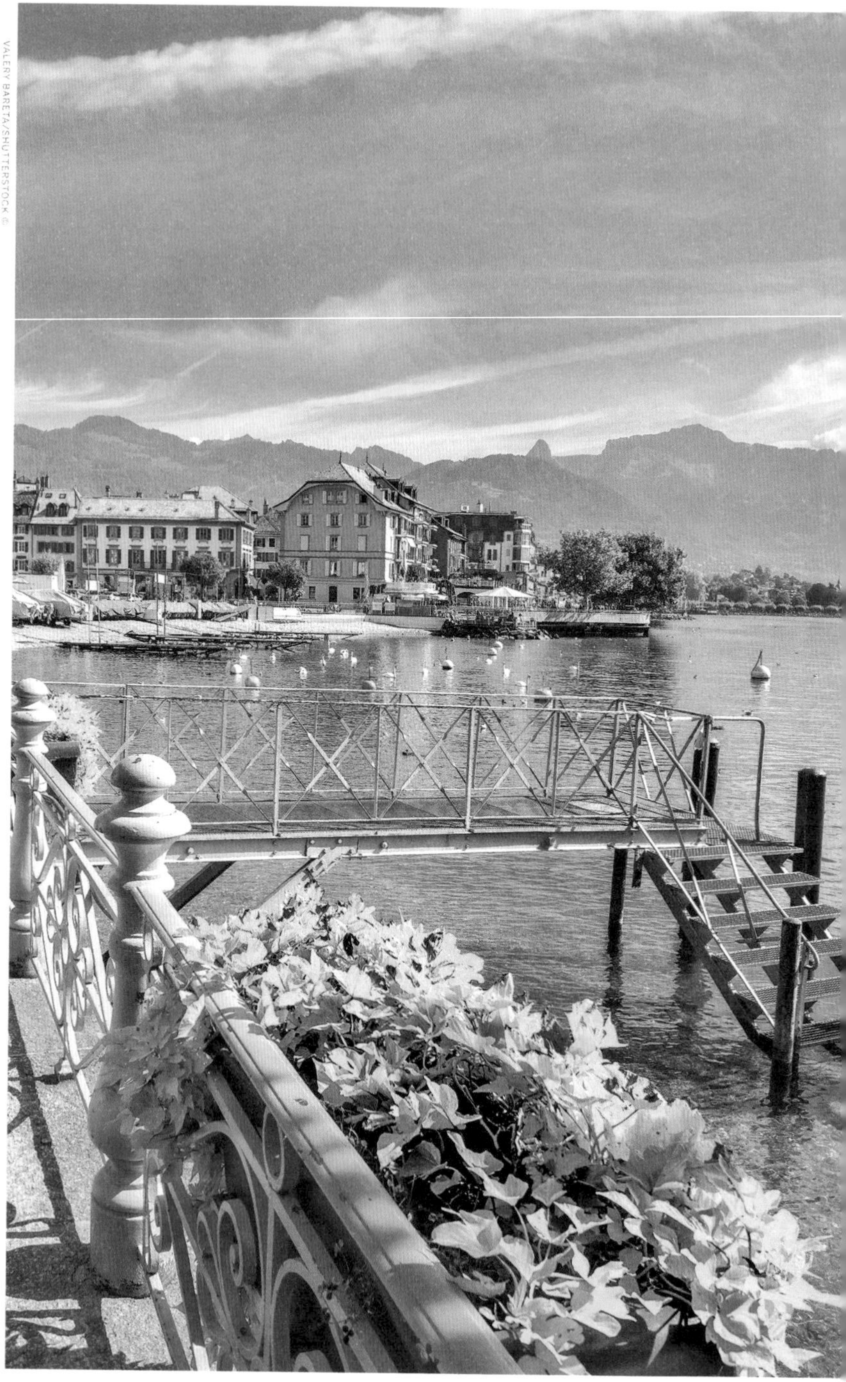

LAKE GENEVA

In This Chapter

Lake Geneva at a Glance...

Welcome to Western Europe's largest lake, known to francophones as Lac Léman and to everyone else as Lake Geneva. Here, in the Swiss canton of Vaud, ancient vineyards and lakeside towns (Lausanne, Montreux, Vevey, Nyon, Aigle) enjoy breathtaking views across the sparkling water to the Alps. In summer, hiking explorations reward nature lovers with perfect air and sublime mountain scenery. In winter, the region becomes a pricey playground for the world's skiing elite. Whenever you visit, don't miss the shore-hugging rail journey from Geneva to Montreux, clacking along past fairy-tale châteaux, luxurious manors, lakeside beaches, and the terraced vineyards of the Lavaux.

Two Days in Lake Geneva

Start with a stroll around **Place de la Palud** (p62), Lausanne's lovely medieval market square. In the afternoon, absorb Olympic history and fine lake views at the **Olympic Museum** (p59). After dinner, join locals for drinks under the bridge at **Les Arches** (p63). On day two, hop a boat to the **Château de Chillon** (p56), everybody's favourite Swiss castle, returning via the gorgeous lakeside footpath to explore Montreux this afternoon.

Four Days in Lake Geneva

Spend day three amid the magnificent terraced vineyards of the Lavaux, learning about – and tasting – local wine at **Lavaux Vinorama** (p60), followed by a walk or a train ride through the vines on the **Lavaux Express** (p61). Dedicate day four to visiting **Chaplin's World** (p58), an engaging new museum in the silent-film star's former home, followed by lunch or a cooking workshop at **Alimentarium** (p59) in Vevey.

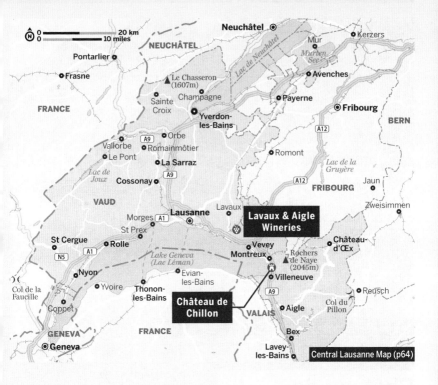

Lavaux & Aigle Wineries

Château de Chillon

Central Lausanne Map (p64)

Arriving at Lake Geneva

Train Regular regional trains ply the routes between Geneva, Nyon, Lausanne, Montreux, Vevey and Aigle. You'll need to change at Lausanne to get to Basel or Zürich.

Air Geneva (Cointrin) Airport (p50) is the closest to the region.

Sleeping

Accommodation around Lake Geneva ranges from the sublime to the ridiculously pricey. You'll be hard pressed to find budget beds outside the region's handful of excellent hostels. Montreux tends to be the most expensive place to stay, but views from many of its lakeside luxury hotels are well worth the coin. If travelling with family or friends, consider renting a holiday house by the lake.

Château de Chillon

Historic, sumptuous and reached by a flower-fringed lakeside footpath, this magnificent stone château built by the Savoys in the 13th century is everything a castle should be.

Great For...

☑ Don't Miss

Lord Byron's name, carved into a pillar in the castle's dungeon.

The Château

Occupying a stunning position on Lake Geneva, the magnificent oval-shaped hulk of 13th-century Château de Chillon is a maze of courtyards, towers and halls filled with arms, period furniture and artwork. The landward side is heavily fortified, but lakeside it presents a gentler face. From the waterfront in neighbouring Montreux, fairy-tale **Chemin Fleuri** – a silky smooth promenade framed by flowerbeds positively tropical in colour and vivacity – snakes dreamily along the lake for 4km to the château.

Chillon was largely built by the House of Savoy and taken over by Bern's governors after Vaud fell to Bern. Don't miss the medieval frescos in the **Chapelle St Georges** and the spooky Gothic **dungeons**.

The fortress gained fame in 1816 when Byron wrote *The Prisoner of Chillon*, a poem

about François Bonivard, thrown into the dungeon for his seditious ideas and freed by Bernese forces in 1536. Painters William Turner and Gustave Courbet subsequently immortalised the castle's silhouette on canvas, and Jean-Jacques Rousseau, Alexandre Dumas père and Mary Shelley all wrote about it.

It's about a 3km easy walk around the lakeshore from Montreux to Chillon, or take bus 201 (10 minutes). CGN (www.cgn.ch) boats and steamers – a wonderful way to arrive – call at Château de Chillon from Lausanne (1¾ hours), Vevey (50 minutes) and Montreux (15 minutes).

What's Nearby
Montreux

The adjacent town of Montreux has been a visitor-magnet for the rich, famous and everyone in-between ever since the 19th century, when writers, artists and musicians (Lord Byron and the Shelleys among them) flocked to this pleasing lakeside resort.

Montreux's main draws include peaceful walks along a lakeshore blessed with 19th-century hotels, a mild microclimate, a hilltop Old Town, Friday-morning lakeside markets, and Queen: The Studio Experience, a lovingly preserved recording studio once used by luminaries including David Bowie, Iggy Pop and the Rolling Stones.

Montreux Jazz Festival

Established in 1967, Montreux's best-known **festival** (www.montreuxjazz.com; ☺Jul), and one of Switzerland's top international events, takes over the town for two weeks in July. Free concerts take place daily (tickets for bigger-name gigs from Sfr60 to Sfr450), and the music is not just jazz: The Strokes, Cat Power, Van Morrison, BB King, Paul Simon, and Sharon Jones and the Dap-Kings have all played here.

Museums of Lake Geneva

The Lake Geneva towns of Lausanne, Vevey and Montreux host an eclectic mix of museums, celebrating everything from the Olympics to the artistic legacy of Queen and Charlie Chaplin.

Great For...

☑ Don't Miss

Mixing your own tracks at Queen's former recording studio, and signing the wall outside.

Chaplin's World

Opened in 2016, this engaging **museum** (www.chaplinsworld.com; Rte de Fenil 2, Corsier-sur-Vevey; adult/child Sfr23/17; ⊙10am-6pm) celebrates the life and work of iconic London-born film star Charlie Chaplin. Split between the neoclassical Manoir de Ban – the Corsier-sur-Vevey mansion where Chaplin spent his last quarter-century – and a purpose-built interactive studio, the exhibits include multimedia displays, excerpts from Chaplin's films, recreations of film sets, family photos and other evocative memorabilia, right down to Chaplin's trademark hat and cane. A tour of the mansion's splendid gardens rounds out the visit.

Allow at least a couple of hours to do this place justice; you can break your visit with lunch at The Tramp, the museum's on-site restaurant.

THE OLYMPIC MUSEUM © CIO. LYDIE NESVADBA

Need to Know

Lausanne, Vevey and Montreux are located only minutes apart, with excellent train connections.

✕ Take a Break

Picnic on the wooden chairs screwed into the rocks on the Alimentarium's lakeshore.

★ Top Tip

Museums listed are open year-round, offering a perfect rainy-day (or snowy-day!) getaway.

Alimentarium

Nestlé's headquarters have been in Vevey since 1814, hence the presence of this **museum** (☏021 924 41 11; www.alimentarium.ch; Quai Perdonnet; adult/child Sfr12/free; ◷10am-5pm Tue-Fri, to 6pm Sat & Sun) dedicated to nutrition and all things edible, past and present. Displays here are clearly meant to entertain as well as inform, starting with the gigantic silver fork that sticks out of the water in front of the lakeside mansion (a great picnic spot).

Particularly fun are the Alimentarium's cooking workshops for both adults and kids, guided tours for families, and gardening workshops. Finish up with a healthy lunch in the museum restaurant.

Olympic Museum

Lausanne's **Musée Olympique** (☏021 621 65 11; www.olympic.org/museum; Quai d'Ouchy 1; adult/child Sfr18/10; ◷9am-6pm daily May–mid-Oct, 10am-6pm Tue-Sun mid-Oct–Apr; P▮) is one of the region's most lavish museums and an essential stop for sports buffs (and kids). State-of-the-art installations recount the Olympic story from its inception to the present day through video, interactive displays, memorabilia and temporary themed exhibitions. Other attractions include tiered landscaped gardens, site-specific sculptural works and a fabulous cafe with champion lake views from its terrace.

Queen: The Studio Experience

Queen recorded seven albums in this lovingly preserved **studio** (www.mercuryphoenix trust.com/studioexperience; Rue du Théâtre 9, Casino Barrière de Montreux; ◷10.30am-10pm) **FREE** near the Montreux waterfront (they also owned the joint from 1979 to 1993). A visit here will give you a strong sense of the band's oeuvre and relationship with the town. Charming paraphernalia (handwritten lyric notes and the like) means this shrine of sorts definitely has a kind of magic. Best of all, it's free!

Lavaux & Aigle Wineries

East of Lausanne lie the steeply terraced vineyards of the Lavaux region – named a Unesco World Heritage Site for its ancient wine-growing roots – and the château-crowned Chablais-producing capital of Aigle.

Great For...

☑ **Don't Miss**

The spectacular lake and vineyard views from La Tour de Gourze (p67).

Lavaux Vinorama

This thoroughly modern **tasting and discovery centre** (☏021 946 31 31; www.lavaux-vinorama.ch; Rte du Lac 2, Rivaz; ⊙10.30am-8.30pm Mon-Sat, to 7pm Sun, closed Mon & Tue Nov-Jun) **FREE**, 5km east of Cully in Rivaz, is fronted by a shimmering 15m-long bay window decorated with 6000 metallic pixels inspired by the veins of a vine leaf. Inside, a film evokes a year in the life of a wine-growing family and, in the state-of-the-art Espace Dégustation, you can sample dozens of different wines.

Pick from wine 'packages' (Sfr13 to Sfr22) and go the whole hog with a platter of local cheeses and cold meats (Sfr12 or Sfr14).

Musée de la Vigne et du Vin

Aigle's beautiful little castle set against the backdrop of the Vaud Alps was built in the 12th century and looks as if it's straight out

Lavaux vineyards

ⓘ Need to Know

The region is especially lively and scenic during the September/October harvest season.

✕ Take a Break

Cap off a day in the vineyards with fondue at Café Tivoli (p66) in Châtel-St-Denis.

★ Top Tip

Taste local tipples at the caveaux des vignerons (wine-growers' cellars) in Lutry (p67).

---

of a fairy-tale. Inside the château, 2000 years of winemaking are evoked in the compelling **Musée de la Vigne et du Vin** (Wine and Vine Museum; www.museeduvin.ch; Pl du Château 1, Aigle; adult/child Sfr11/5; ☺10am-6pm Jul & Aug, closed Mon Apr-Jun, Sep & Oct, 10am-4pm Tue-Sun Jan-Mar, Nov & Dec), a thoroughly modern wine museum. The six hands-on digital experiments – indulge in your own Chasselas grape harvest, make wine etc – in the 'lab' are particularly fun.

Domaine du Daley

Vines have been cultivated at this wine estate near Lutry since 1392, making it the region's oldest winery – and a lovely spot for a memorable *dégustation* (tasting).

Lavaux Express

A fun and easy way to lose yourself in green vines and blue lake views is aboard the **Lavaux Express** (📞0848 848 791; www.lavauxexpress.ch; Quai Gustave Doret 1, Lutry; adult/child Sfr15/12; ☺Tue-Sun Apr-Oct) – a tractor-pulled tourist train that chugs through the Lavaux's vineyards and villages. Pick from two routes: Lutry CGN boat pier up to the wine-growing villages of Aran and Grandvaux (one hour return); or Cully pier to Riex, Epesses and Dézaley (1¼ hours).

Vineyard Walking Trails

From the village of Chardonne, uphill from Corseaux, there are some lovely walking trails, including the easy Boucle Chardonne (2.8km) that starts and ends at the Golden-Pass funicular station and swoops in a circle through pea-green vines.

Another beautiful 5.5km walking trail winds east through vines and the tiny hamlets of Le Châtelard and Aran to the larger wine-making villages of Grandvaux and Riex. For staggering vine and lake views, hike up to La Conversion (3.8km) above Lutry and continue on the high trail to Grandvaux (4km).

Lausanne

Surrounded by vineyards, rolling down a trio of hillsides to the lakeshore, Lausanne is Switzerland's fourth-largest city. It is known for its upbeat vibe, perhaps on account of its dramatic vistas of the lake and its high-brow though party-hearty student population.

◎ SIGHTS

Cathédrale de Notre Dame   Cathedral

(Map p64; ☏021 316 71 60; www.cath-vd.ch/cvd_parish/notre-dame; Pl de la Cathédrale; ◷9am-7pm Apr-Sep, to 5.30pm Oct-Mar) Lausanne's Gothic cathedral, Switzerland's finest, stands proudly at the heart of the Old Town. Raised in the 12th and 13th centuries on the site of earlier, humbler churches, it lacks the lightness of French Gothic buildings but is remarkable nonetheless. Pope Gregory X, in the presence of Rudolph of Habsburg (the Holy Roman Emperor), consecrated the church in 1275.

Place de la Palud   Square

(Map p64) In the heart of the Vieille Ville (Old Town), this pretty-as-a-picture 9th-century medieval market square was once bogland. For five centuries it has been home to the city government, now housed in the 17th-century **Hôtel de Ville** (town hall; Map p64; Pl de la Palud 2). Opposite, you'll find the **Fontaine de la Justice** (Justice Fountain; Map p64; Place de la Palud), from where, atop a brightly painted column, the allegorical figure of Justice herself, clutching scales and dressed in blue, presides over the square.

Bear left along Rue Mercière to pick up **Escaliers du Marché** (Map p64), a timber-canopied staircase with a tiled roof that heads up to Rue Pierre Viret and beyond to the Cathédrale de Notre Dame.

✪ ACTIVITIES

Guides d'Accueil MdA   Walking

(Map p64; ☏021 320 12 61; www.lausanne-a-pied.ch; Pl de la Palud; adult/child Sfr10/free; ◷May-Sep) Walking tours of Lausanne's Old Town, departing from in front of the Hôtel de Ville

Lausanne

(town hall) on Place de la Palud. Themed tours for up to five people on demand. English language tours are held daily and no reservations are required. Check the homepage for specifics.

🅐 SHOPPING

Marché du Centre-ville   Market

(Lausanne Market; Map p64; Place de la Riponne; ⊙Wed & Sat 8am-2pm) The pedestrianised streets of the Old Town around the Place de la Riponne, in the foreground of the **Palais de Rumine** (Map p64; ☑021 316 33 10; http://musees.vd.ch/palais-de-rumine/accueil/; Pl de la Riponne 6; ⊙11am-6pm Tue-Thu, to 5pm Fri-Sun) **FREE**, come to life every Wednesday and Saturday with purveyors of quality regional produce such as fruit, vegetables, cheeses and meats. It's a great spot to stock up on picnic provisions or to try local snacks such as *taillé aux greubons* (flaky pastry cooked with pork fat). From early November to Christmas Eve it's also the location of Lausanne's bustling **Christmas market**.

There's also a flea market, **Marché de Chaudero** (Place Chauderon Flea Market; Map p64; Pl Chauderon; ⊙9am-7pm Tue & Thu) **FREE**, and a craft market, **Marché à la Place de la Palud** (Place de la Palud Crafts Market; Map p64; Pl de la Palud; ⊙10.30am-7pm 1st Fri of the month).

🅧 EATING

Eat Me   Tapas $

(Map p64; ☑021 311 76 59; www.eat-me.ch; Rue Pépinet 3; small plates Sfr10-20; ⊙noon-2pm & 5pm-midnight Tue-Sat; 🛜🍴) Eat Me's tagline of 'The world on small plates' will give you an idea of what this fun, immensely popular and downright delicious resto-bar is all about: global tapas, basically, with everything from baby burgers (sliders) to sashimiviche (Sichuan sashimi à la ceviche!) and shrimp lollipops. Everything is well priced and it's just downright fun. Bring your friends!

Bridge Bars

Where there's a bridge, there's a bar. At least that's how it works in artsy Lausanne where the monumental arches of its bridges shelter the city's most happening summertime bars.

Les Arches (Map p64; www.lesarches.ch; Pl de l'Europe; ⊙11am-midnight Mon-Wed, to 1am Thu, to 2am Fri & Sat, 1pm-midnight Sun) Occupying four arches of Lausanne's magnificent Grand Pont (built between 1839 and 1844) above Place de l'Europe, this is the perfect port of call for that all-essential, after-work drink in the warm evening sun or for that final drink before bed.

Terrasse des Grandes Roches (Map p64; ☑021 312 34 18; http://lesgrandes-roches.ch; Escaliers des Grandes-Roches; ⊙2pm-midnight Apr-Sep) Mid-evening, Lausanne's hipsters move to this fabulous terrace complete with pool table, table football, palm trees and deckchairs beneath an arch of the Bessières Bridge, built between 1908 and 1910. Steps lead up to it from Rue Centrale and down to it from opposite MUDAC (Museum of Contemporary Design and Applied Arts; Map p64; ☑021 315 25 30; www.mudac.ch; Pl de la Cathédrale 6; adult/child Sfr10/free, 1st Sat of month free; ⊙11am-6pm Tue-Sun) on Rue Pierre Veret.

Grand Pont, Lausanne
WESTEND61/GETTY IMAGES ©

Central Lausanne

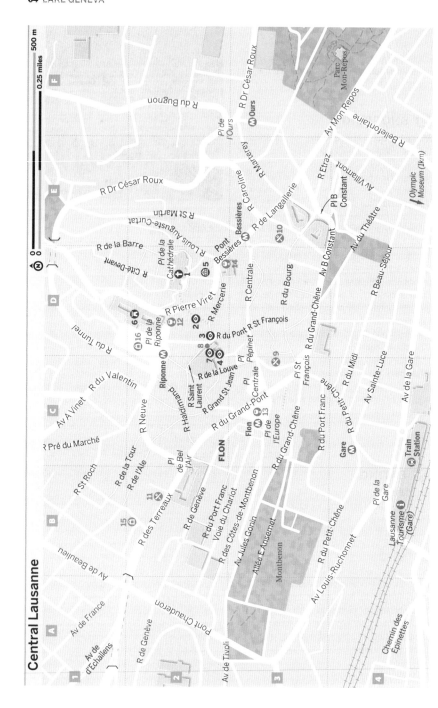

Central Lausanne

◎ Sights

◎ Activities, Courses & Tours

◎ Eating

◎ Drinking & Nightlife

◎ Shopping

Holy Cow   Burgers $

(Map p64; ☎021 312 24 04; www.holycow.ch; Rue Cheneau-de-Bourg 17; burger with chips & drink Sfr14-26; ☺11am-11pm; ♠) A Lausanne success story, with branches in Geneva, Zürich and France, its burgers (beef, chicken or veggie) feature local ingredients, creative toppings and witty names. Grab an artisanal beer, sit at a shared wooden table, and wait for your burger and fab fries to arrive in a straw basket. A second outlet can be found at **Rue des Terreaux** (Map p64; Rue des Terreaux 10).

◉ DRINKING & NIGHTLIFE

Great Escape   Pub

(Map p64; ☎021 312 31 94; www.the-great.ch; Rue de la Madeleine 18; ☺11.30am-late Mon-Fri, from 10am Sat, from noon Sun) Everyone knows the Great Escape, a busy student pub with pub grub (great burgers) and an enviable terrace with a view over Place de la Riponne. From the aforementioned square, walk up staircase Escaliers de l'Université and turn right.

ℹ INFORMATION

Lausanne Tourisme (Map p64; ☎021 613 73 73; www.lausanne-tourisme.ch; Pl de la Gare 9; ☺9am-7pm) At Lausanne station; a good spot to pick up detailed information and maps.

Nyon

A pretty lakeside town, half-way between Geneva and Lausanne, Nyon offers a good museums and festivals galore. Surrounded by vineyards and sloping casually downhill to the edge of Lake Geneva, Nyon makes a lovely, quieter alternative base to its bigger neighbours on either side.

◎ SIGHTS

Château de Nyon   Chateau

(☎022 316 42 73; www.chateaudenyon.ch; Pl du Château; adult/child Sfr8/free; ☺2-5pm Tue-Sun Nov-Mar, from 10am Mar-Nov; ℗♠) Nyon's castle was started in the 12th century, modified 400 years later and now houses the town's historical museum and a rare collection of fine porcelain. Beneath the castle in its ancient cellars, you'll find **Le Caveau de Nyon** (☎022 361 95 25; www.caveaudenyon.ch; ☺2-9pm Fri & Sat, 11am-8pm Sun) where you can taste different Nyon wines by local producers.

Château de Coppet   Chateau

(☎022 776 10 28; www.chateaudecoppet.ch; Rue de la Gare 2, Coppet; adult/child Sfr8/6; ☺2-6pm Apr-Oct; ℗) This is the former home of Jacques Necker, Louis XVI's banker and minister of finance, before it was handed down to his daughter, Madame de Staël, after she was exiled from Paris by Napoleon. It remains the little town of Coppet's

Fondue Moitié-Moitié

The township of Châtel-St-Denis, 13km northeast of Vevey, warrants a visit solely to sample its legendary fondue *moitié-moitié* (made from a combination of Gruyère and Vacherin Fribourgeois cheeses).

Indulge at the well-known, family-run and very traditional **Café Tivoli** (📞021 948 70 39; www.cafetivoli.ch; Pl d'Armes 18, Châtel-St-Denis; fondue per person Sfr25; ⏰11.30am-2pm & 6-9.30pm Mon-Fri, 11.30am-9.30pm Sat, 11.30am-9pm Sun), where you pay a per-person fee for your share of the *caquelon* (fondue pot), or across the street at the quaint, cafeteria-style **La Crémerie** (📞021 948 71 87; www.lacremerie.ch; Pl d'Armes 21, Châtel-Saint-Denis; mains Sfr18-32; ⏰7am-11pm Mon-Sat, to 8pm Sun; 🅿🖋👪) with its wonderful staff and adjacent *laiterie* (dairy) – basically a cheese shop selling every dairy product you can think of.

crowning glory. Visitors can tour the rooms, sumptuously furnished in Louis XVI style, where de Staël entertained the likes of Edward Gibbon and Lord Byron.

⊗ EATING

La Plage de Nyon   Swiss $
(📞022 362 61 01; www.laplagedenyon.ch; Rte de Genève 12; small plates Sfr5-18, mains Sfr18-38; 👪) In the warmer months you'll love the refreshingly chilled-out vibe of this casual 'beachfront' kitchen. It uses seasonal ingredients and lake-fresh fish to produce healthy, seafood-centric small and share plates that taste great, plus heartier choices such as fondue (yum!) – all from a killer location on the waterfront. Highly recommended.

Hôtel-Restaurant de la Plage   Swiss $$
(📞022 364 10 35; www.hoteldelaplage.info; Chemin de la Falaise, Gland; mains Sfr34-86;

⏰noon-2pm & 7-9.30pm Tue-Sun Feb–mid-Dec; 🅿👪) This low-key lakeside hotel in Gland, 7km northeast of Nyon, gets packed on account of its rendition of Lake Geneva's ubiquitous *filets de perche* (perch fillets), pan-fried in a divinely buttery, herbed secret-recipe sauce; fries and green salad included. Unless you specify otherwise, you automatically get two (very large) servings per person.

Vevey

There's something very special about Vevey that's hard to put your finger on, and that only those in the know would understand. Perhaps that's what gives the place its charm; a certain understated swankiness that's a little bit stuck in the 1970s and a little bit chic and cutting edge.

Villa Le Lac   Historic Site
(www.villalelac.ch; Route de Lavaux 21; adult/child Sfr12/6; ⏰10am-5pm Fri-Sun Jun-Sep) Declared a World Heritage Site in 2016, Villa le Lac, built by world-renowned Swiss-born architect Le Corbusier between 1923 and 1924, is a must for architecture buffs. The little white lakefront house with its functional rooftop sun deck and ribbon windows is the perfect overture to the great modern architect's better-known concrete building theme. His mother lived here from 1924 until 1960, followed by his brother until 1973. Visiting exhibitions are hosted each summer.

Mont Pélerin   Mountain
Ride the **GoldenPass** (📞021 989 81 90; www.goldenpass.ch/en/) funicular from Vevey (Sfr14, 11 minutes, every 20 minutes) through vineyards to the village of Chardonne, and onwards to the foot of this, the Lavaux's highest mountain (1080m). View not yet good enough? From the top funicular station, hike to the satellite-dish-encrusted communication tower near the top of Mont Pélerin and hop in the **Ascenseur Plein Ciel** (www.mob.ch; Mont Pélerin; adult/child Sfr5/3; ⏰8am-6pm Apr-Oct) for even more elevation and even better views.

Lavaux vineyards

Denis Martin — Swiss $$$

(021 921 12 10; www.denismartin.ch; Rue du Château 2; tasting menu from Sfr320; from 7pm Tue-Sat, closed 3 weeks Jul & Aug & 2 weeks Dec & Jan) Charismatic and engaging, chef Denis Martin is one of the country's biggest names in Swiss contemporary cooking and molecular cuisine. His tasting menu – think Michelin-starred – is a thrilling succession of 20-odd different bite-sized taste sensations, served in a traditional 17th-century mansion a block from the lake. Reservations essential.

Cully

Lakeside Cully, 5km east of Lutry, is a lovely village for a waterfront meander and early-evening mingle with vignerons (wine-growers) in its numerous vineyards.

Old stone **La Tour de Gourze** (www.gourze.ch; Rte de la Tour-de-Gourze), built in the 12th century as a defence tower, peers out on Lavaux vines, Lake Geneva, the Vaud and the Jura beyond from its hilltop perch at 924m. Hike or take the narrow lane that twists up to the tower from Chexbres.

Lutry

This captivating medieval village, just 4km east of Lausanne, was founded in the 11th century by French monks. Lutry celebrates its annual wine harvest with parades and tastings during the last weekend in September.

Plage de Curtinaux — Beach

(Lutry Beach; Buvette de la Plage) In summer, there's a pebble-and-grass beach at the eastern end of Lutry town with *buvette* (snack bar and tables), stand-up paddle-board hire and pontoons. It's popular with locals and visitors from Lausanne.

Caveau des Vignerons — Wine

(078 661 26 25; Grand Rue 23; 5-9pm Tue-Fri, 11am-2pm & 5-9pm Sat) The traditional charms (low ceiling, barrel tables) of this low-key cellar attract locals and tourists alike. The two main wine types available in the area are Calamin and Dézaley, and most of the whites (about three-quarters of all production) are made with the Chasselas grape.

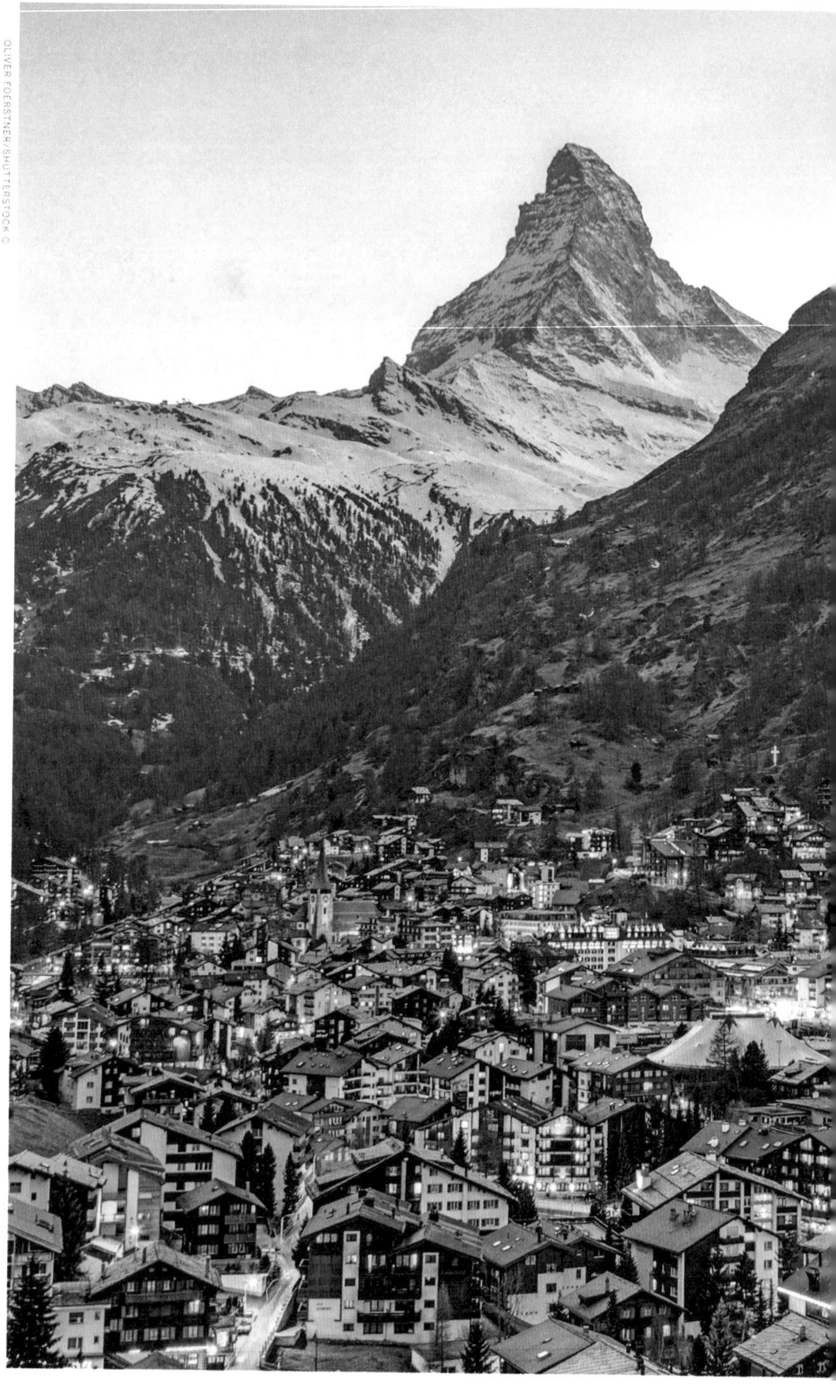

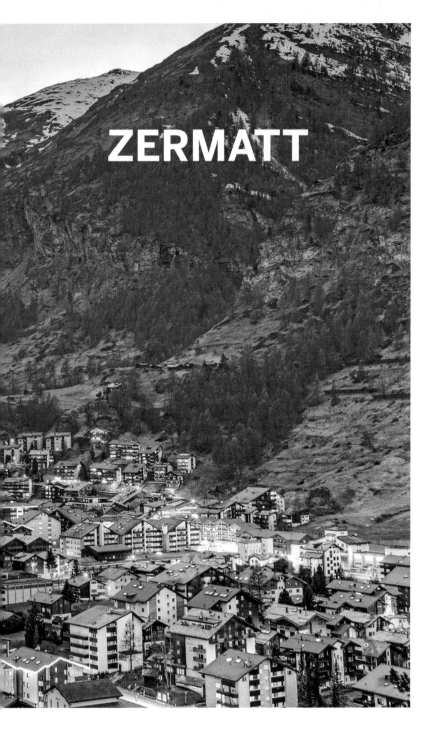

ZERMATT

Zermatt at a Glance...

You'll sense the anticipation on the train from Täsch: couples gaze wistfully out the window, kids stuff in Toblerone, and everyone rummages for their camera. Then, arriving in Zermatt, all give little whoops of joy at the Matterhorn's mesmerising pop-up-book effect.

Since the mid-19th century, Zermatt has starred among Switzerland's glitziest resorts. British climber Edward Whymper reached the Matterhorn's summit first in 1865, Theodore Roosevelt climbed it in 1881, and a young Winston Churchill scaled Monte Rosa (4634m) in 1894. Today, spellbound skiers and hikers cruise the surrounding high country, while style-conscious darlings flash designer threads in the town's swish bars.

Two Days in Zermatt

Stroll Zermatt's car-free streets, relishing your first glimpses of the Matterhorn and contemplating the mountain's illustrious history at the **Matterhorn Museum** (p78). Climb by funicular to **Sunnegga** (2288m; p78), then hike down to **Chez Vrony** (p81) for lunch. On day two, take the **Gornergratbahn** (p72) to **Gornergrat** (3089m) for breathtaking mountain perspectives; on the downhill journey, disembark midway for a return hike to Zermatt.

Four Days in Zermatt

On day three, soar to 3883m on the **Matterhorn Glacier Paradise** (p72) cable car, taking in the otherworldly beauty of a dozen-plus glaciers and a slew of 4000m peaks. On day four, plunge again into Zermatt's great outdoors, heading up to Plateau Rosa on the Theodul glacier for a spot of summer skiing, or hiking the **Matterhorn Glacier Trail** (p73) for unforgettable close-up views of the Matterhorn.

Zermatt Map (p80)

Matterhorn

Arriving in Zermatt

Zermatt Train Station Direct trains arrive hourly from Brig (1½ hours) and Visp (70 minutes). It is also the start/end point of the Glacier Express.

Matterhorn Terminal Täsch Motorists must park at Täsch and take the Zermatt Shuttle train 5km south to Zermatt.

Zürich/Geneva Airports Direct trains run hourly to Visp (2½ hours), transfer point for Zermatt trains.

Sleeping

Zermatt is packed with accommodation, from hostels and mountain huts to boutique chalets and designer hotels. Book well ahead in winter, and bear in mind that nearly everywhere closes between May and mid to late June, and from mid-October to November or early December. Many places will pick you and your bags up at the station in an electro-shuttle. Check when you book.

The Matterhorn

Rising like a shark's fin above Zermatt, the Matterhorn (4478m) has long seduced visitors with its hypnotic beauty, which demands to be admired, ogled and photographed from every conceivable angle.

Great For...

☑ Don't Miss

The Gornergratbahn's spectacular sunrise and sunset excursions, offered weekly throughout the summer.

The Matterhorn by Cog Railway

Europe's highest cogwheel railway, the **Gornergratbahn** (Map p80; www.gornergrat. ch; Bahnhofplatz 7; adult/child round trip Sfr94/47; ☺7am-7.15pm), has climbed through picture-postcard scenery to Gornergrat (3089m) – a 30-minute journey – since 1898. On the way up, sit on the right-hand side of the train to gawp at the Matterhorn. Tickets allow you to get on and off en route; there are restaurants at Riffelalp (2211m) and Riffelberg (2582m).

The Matterhorn by Cable Car

Views from Zermatt's cable cars are all remarkable, but the **Matterhorn Glacier Paradise** (Map p80; www.matterhornparadise. ch; Schluhmattstrasse; adult/child return Sfr100/50; ☺8.30am-4.20pm) steals the show. Ride Europe's highest-altitude cable car

View of the Matterhorn from Gornergrat

❶ Need to Know
Dinky electro-taxis zip around Zermatt, noiselessly taking pedestrians by surprise – watch out!

✗ Take a Break
For soul-nourishing Swiss comfort food and prime Matterhorn views, hit the sundeck at Chez Vrony (p81).

★ Top Tip
To see the Matterhorn spectacularly reflected in Riffelsee, walk 10 minutes downhill from the Gornergratbahn's Rotenboden station.

to 3883m and gawp at 14 glaciers and 38 mountain peaks over 4000m from the Panoramic Platform. Don't miss snow tubing and visiting the Glacier Palace, an ice palace complete with glittering ice sculptures and an ice slide to swoosh down.

Walking the Matterhorn
For Matterhorn close-ups, nothing beats the highly dramatic **Matterhorn Glacier Trail** (two hours, 6.5km) from Trockener Steg (midpoint of the Matterhorn Glacier Paradise cable car) to Schwarzsee; 23 information panels en route provide a comprehensive crash course on glaciers.

Climbing the Matterhorn
Some 3000 alpinists summit Europe's most photographed, 4478m-high peak each year. You don't need to be superhuman to do it, but you do need to be a skilled climber in tip-top physical shape and have a week to acclimatise before making the iconic ascent up sheer rock and ice.

No one attempts the Matterhorn without local know-how. An excellent source of mountain guides is Zermatters (p79); client–guide ratios are 1:1. Mid-July to mid-September is the best season to attempt the ascent. You'll probably be required to do training climbs first, to prove you're 100% up to it. The Matterhorn claims more than a few lives each year.

Skiing the Matterhorn
Zermatt is cruising heaven, with mostly long, scenic red runs, plus a smattering of blues for ski virgins and knuckle-whitening blacks for experts. The main skiing areas in winter are **Rothorn**, **Stockhorn** and **Klein Matterhorn** – 52 lifts, 360km of ski runs in all with a link from Klein Matterhorn to the Italian resort of **Cervinia** and a freestyle park with half-pipe for snowboarders.

Summer skiing and boarding (gravity park at **Plateau Rosa** on the Theodul glacier) is Europe's most extensive.

Glacier Express

One of Europe's mythical train journeys, the Glacier Express links two of Switzerland's oldest, glitziest mountain resorts – Zermatt and St Moritz – and the Alpine scenery in between is truly magnificent.

Great For...

☑ Don't Miss

The 65m-high Landwasser Viaduct between Chur and St Moritz, one of Switzerland's most photographed sights.

Glacier Express Basics

Charting an eight-hour, 290km course through the heart of the Swiss Alps, the Glacier Express is one of Switzerland's classic experiences. While it's not all hardcore mountain porn (witness the 191 tunnels en route), there are some spectacularly scenic stretches, most notably the one-hour ride from Disentis to Andermatt across the Oberalp Pass (2033m). Before setting off, it pays to know a few nuts and bolts:

● Check the weather forecast. A blue sky enhances the experience immeasurably.

● The complete trip takes almost eight hours. If you're travelling with children or can't bear the thought of sitting all day, opt for just a section of the journey.

● Windows in the stylish panoramic carriages can't be opened, making it tricky

Crossing the Landwasser Viaduct

Need to Know

www.glacierexpress.ch; adult/child one way St Moritz–Zermatt Sfr153/76.50, obligatory seat reservation summer/winter Sfr33/13; on-board 3-course lunch Sfr45; 3 trains daily May-Oct, 1 daily mid-Dec–Feb

Take a Break

Unexceptional three-course lunches are served on board; alternatively, bring your own picnic.

Top Tip

For the best views, sit on the south-facing side of the train.

Fiesch Sitting in the Rhône Valley at 1049m, Fiesch is a ski village in winter and a hiking and paragliding centre in summer. Most visitors come to take the cable cars up to Eggishorn (2927m) for riveting views of the spectacular Aletsch Glacier.

Andermatt Blessed with austere mountain appeal, Andermatt is a skiing and mountain-biking mecca at the junction of three passes: the St Gotthard Pass (2106m) linking Lucerne with Ticino; the Furka Pass (2431m) corkscrewing west to Valais; and the Oberalp Pass (2044m) looping east to Graubünden.

Disentis/Mustér This small, primarily Romansch-speaking village in western Graubünden is home to the massive Benedictine monastery, Kloster Disentis.

Chur The Alps rise like an amphitheatre around Chur, Graubünden's biggest city and the country's oldest, inhabited since 3000 BC. Chur's Altstadt (Old Town) is like a vibrant gallery, with arty boutiques, authentic restaurants and relaxed bars.

to take good photos. If this is the reason you're aboard, take a regional express SBB train, which follows the same route: it's cheaper; no reservation is required; windows can be opened; and you can mingle with locals and stretch your legs when changing trains.

○ Children aged under six travel free on their parent's lap.

○ The train runs thrice daily May to October, and once daily mid-December to February.

Stops from West to East

Break your journey at any of these stops.

Brig An important crossroads since Roman times, lively Brig is dotted with cobbled squares, alfresco cafe terraces and candy-hued townhouses.

Walking Tour: Aletsch Glacier

This high-Alpine walk is a nature-gone-wild spectacle of moors, jagged mountains and deeply crevassed glaciers.

Start Fiescheralp
End Bettmeralp
Distance 17km
Duration 5 to 6 hours

Olmenhorn
(3314m)

5 At **Roti Chumma** (2369m), fork right onto a magnificent route above a seemingly endless sweep of ice.

Grosser Aletschgletscher
(Aletsch Glacier)

Wysses Löub

6 From Biel saddle (2292m), head southwest along a tarn-speckled ridge and grassy slopes to **Moosfluh** (2333m).

Greichergrat

6

Bettmersee

7 Bettmeralp
FINISH

Aletschwald

Riederalp

Riederalp

7 From the ridge, descend to the inky-blue Blausee (2204m), then continue to Bettmersee and **Bettmeralp**.

Betten

0 ——————— 2 km
0 ——————— 1 mile

Fieschergletscher

Platta

4

Vordersee

3 Cross rocky ledges to the tiny Märjela valley, continuing to the **Gletscherstube mountain hut** (2363m).

3

2 Wind above the Fieschertal, cross **Unners Tälli** gully, and climb to a small wooden cross.

2

Eggishorn (2927m)

5

Elselicka (2722m)

START
Fiescheralp **1**

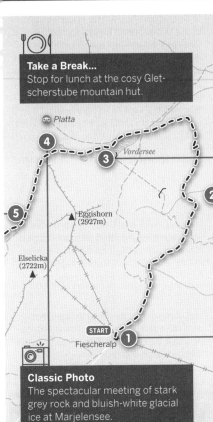

1 Northeast of **Fiescheralp cable-car station** (2212m), fine views unfold immediately along the flat dirt trail.

4 Make your way to the **Märjelensee** (2300m), dramatically bordered by the Aletsch Glacier's icy edge.

Rhône

Grengiols

◉ SIGHTS

Meander main-strip Bahnhofstrasse, with its flashy boutiques and the stream of horse-drawn sleds or carriages and electric taxis, then head downhill towards the noisy Vispa River along Hinterdorfstrasse. This old-world street is crammed with 16th-century pig stalls and archetypal Valaisian timber granaries propped up on stone discs and stilts to keep out pesky rats; look for the fountain commemorating Ulrich Inderbinen (1900–2004), a Zermatt-born mountaineer who climbed the Matterhorn 370 times, the last time at age 90. Nicknamed the King of the Alps, he was the oldest active mountain guide in the world when he retired at the ripe old age of 95.

Sunnegga   Viewpoint
(Map p80; www.matterhornparadise.ch; adult/child one way Sfr12/6, return Sfr24/12; 👪) Take the Sunnegga Express 'tunnel funicular' up to Sunnegga (2288m) for amazing views of the Matterhorn. This is a top spot for families – take the Leisee Shuttle (free) down to the lake for beginner ski slopes at Wolli's Park in winter, and a children's playground plus splashing around in the lake in summer. A marmot-watching station is a few minutes' walk from Sunnegga. It's a relatively easy downhill walk back to Zermatt (via Findeln) in about 1½ hours.

Matterhorn Museum   Museum
(Map p80; ☏027 967 41 00; www.zermatt.ch/museum; Kirchplatz; adult/child Sfr10/5; ⏰11am-6pm Jul-Sep, 3-6pm Oct–mid-Dec, 3-7pm mid-Dec–Mar, 2-6pm Apr-Jun) This crystalline, state-of-the-art museum provides fascinating insight into Valaisian village life, mountaineering, the dawn of tourism in Zermatt and the lives the Matterhorn has claimed. Short films portray the first successful ascent of the Matterhorn on 14 July 1865 led by Edward Whymper, a feat marred by tragedy on the descent when four team members crashed to their deaths in a 1200m fall. The infamous rope that broke is exhibited.

The entire town centre is packed with restaurants

Brown Cow Pub (Hotel Post; p81)

SAHACHATZ/SHUTTERSTOCK ©

Mountaineers' Cemetery   Cemetery
(Map p80; Kirchstrasse) A walk in Zermatt's pair of cemeteries – the Mountaineers' Cemetery in the garden of Zermatt's **St Mauritius Church** (Map p80; Kirchplatz) and the main cemetery across the road – is a sobering experience. Numerous gravestones tell of untimely deaths on Monte Rosa, the Matterhorn and Breithorn.

ACTIVITIES

Zermatters   Skiing, Hiking
(Snow & Alpine Center; Map p80; ☑027 966 24 66; www.zermatters.ch; Bahnhofstrasse 58; ☺8am-noon & 3-7pm Dec-Apr, 9am-noon & 3-7pm Jul-Sep) This centre houses the ski-school and mountain-guides office. It arranges guided climbs to major 4000ers including Breithorn, to Riffelhorn (for Matterhorn practice) and, for experts willing to acclimatise for a week, Matterhorn. Its program also covers multiday hikes, glacier hikes, snowshoeing and ice climbing.

Air-Taxi   Paragliding
(Map p80; ☑027 967 67 44; www.paragliding-zermatt.ch; Bachstrasse 8; flights from Sfr170) For sky-high mountain views to make you swoon, ride warm thermals alone or in tandem (both summer and winter flights) with Zermatt's paragliding school.

Forest Fun Park   Adventure Sports
(☑027 968 10 10; www.zermatt-fun.ch; Zen Steckenstrasse 110; adult/child Sfr33/23; ☺10am-7pm Jun-Oct; ♠) Let rip Tarzan-style in the forest with zip-lines, river traverses, bridges and platforms all graded according to difficulty. The easiest of the three trails is for children from age four.

Dorsaz Sport   Scooter Rental
(Map p80; www.dorsaz-sport.ch; Schluhmatt-strasse; scooter 1/2/3hr Sfr20/32/39; ☺8am-5.30pm; ♠) This sports shop next to the Matterhorn Glacier Paradise cable car rents chunky off-road dirt scooters (with helmet) to race down the mountain. Ride the cable car as far as Füri (1867m) or right up to Schwarzsee (2583m) then scoot back

Hiking Around Zermatt

Zermatt is a hiker's paradise, with 400km of summer trails through some of the most incredible scenery in the Alps – the tourist office (p83) has trail maps.

For those doing lots of walking, local excursion passes offer a convenient way to get into the high country. A Peak Pass, offering unlimited use of the Schwarzsee, Rothorn and Matterhorn Glacier Paradise cable cars plus the Gornergratbahn cog railway (p72), costs Sfr220 for three days or Sfr315 for a week. To find your perfect walk, search by duration, distance and difficulty on the hiking page of the excellent tourist-office website (www.zermatt.ch).

IOANA CATALINA E/SHUTTERSTOCK ©

down. Families should only go up as far as Füri; minimum age for children is nine.

EATING
You won't go hungry in Zermatt. The entire town centre is packed with restaurants, with the greatest concentration along busy Bahnhofstrasse.

Snowboat Bar & Yacht Club   International $
(Map p80; ☑027 967 43 33; www.zermatt snowboat.com; Vispastrasse 20; mains Sfr22-39; ☺noon-midnight) This hybrid eating-drinking riverside address, with deckchairs sprawled across its rooftop sun terrace, is a blessing. When fondue tires, head here for barbecue-sizzled burgers (not just beef, but crab and

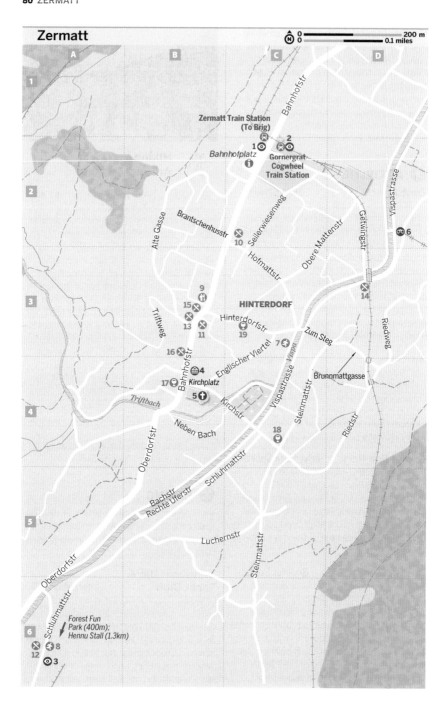

Zermatt

veggie burgers, too), super-power creative salads (the Omega 3 buster is a favourite) and great cocktails. The vibe? 100% friendly, fun and funky.

Bayard Metzgerei · Swiss $
(Map p80; ☎027 967 22 66; www.metzgerei -bayard.ch; Bahnhofstrasse 9; sausage Sfr6; ⊙noon-6.30pm Jul-Sep, 4-6.30pm Dec-Mar) Join the line for a street-grilled sausage (pork, veal or beef) and chunk of bread to down with a beer on the hop – or at a bar stool with the sparrows in the alley – from this first-class butcher's shop.

Brown Cow Pub · Pub Food $
(Map p80; ☎027 967 19 31; www.hotelpost.ch; Bahnhofstrasse 41; ⊙9am-2am, kitchen 9am-10.30pm) Dozens of dining joints line Bahnhofstrasse, including this busier-than-busy pub, one of several eating spots inside the legendary **Hotel Post**. The Brown Cow serves pub grub (hot dogs from Sfr9, burgers from Sfr16) all day.

Stefanie's Crêperie · Crêpes $
(Map p80; Bahnhofstrasse 60; crêpes sweet Sfr5-10, savoury Sfr11-14; ⊙1-10pm) Perfectly thin, light crepes – topped with a good choice of sweet or savoury toppings – served to go on the main street. Just up from the Snow & Alpine Center.

Klein Matterhorn · Pizza $
(Map p80; ☎027 967 01 42; www.klein matterhorn-zermatt.com; Schluhmattstrasse 50; pizza Sfr17-22; ⊙8am-midnight, kitchen 11.30am-10pm) For first-rate Italian pizza in the sun with a Matterhorn view, this simple pizzeria and cafe-bar opposite the Matterhorn Glacier Express cable-car station is the address.

Chez Vrony · Swiss $$
(☎027 967 25 52; www.chezvrony.ch; Findeln; breakfast Sfr15-28, mains Sfr25-45; ⊙9.15am-5pm Dec-Apr & mid-Jun–mid-Oct) Ride the Sunnegga Express funicular to 2288m, then ski down or summer-hike 15 minutes to Zermatt's tastiest slope-side address in the Findeln hamlet. Delicious dried meats, homemade cheese and sausage come from Vrony's own cows that graze away the summer on the high Alpine pastures (2100m) surrounding it, and the Vrony burger (Sfr31) is legendary. Advance reservations essential in winter.

Whymper Stube · Swiss $$
(Map p80; ☎027 967 22 96; www.whymper -stube.ch; Bahnhofstrasse 80; raclette Sfr9, fondue from Sfr25; ⊙11am-11pm Nov-Apr & Jun–mid-Oct) This cosy bistro, attached to the **Monte Rosa Hotel** from which Whymper left to climb the Matterhorn in 1865, is legendary for its excellent raclette and fondues. The icing on the cake is a segmented pot bubbling with three different cheese fondues. Service is relaxed and friendly, tables are packed tightly together, and the place – all inside – buzzes come dusk.

Top Three Sky-High Sleeps

Zermatt is all about big views, and there's no better way to get to the heart of this than to sleep above the clouds.

Kulmhotel Gornergrat (☎027 966 64 00; www.gornergrat-kulm.ch; d incl half-board from Sfr295/335; ☺mid-May–mid-Oct & mid-Dec–Apr; ☎) At the top of the Gornergrat cogwheel railway (p72), this century-old hotel (Switzerland's highest at 3100m) appeals to those who like the atmosphere and views of an Alpine hut, but shiver at the thought of thin mattresses and icy water. The sleek rooms offer downy duvets, picture-perfect panoramas, and magical solitude after the crowds have left.

Berggasthaus Trift (☎079 408 70 20; www.zermatt.net/trift; dm/d incl half-board Sfr70/164; ☺Jul-Sep) An outstanding two-hour hike from Zermatt leads to this 2337m-high, family-run mountain haven. At the foot of Triftgletscher, it offers simple, cosy rooms and a great terrace to kick back on, while admiring the mesmeric glacial landscape. Bookings essential.

Monte Rose Hütte (☎027 967 21 15; www.section-monte-rosa.ch; dm Sfr45, incl half-board Sfr85) Hardcore climbers adore this solar-powered, crystalline hut, deemed the height of state-of-the-art Alpine self-sufficiency. Perched on the edge of the Monte Rose glacier at 2883m, it's only accessible via a four-hour glacial trail (for serious mountaineers with a guide).

Kulmhotel Gornergrat

Le Gitan – Zermatterstübli   Swiss $$

(Map p80; ☎027 968 19 40; www.legitan.ch; Bahnhofstrasse 64; mains from Sfr23; ☺noon-3pm & 7-10pm) Le Gitan stands out for its elegant chalet-style interior and extra-tasty cuisine. Plump for a feisty pork or veal sausage with onion sauce and rösti, or dip into a cheese fondue – with Champagne (yes!), or, if you're feeling outrageously indulgent, Champagne and fresh truffles. End with coffee ice cream doused in kirsch, or apricot sorbet with *abricotine* (local Valais apricot liqueur).

🍷 DRINKING & NIGHTLIFE

Still fizzing with energy after schussing down the slopes? Zermatt pulses in party-mad après-ski huts, suave lounge bars and Brit-style pubs. Most close (and some melt) in low season.

Hennu Stall   Bar

(☎027 966 35 10; www.facebook.com/HennustallZermatt; Klein Matterhorn; ☺2-10pm Dec-Apr) Last one down to this snowbound 'chicken run' is a rotten egg. Hennu is the wildest après-ski shack on Klein Matterhorn, located below Fri on the way to Zermatt. Order a caramel vodka and take your ski boots grooving to live music on the terrace. A metre-long 'ski' of shots will make you cluck all the way down to Zermatt.

Z'alt Hischi   Bar

(Map p80; ☎027 967 42 62; www.hischibar.ch; Hinterdorfstrasse 44; ☺9.30pm-2am Fri & Sat) Squirrelled away in an old wooden chalet, wedged between 17th-century granaries and pig stalls on Zermatt's most photographed street, this bijou watering hole demands at least one late-night drink.

Elsie Bar   Wine Bar

(Map p80; ☎027 967 24 31; www.elsiebar.ch; Kirchplatz 16; ☺4pm-1am) In a building originally erected in 1879, this elegant, old-world wine bar with wood-panelled walls, across from the church, has been known as Elsie's

Bahnhofstrasse, outside Le Gitan – Zermatterstübli

since 1961. Oysters, caviar and snails are on the winter menu, along with a top selection of wine and whisky.

Papperla Pub   Pub

(Map p80; www.julen.ch; Steinmattstrasse 34; ⊙2pm-2am; 🛜) Rammed with sloshed skiers in winter and happy hikers in summer, this buzzing pub with red director chairs on its pavement terrace blends pulsating music with lethal Jägermeister bombs, good vibes and pub grub (from 5pm). Its downstairs **Schneewittli club** rocks until dawn in season.

🛈 INFORMATION

Tourist Office (Map p80; 🕾027 966 81 00; www. zermatt.ch; Bahnhofplatz 5; ⊙8.30am-6pm; 🛜) A wealth of information, with iPads to surf on and free wi-fi.

🛈 GETTING THERE & AWAY

CAR & MOTORBIKE

Zermatt is car-free. Motorists have to park in the **Matterhorn Terminal Täsch** (🕾027 967 12 14; www.matterhornterminal.ch; Täsch; per 24hr Sfr15.50) and ride the Zermatt Shuttle train (return adult/child Sfr16.80/8.40, 12 minutes, every 20 minutes from 6am to 9.40pm) the last 5km up to Zermatt. Täsch is 31km south of Visp.

TAXI

Electro-taxis zip around town, transporting goods and the weary. Pick one up at the main rank in front of the train station on Bahnhofstrasse.

TRAIN

All trains, including regular Matterhorn Gotthard Bahn service to Visp (Sfr37, 70 minutes) and Brig (Sfr38, 1½ hours), as well as the Glacier Express (p74) to/from St Moritz, terminate at the Bahnhof at Zermatt's northern edge.

ST MORITZ &
GRAUBÜNDEN

In This Chapter

St Moritz & Graubünden at a Glance...

Switzerland's original winter wonderland and the cradle of Alpine tourism, St Moritz has been luring royals and celebrities since 1864 with its shimmering aquamarine lake, emerald forests and aloof mountains. The surrounding canton of Graubünden is replete with other world-class resorts offering sensational skiing, including Davos and Klosters to the north.

Ask any local what makes Graubünden special and they'll likely wax lyrical about how wild it is. Wherever you go, the region's raw natural beauty begs outdoor escapades, reaching its zenith in the brooding Alpine grandeur of the wonderfully remote Swiss National Park.

Two Days in St Moritz & Graubünden

Begin day one with coffee and Engadine nut tart at **Hanselmann** (p99) in St Moritz' chic village centre; then head for the hills for a day of skiing, hiking, cycling or braving Celerina's hair-raising **Cresta Toboggan Run** (p91). Continue exploring St Moritz' mountain majesty on day two, or seek fresh Alpine perspectives in nearby **Davos** and **Klosters**.

Four Days in St Moritz & Graubünden

On day three, immerse yourself in the wild beauty of the **Swiss National Park** (p88). Stop first at the **Swiss National Park Centre** (p89) in Zernez to pick up maps and learn what guided hikes are on offer. On day four, hop aboard the **Glacier Express** (p74) or the **Bernina Express** (p101) for romantic visions of Graubünden's beauty through panoramic train windows.

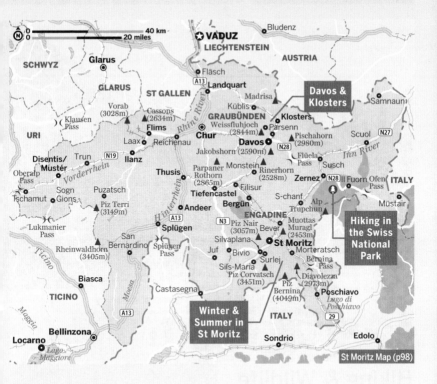

St Moritz Map (p98)

Arriving in St Moritz & Graubünden

St Moritz Train Station Trains run at least hourly from Zürich to St Moritz (Sfr77, three to 3½ hours), changing at Landquart or Chur. Between mid-December and late October, the celebrated Glacier Express makes its scenic eight-hour journey between St Moritz and Zermatt (one to three times daily).

Zürich Airport Take a direct train to Landquart or Chur and change for St Moritz (total journey time 3¾ hours).

Sleeping

St Moritz and surrounding resorts have plenty of quality accommodation, from hostels to family-run lodges to five-star hotels. Book early for the winter season. Rates drop up to 30% in summer, when many hotels throw in free mountain transport for guests. St Moritz virtually shuts down in the shoulder seasons.

Hiking & Wildlife in the Swiss National Park

A stunning collection of peaks, glaciers, woodlands, pastures, waterfalls, high moors and lakes, the Swiss National Park has been a refuge for nature gone wild since its inception in 1914.

Great For...

☑ **Don't Miss**

The excellent ranger-led hikes offered by the Swiss National Park Centre in Zernez.

Switzerland's First & Only National Park

Established more than a century ago, the **Swiss National Park** (www.nationalpark.ch) **FREE** was the Alps' first national park and is still the only protected area of its kind in Switzerland. Covering 172 sq km, the park remains true to its original conservation ethos, with the aim of protecting, researching and informing. Admission to the park and its car parks is free.

Given that nature has been left to its own devices here for a century, the Swiss National Park is a glimpse of the Alps before the dawn of tourism. There are some 80km of well-marked hiking trails, where, with a little luck and a decent pair of binoculars, ibex, chamois, marmots, deer, bearded vultures and golden eagles can be sighted.

❶ Need to Know

Public transport in the park is limited; plan ahead, or bring your own wheels.

✕ Take a Break

Hotel Parc Naziunal Il Fuorn (☐081 856 12 26; www.ilfuorn.ch; mains from Sfr21; ⏱closed Nov, 2nd half Jan & Easter-late Apr; ℗🛜) serves heart-warming Swiss comfort food in the heart of the national park.

★ Top Tip

Golden larches and rutting deer make autumn an engaging time to visit.

Conservation is paramount here, so stick to footpaths and respect regulations prohibiting camping, littering, lighting fires, cycling, and disturbing flora and fauna. Take only photographs, leave only footprints.

The Swiss National Park Centre

The **Swiss National Park Centre** (☐081 851 41 41; www.nationalpark.ch; exhibition adult/child Sfr7/3; ⏱8.30am-6pm Jun-Oct, 9am-noon & 2-5pm Nov-May) should be your first port of call for information on activities and accommodation. At this hands-on information centre in the village of **Zernez**, an audioguide gives you the low-down on conservation, wildlife and environmental change. Staff can provide details on hikes in the park, including the three-hour hike from S-chanf to Alp Trupchun (particularly popular in autumn, when you might spy rutting

deer) and the less strenuous, family-friendly Naturlehrpfad circuit near Il Fuorn, where bearded vultures can often be sighted. It sells an excellent 1:50,000 park map (Sfr14, or Sfr20 with guidebook), which covers 21 walks through the park.

Guided Tours

You can easily head off on your own, but you might get more out of one of the informative guided hikes (Sfr25) run by the centre from late June to mid-October. These include wildlife-spotting treks to the Val Trupchun and high-Alpine hikes to the Offenpass and Lakes of Macun. Most are in German, but many guides speak a little English. Book ahead by phone or at the park office in Zernez.

Getting to the Park

Postal bus 811 runs every hour or two from Zernez train station to Il Fuorn in the heart of the national park (Sfr9.80, 25 minutes). Zernez itself is a 45- to 55-minute train ride from St Moritz (Sfr19.60).

Winter & Summer in St Moritz

Switzerland's original winter wonderland, chic St Moritz has been packing in ski-season crowds since 1864. When the snow melts, everyone's focus shifts to warm-weather adventures, including hiking, kitesurfing and mountain biking.

Great For...

☑ Don't Miss

St Moritz' offbeat winter sports events, including snow polo and horse races on ice.

Winter Activities

Skiing in St Moritz is superb, with one ski pass covering a huge area of lifts and slopes around St Moritz village and the Engadine and Bernina valleys. Either stick close to town using the **Corviglia Funicular** to access the ski areas above St Moritz-Dorf or head further afield for a mind-boggling array of places to play on the snow. There's also an abundance of cross-country ski trails in the valleys.

The family-friendly ski area of Corviglia/Piz Nair, located above Celerina, is part of the St Moritz Ski Resorts group with the glizty, royal-welcoming village just a three-minute train ride away.

St Moritz Ski Resorts

With 350km of slopes, ultramodern lifts and spirit-soaring views, skiing in St Moritz is second to none, especially for confident

Skiing, St Moritz

ⓘ Need to Know

Switzerland's two most scenic train routes, the Glacier Express and the Bernina Express, intersect in St Moritz.

✕ Take a Break

Tuck into fondue or raclette at Gondolezza (p100), a ski gondola-turned-restaurant in Pontresina.

★ Top Tip

Summer hotel guests staying two nights or more travel free on local cable cars, chairlifts and funiculars.

is a must-ski for freeriders and fans of jaw-dropping descents.

Schweizer Skischule

The first **Swiss ski school** (Map p98; ☏081 830 01 01; www.skischool.ch; Via Stredas 14; ⏰8am-noon & 2-6pm Mon-Sat, 8-9am & 4-6pm Sun) was founded in St Moritz in 1929. Today you can arrange skiing or snowboarding lessons here – check out the website for details.

Celerina Bob Run

Celerina is synonymous with its 1722m Olympic **bobsleigh run** (☏081 830 02 00; www.olympia-bobrun.ch), which is the world's oldest, dating to 1904, and made from natural ice. A hair-raising 75-second,135km/h guest ride costs a cool Sfr250, but the buzz is priceless. Don't worry, you'll be safely ensconced between a pilot and a brakeman.

Cresta Run

Celerina's heart-stopping, head-first 1km tobogganing course, **Cresta Run** (www.cresta-run.com) was created by British visitors in 1885. A set of five rides, including

intermediates. The general ski pass covers all the slopes, including Silvaplana, Sils-Maria, Celerina, Zuoz, Pontresina and Diavolezza.

If cross-country skiing is more your scene, you can glide across plains and through woods on 220km of groomed trails.

For groomed slopes with big mountain vistas, head to **Corviglia** (2486m), accessible by funicular from St Moritz-Dorf. From St Moritz-Bad a cable car goes to **Signal** (shorter queues), giving access to the slopes of Piz Nair. Above nearby Silvaplana, there's varied skiing at **Corvatsch** (3303m), including spectacular glacier descents and the gentle black run Hahnensee, all served by the **Corvatsch 3303 cable car** (☏081 838 73 73; www.corvatsch.ch; Via dal Corvatsch; return adult/child Sfr60/30) and offering unbelievable vistas. Silhouetted by glaciated 4000ers, **Diavolezza** (2978m)

tuition, costs Sfr600 (and Sfr51 per ride thereafter). This is different from a bob-sleigh run. Here, the rider goes down alone, in a head-first lying position, using rakes on the end of special boots to brake and steer.

Snow Polo World Cup

In late January, St Moritz' frozen lake is the centre of attention for the **Snow Polo World Cup** (www.snowpolo-stmoritz.com).

WhiteTurf

Jockeys saddle up for horse races on ice at the **WhiteTurf** (www.whiteturf.ch) in February.

Summer Activities

In summer, get out and stride one of the region's excellent hiking trails, such as the Corvatsch *Wasserweg* (water trail) linking six mountain lakes. Soaring above St Moritz, **Piz Nair** (3057m) commands views of the jewel-coloured lakes that necklace the valley below. For head-spinning views of the Pers glacier and the Bernina Alps, tack-le the vertiginous, 2½-hour **Piz Trovat** *via ferrata* (route with fixed cables and rungs) at Diavolezza; equipment hire is available at the base station. The tourist office has a map providing more suggestions (in English) for walking in Oberengadin.

Muottas Muragi to Pontresina Hike

Save this spectacular hike, known as the Climate Trail, for a good day. It involves taking the Muottas Muragl Bahn funicular up to Punt Muragl at 2454m, then hiking across the mountains above Pontresina to Alp Languard (2330m), then taking the chairlift down into Pontresina. There are 18 information boards along the 9km route, which will take around 2½ to three hours.

Piz Nair

Murtel to Val Roseg Hike

For a superb day hike, ride the Corvatsch cable cars to 3303m, check out the views, then return down to the mid-station of Murtèl (2702m). Hike east for 45 minutes to Fuorcla Surlej (2760m), the hut you can see on the ridge line. From there, it's a 1½-hour hike down to Hotel Roseg Gletscher in the Roseg Valley.

From there, either walk (1½ hours) or take a horse-drawn carriage (50 minutes) out to Pontresina station, 10 minutes by bus or train from St Moritz.

🏃 Don't Miss

St Moritz hosts the notoriously gruelling Engadine Ski Marathon (www.engadin-skimarathon.ch) in early March, when cross-country skiers skate 42km from Maloja to S-chanf.

BRIGITTE BLATTLER/SHUTTERSTOCK ©

Clean Energy Tour

Beginning at Piz Nair, this 2½-hour **hike** (www.clean-energy.ch) presents different kinds of renewable energy in natural settings. You'll hike down from Chantarella along the flower-speckled Heidi Blumenweg, then along Schellenursliweg past Lord Norman Foster's wood-tiled **Chesa Futura** (Map p98; www.fosterandpartners.com/projects/chesa-futura; Via Tinus 25). Built between 2000 and 2004, this ecofriendly 'House of the Future' is an apartment building of breathtaking architectural design, once described as 'a massive pumpkin'.

Biking in St Moritz

The St Moritz region is exhilarating biking terrain, criss-crossed by 400km of trails. One of the finest routes is the five-hour **Suvretta Loop** at Corviglia, taking in forests and meadows en route to the Suvretta Pass (2615m), before making a spectacular descent to Bever. You can hire mountain bikes, e-bikes and children's bikes from **Engadin Bikes** (📞081 828 98 88; www.engadinbikes.com; Via dal Bagn 1, St Moritz; ⊙8.30am-12.30pm & 1.30-6.30pm Mon-Fri, to 5.30pm Sat).

Kitesurfing in Silvaplana

Only 5km southwest of St Moritz, the lively resort village of Silvaplana (Silvaplauna in Romansch) is a gorgeous place to play. Thanks to its startlingly turquoise, wind-buffeted lake, Silvaplanasee, it's renowned as a kitesurfing and windsurfing mecca, and brightly coloured kites and sails dot the lake once the weather warms up a bit. Slip into a wetsuit at **Kite Sailing School Silvaplana** (📞081 828 97 67; www.kitesailing.ch; Silvaplana; intro/2-day/5-day course Sfr190/350/800; ⊙9am-6.30pm), which offers equipment hire and has introductory lessons.

★ Top Tip

St Moritz has some of the top restaurants in the Alps. If you're on a budget, you might want to spend more time in St Moritz-Bad than St Moritz-Dorf.

Davos & Klosters

These neighbouring resorts are a study in contrasts. Davos, known for its après-ski parties and monster ski runs, is more cool than quaint, while nearby Klosters seduces slaloming celebrities with its picture-postcard looks.

Great For...

☑ Don't Miss

In August, don't miss Davos' traditional *Schwingen* (Swiss wrestling; p99) competition.

Skiing in Davos & Klosters

Davos and Klosters share 320km of **ski runs** (www.davos.ch; Regional Pass 2/6 days Sfr139/332), and some glorious off-piste terrain. They operate together, but if you're staying in Davos, the Jakobshorn lifts on the south side of the valley are superb. Also on the south side is family-friendly Rinerhorn.

On the north side, **Parsenn**, with a huge variety of terrain, is accessible from both Davos and Klosters. The vast area reaches as high as Weissfluhjoch (2844m), from where you can ski to Küblis, more than 2000m lower and 12km away. **Schatzalp/Strela** focuses on 'decelerated' skiing on gentle slopes. It's all magnificent!

If you're staying in Klosters, **Madrisa**, up the eastern side of the valley, is family-friendly, with long, sunny runs, mostly above the treeline.

Parasailing over Davos

❶ Need to Know
From St Moritz, the 1½-hour ride to Davos or Klosters requires a change of train.

✖ Take a Break
Feast on fondue or rösti on the sunny terrace at Strela-Alp (p100), atop the Schatzalp funicular.

★ Top Tip
A Davos Klosters regional pass lets you ski carefree on every slope in the area.

Davos' **Schweizer Schneesportschule** (☑081 416 24 54; www.ssd.ch; Promenade 157) is one of the best ski schools in the country.

Sleigh Rides & Tobogganing
When the flakes are falling, nothing beats a **horse-drawn sleigh ride** (☑081 422 18 73; www.pferdekutschen.ch; Doggilochstrasse 1), organised through Klosters' tourist office; expect to pay around Sfr80 per hour. Kid-friendly winter activities include the bumpy downhill **toboggan run** (Madrisa; day ticket adult Sfr37, child Sfr15-26; ⊙8.15am-4pm Dec-Apr) from Madrisa to Saaseralp.

Mountain Biking
Intrepid souls can test their skills on the tables, curves and jumps of **Davos Bike Park** (☑081 416 18 68; www.davos.ch/bikepark; Flüelastrasse; ⊙dawn-dusk Jul-Oct). For more thrills, try the **Gotschna Freeride** (www.davos.ch/en/

summer/activities/bike/mountain-bike/gotschna-freeride; ⊙Jun-Oct), a breathtakingly steep 5.7km trail from Gotschna middle station to Klosters; with more than 200 banked curves, jumps and waves, it's freeride heaven.

Adventure Sports
Daredevils eager to leap off Jakobshorn or Gotschnagrat can book tandem flights (Sfr175) at **Luftchraft – Flugschule Davos** (☑079 623 19 70; www.luftchraft.ch; Mattas-trasse 9), a reputable Davos paragliding outfitter. Tailor your own white-water rafting or canyoning adventure with Klosters' **R&M Adventure** (☑079 384 29 36; www.ramadventure.ch; Landstrasse 171).

Swimming
In Klosters, enjoy views of the Silvretta Alps as you splash at **Strandbad Klosters** (Doggilochstrasse 51; adult/child Sfr7/5; ⊙9am-7pm May-Sep), a heated outdoor pool complete with kids' play area, volleyball court and climbing wall suspended above the diving pool. In Davos, try **Eau-là-là** (www.eau-la-la.ch; Promenade 90; pool adult/child Sfr10/7, day spa Sfr28; ⊙10am-10pm Mon-Sat, to 6pm Sun), a leisure centre with heated outdoor pools, kids' areas and a spa with mountain views.

Walking Tour: Valleys & Lakes

This highly rewarding day walk leads from the main valley of the Engadine into the lakeland of the Macun Basin.

Start Lavin
End Zernez
Distance 16km
Duration 7½ to 8½ hours

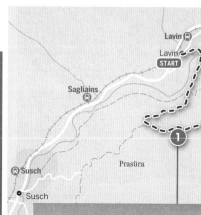

1 From Lavin, cross the En (Inn) River and twist up to **Plan Surücha** (1577m).

7 Traverse coniferous forest via La Rosta and God Baselgia, emerging into grassy fields above **Zernez**.

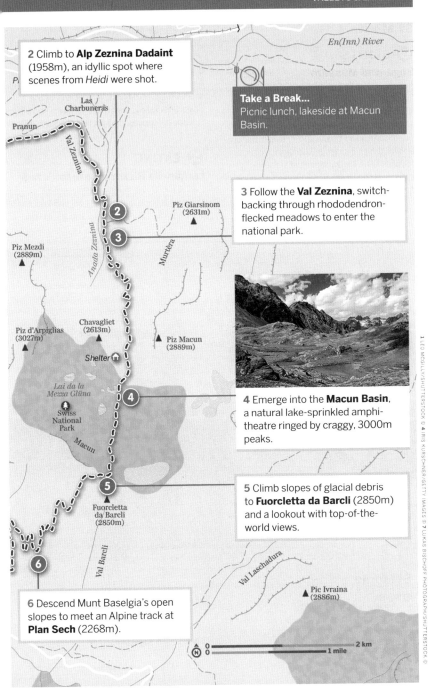

En(Inn) River

2 Climb to **Alp Zeznina Dadaint** (1958m), an idyllic spot where scenes from *Heidi* were shot.

Las Charbuneras

Pranun

Val Zeznina

Take a Break...
Picnic lunch, lakeside at Macun Basin.

Piz Giarsinom (2631m) ▲

Anada Zeznina

Murtera

3 Follow the **Val Zeznina**, switch-backing through rhododendron-flecked meadows to enter the national park.

Piz Mezdi (2889m) ▲

Piz d'Arpiglias (3027m) ▲

Chavagliet (2613m) ▲

Piz Macun (2889m) ▲

Shelter

Lai da la Mezza Glüna

Swiss National Park

Macun

4 Emerge into the **Macun Basin**, a natural lake-sprinkled amphi-theatre ringed by craggy, 3000m peaks.

5 Climb slopes of glacial debris to **Fuorcletta da Barcli** (2850m) and a lookout with top-of-the-world views.

Fuorcletta da Barcli (2850m)

Val Barcli

Val Laschadura

Pic Ivraina (2886m) ▲

6 Descend Munt Baselgia's open slopes to meet an Alpine track at **Plan Sech** (2268m).

0   2 km
0   1 mile

Ⓝ

1 LEO MCGILLY/SHUTTERSTOCK © 4 IRIS KURSCHNER/GETTY IMAGES © 7 LUKAS BISCHOFF PHOTOGRAPHY/SHUTTERSTOCK ©

St Moritz

⊙ SIGHTS

Segantini Museum   Museum

(Map p98; www.segantini-museum.ch; Via Somplaz 30; adult/child Sfr10/3; ☉10am-noon & 2-6pm Tue-Sun, closed 20 Oct-10 Dec & 20 Apr-20 May) Housed in an eye-catching stone building topped by a cupola, this museum shows the paintings of Giovanni Segantini (1858–99). The Italian artist beautifully captured the dramatic light and ambience of the Alps on canvas.

Engadiner Museum   Museum

(Map p98; ☏081 833 43 33; www.engadiner-museum.ch; Via dal Bagn 39; adult/child Sfr13/free; ☉10am-6pm Wed-Mon 20 May-20 Oct, 2-6pm Dec-Apr) For a peek at the archetypal dwellings and humble interiors of the Engadine Valley, visit this museum showing traditional stoves and archaeological finds.

⊗ EATING

Laudinella Pizzeria Caruso Pizza $

(☏081 836 06 29; www.laudinella.ch; Via Tegiatscha 17; pizza from Sfr13.50; ☉noon-2am; ⊕) Pizza lovers rave about the thin-crust

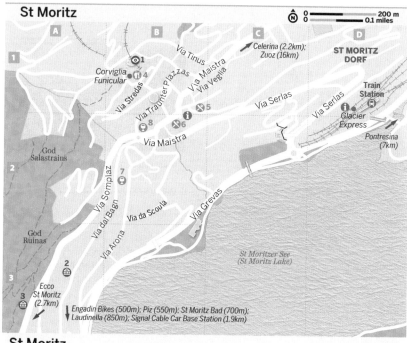

St Moritz

⊙ Sights

Neapolitan numbers that fly out of the
wood-oven at Hotel Laudinella's pizzeria,
which range from a simple Margherita to
the gourmet Domenico with truffles and
beef. Laudinella also offers delivery service.

Hanselmann
Cafe $

(Map p98; ☑081 833 38 64; www.hanselmann.
ch; Via Maistra 8; pastries & cakes Sfr3-6, snacks
& light meals Sfr12-24; ☺7.30am-7pm) You
can't miss the lavishly frescoed facade
of St Moritz' celebrated bakery and tea
room, famous for its caramel-rich, walnut-
studded Engadine nut tart.

Chesa Veglia
Italian $$$

(Map p98; ☑081 837 28 00; www.badruttspalace.
com; Via Veglia 2; pizza/mains from Sfr25/45;
☺noon-11.30pm) This slate-roofed, chalk-
white chalet restaurant dates from 1658.
The softly lit interior is all warm pine and
creaking wood floors, while the terrace
affords lake and mountain views. Go for
pizza or regional specialities such as *Bünd-
ner Gerstensuppe* (creamy barley soup)
and venison medallions with *Spätzli* (egg
noodles).

Ecco St Moritz
Italian $$$

(☑081 836 63 00; www.giardino-mountain.ch;
Giardino Mountain, Champfèr; menus Sfr190-240;
☺7pm-midnight Wed-Sun) The pinnacle of St
Moritz' dining scene, Ecco St Moritz is where
chef Rolf Fliegauf gives flight to culinary fantasy when the flakes fall in winter. A sublime
gold-and-white interior is the backdrop for
exquisitely presented dishes with strong, as-
sured flavours that revolve around primary
ingredients – Wagyu beef and horseradish,
lime, caramel, fig and the like.

DRINKING & NIGHTLIFE
Roo Bar
Bar

(Map p98; ☑081 837 50 50; www.facebook.
com/RooBarStMoritz; Via Traunter Plazzas 7;
☺2-10pm) Snow bums fill the terrace of this
après-ski joint at Hauser's Hotel. Hip-hop,
techno and hot chocolate laced with rum
fuel the party.

 **Extreme Sports,
Swiss-style**

Swiss craziness peaks in August at
Sertig Schwinget near Davos, where
Schwingen (Swiss wrestling) champs
do battle in the sawdust. See www.
davos.ch for details.

Schwingen match
MARTIN LEHMANN/SHUTTERSTOCK ©

Bobby's Pub
Pub

(Map p98; ☑081 834 42 83; www.bobbys-pub.ch;
Via dal Bagn 50a; ☺9am-1am Mon-Fri, 11am-1am
Sat, noon-1am Sun) This friendly English-style
watering hole serves 20 different international brews and is one of the few places
open year-round.

ℹ INFORMATION

The main **tourist office** (Map p98; ☑081 837 33
33; www.stmoritz.ch; Via Maistra 12; ☺9am-
6.30pm Mon-Fri, to 6pm Sat) is in St Moritz-Dorf,
but if you're coming by train, visit the **sub-office**
(Map p98; St Moritz train station; ☺10am-2pm &
3-6.30pm) in the train station.

ℹ GETTING THERE & AWAY

Regular SBB trains run at least hourly from
Zürich to St Moritz (Sfr77, three to 3½ hours),
with one change (at Landquart or Chur).

Two of Switzerland's most celebrated scenic
trains, the Glacier Express (p74) to Zermatt and
the Bernina Express (p101) between Chur and
Tirano, also both stop in at St Moritz.

Alp Grüm station on the Bernina Express railway

Pontresina

At the mouth of Val Bernina, Pontresina is a low-key alternative resort to St Moritz, only 8km away. It's a brilliant place to stay, especially if you are into the outdoors.

To sit in a former gondola car and dine out on top-notch fondue, head up to the back of Pontresina to find **Gondolezza** (081 839 36 26; www.hotelsteinbock.ch/en/kulinarik/en-gondolezza; Via Maistra 219; fondue from Sfr29/32; ☺from 5pm winter, 2pm summer) and its accompanying terrace.

Davos

◉ SIGHTS

Kirchner Museum   Museum
(081 410 63 00; www.kirchnermuseum.ch; Promenade 82; adult/child Sfr12/5; ☺11am-6pm Tue-Sun) This giant cube of a museum showcases the world's largest Ernst Ludwig Kirchner (1880–1938) collection. The German expressionist painted extraordinary scenes of the area. When the Nazis classified Kirchner as a 'degenerate artist' and emptied galleries of

his works, he was overcome with despair and took his own life in 1938.

🍴 EATING

Kaffee Klatsch   Cafe $
(☑081 413 30 16; Promenade 72; light meals from Sfr19; ☺7.30am-9pm Mon-Sat, 8am-9pm Sun, shorter hours in low season) ♪ Mellow music creates a relaxed feel in this arty cafe. Try the delicious homemade Swiss muesli for breakfast, or stop by for cake with a speciality coffee like vanilla bean or Heidi latte (made with roasted organic oats).

Strela-Alp   Swiss $
(☑081 413 56 83; www.schatzalp.ch; Schatzalp; mains from Sfr17; ☺9am-6pm Jul–mid-Oct, to 5pm mid-Oct–Jun; 👪) Expansive mountain views, a sunny terrace and Swiss grub, like rösti and fondue, await at this rustic haunt, a 10-minute walk from Schatzalp funicular top station. This is a superb spot to come for lunch.

Montana Stube   Swiss $$
(☑081 420 71 77; www.montanastube.ch; Bahnhofstrasse 2, Davos Dorf; mains from Sfr24;

⊗5-11pm Wed-Sat; 🎿) Warm and woody, the Montana Stube is a convivial spot for dinner in Davos Dorf. Heavy on the meat and cheese, the menu is Swiss through and through. The fondue chinoise is highly recommended.

🍷 DRINKING

Jatzhütte   Bar

(☎081 413 73 61; www.jatzhuette.ch; Jakobshorn; ⊗from 2.30pm) Perched at 2560m at the top of Jakobshorn, this is Davos' wackiest après-ski joint. Those who dare to partially bare can soak in a 39°C whirlpool framed by icy peaks. Or take your ski boots grooving inside.

Mountain's Akt   Bar

(☎079 829 79 16; www.facebook.com/mountains akt; Promenade 64; ⊗3pm-1am Tue-Thu & Sun, to 4am Fri & Sat; 🛜) DJs spin house and electro at the weekend at this funky bar. There's a great selection of beers from Kilkenny to Leffe. The summer beer garden becomes a snow bar in winter.

ℹ INFORMATION

Tourist Office (☎081 415 21 21; www.davos. ch; Tourismus- und Sportzentrum, Talstrasse 41; ⊗8.30am-6pm Mon-Fri, 1-5pm Sat, 9am-1pm Sun) The most central branch of the tourist office is in Davos Platz. It's well stocked.

ℹ GETTING THERE & AWAY

For trains to Zürich (Sfr28, 2½ hours), change at Landquart. For St Moritz (Sfr30, 1½ hours), take the train at Davos Platz and change at Filisur.

Klosters

No matter whether you come in summer to hike in the flower-speckled mountains or in winter when the log chalets are veiled in snow and icicle-hung – Klosters is postcard stuff. Indeed, the village has attracted a host of slaloming celebrities and royals with its gorgeous looks and paparazzi-free slopes.

Bernina Express

One of Switzerland's most spectacular train rides, the **Bernina Express** (www. berninaexpress.ch; one-way Chur–Tirano Sfr64; ⊗mid-May–early Dec) connects the German- and Italian-speaking regions of Graubünden, climbing high into the glaciated realms of the Alps and traversing 55 tunnels and 196 bridges on its four-hour journey from Chur to St Moritz to Tirano. The Thusis–Tirano section is a Unesco World Heritage Site. From Tirano, a connecting bus (Sfr34) continues west to Lugano in the Italian-speaking canton of Ticino.

Kaffee Klatsch Easy   Cafe $

(☎081 422 66 30; www.kaffeeklatsch-klosters. ch; Bahnhofstrasse 8; lunch mains from Sfr16.50; ⊗8am-6pm Mon-Sat; 🛜) Catchy Kaffee Klatsch has two operations in Klosters, with Easy, next to the Co-op on Bahnhofstrasse, being a cafe, open during the day for breakfast, lunch, snacks and divine desserts. Everything is homemade. **Kaffee Klatsch Lounge** (Gotschnastrasse 21; lunch mains from Sfr11.90), on the other side of the tracks next to the Goschna Ski Lift, is open 8.30am to 6pm Friday to Sunday.

ℹ INFORMATION

Tourist Office (☎081 410 20 20; www.davos.ch/ klosters; Alte Bahnhofstrasse 6; ⊗8.30am-noon & 2-6pm Mon-Fri, 9am-5pm Sat, 9am-1pm Sun) Located in the centre of the village.

ℹ GETTING THERE & AROUND

Klosters is on the same train route between Landquart and Filisur as Davos. Klosters and Davos are linked by free buses for those with Guest Cards or ski passes.

CENTRAL
SWITZERLAND

In This Chapter

Central Switzerland at a Glance...

To the Swiss, Central Switzerland – green, mountainous and soothingly beautiful – is the country's geographical, political and spiritual heartland, where hero William Tell gave a rebel yell against Habsburg rule and the Confoederatio Helvetica's founding document was signed in 1291.

The region's focal point is Lake Lucerne: enigmatic in the cold mist of morning, molten gold in the dusky half-light. The dreamy city of Lucerne is small enough for old-world charm yet big enough to harbour designer hotels and world-class artworks. From here, cruise across to lakeside resorts such as Weggis and Brunnen, hike Mt Pilatus and Mt Rigi, or head to Engelberg for powdery off-piste perfection.

Two Days in Central Switzerland

Start day one in classic style, strolling across **Kapellbrücke** (p106), Lucerne's flower-bedecked covered bridge, and wandering among the painted facades of the old town. Afterwards, cruise across the lake and spend the afternoon exploring the **Verkehrshaus** (p107), Lucerne's family-friendly transport museum. On day two, visit other top city-centre attractions, including the **Sammlung Rosengart** (p107) art museum and the captivating **Lion Monument** (p108).

Four Days in Central Switzerland

Spread out and explore the lake on day three. If the weather's clear, make a beeline for the summit of **Mt Pilatus** (p110), **Mt Rigi** (p111) or **Stanserhorn** (p110). Otherwise, cruise across the lake to genteel Weggis or the **Swiss Knife Valley Museum** (p121) in Brunnen. On day four, take a train to **Engelberg** to discover glaciated **Mt Titlis** (p112), whose surrounding meadows have inspired countless Bollywood love scenes.

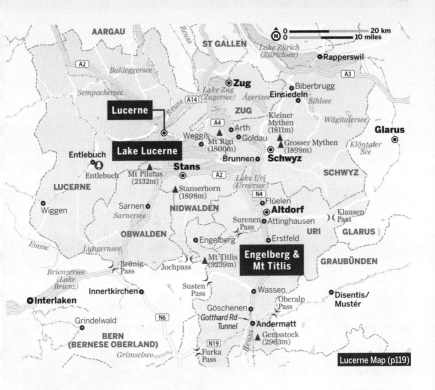

AARGAU

Reuss

ST GALLEN

Lake Zürich
(Zürichsee)

Rapperswil

0   20 km
0   10 miles

A2

Baldeggersee

Sempachersee

A3

Zug

Biberbrugg

Lake Zug
(Zugersee)   Ägerisee   Einsiedeln

Sihlsee

A14

Lucerne

ZUG

Wägitalersee

Kleiner
Mythen
(1811m)

A4   Arth

Weggis   ▲   Goldau
Mt Rigi
(1800m)

Grosser Mythen
(1898m)

Klöntaler
See

Glarus

Lake Lucerne

Entlebuch

Brunnen   **Schwyz**

Entlebuch   ▲ Mt Pilatus
(2132m)   **Stans**   A2   Lake Uri
(Urnersee)   **SCHWYZ**

LUCERNE

Stans

▲ Stanserhorn
(1898m)   N4   Flüelen

Wiggen   Sarnen   **NIDWALDEN**   **Altdorf**   Klausen
Pass

Sarnersee   Surenen   Attinghausen
Pass   **URI**   **GLARUS**

OBWALDEN   Engelberg   Erstfeld

Emme   Lungernsee   ▲ Mt Titlis
(3239m)   **Engelberg &
Mt Titlis**

Brienzersee
(Lake
Brienz)   Brünig
Pass   Jochpass   **GRAUBÜNDEN**

Innertkirchen   Susten
Pass   Wassen   Disentis/
Mustér

Interlaken   Oberalp
Pass

Göschenen

Grindelwald   N6   Gotthard Rd
Tunnel   Andermatt

**BERN
(BERNESE OBERLAND)**   N19   Gemsstock
(2963m)

Grimselsee   Furka
Pass

Reuss

Lucerne Map (p119)

Arriving in Central Switzerland

Air The nearest major airport is Zürich, with frequent train connections to Lucerne (Sfr30, 65 minutes).

Train Lucerne is the regional transport hub, served regularly by trains from other Swiss cities including Interlaken, Bern, Lugano and Zürich.

Sleeping

Central Switzerland is easy to get around, and Lucerne, at the centre of the action, is the most convenient home base. There are wonderful lodging options, both for those with deep pockets and those on a budget, but book early, especially once June rolls around. The ski resorts are full-on in winter, less so once the snow melts.

Lucerne

Recipe for a gorgeous Swiss city: take a cobalt, mountain-fringed lake, add a well-preserved medieval Old Town, and sprinkle with covered bridges, sunny plazas, candy-coloured houses and waterfront promenades. Voilà!

Great For...

☑ **Don't Miss**

Inseli, Lucerne's beloved lakeside park, where half the town lounges on a sunny day.

Kapellbrücke

You haven't really been to Lucerne until you have strolled the creaky 14th-century **Kapellbrücke** (Chapel Bridge; Map p119), spanning the Reuss River in the Old Town. The octagonal water tower is original, but its gabled roof is a modern reconstruction, rebuilt after a disastrous fire in 1993. As you cross the bridge, note Heinrich Wägmann's 17th-century triangular roof panels, showing events from Swiss history and mythology. The icon is at its most photogenic when bathed in soft golden light at dusk.

Spreuerbrücke

Downriver from Kapellbrücke, this 1408 **bridge** (Map p119; btwn Kasernenplatz & Mühlenplatz) is dark and small but entirely original. Lore has it that this was the only bridge where Lucerne's medieval villagers

🛈 Need to Know

Lucerne's train station and ferry boat dock are conveniently located a few paces apart.

✖ Take a Break

Break for snacks and drinks at Luz Seebistro (p119), a fin-de-siècle boathouse on the lakeshore.

★ Top Tip

Lucerne's old town abounds in elegantly adorned facades; look for the golden pretzel outside the baker's guild.

collection are some 200 photographs by David Douglas Duncan, documenting the last 17 years of Picasso's life.

Verkehrshaus

A great kid-pleaser, the fascinating interactive **Verkehrshaus** (Swiss Museum of Transport; ☑0900 333 456; www.verkehrshaus. ch; Lidostrasse 5; adult/child Sfr30/15; ☉10am-6pm Apr-Oct, to 5pm Nov-Mar; 🚼) is deservedly Switzerland's most popular museum. Alongside rockets, steam locomotives, aeroplanes, vintage cars and dugout canoes are hands-on activities, such as pedalo boats, flight simulators, broadcasting studios and a walkable 1:20,000-scale map of Switzerland.

The museum also shelters a **planetarium** (www.verkehrshaus.ch/en/planetarium; adult/child Sfr15/9; ☉hours vary), Switzerland's largest **3D cinema** (www.filmtheater.ch; adult/child Sfr18/14) and the **Swiss Chocolate Adventure** (www.verkehrshaus.ch/en/swiss-chocolate-adventure; adult/child Sfr15/9), a 20-minute ride that whirls visitors through multimedia exhibits on the origins, history, production

were allowed to throw *Spreu* (chaff) and leaves into the river. Here, the roof panels consist of artist Caspar Meglinger's movie-storyboard-style sequence of paintings, *The Dance of Death*, showing how the plague affected all levels of society.

Sammlung Rosengart

Lucerne's blockbuster cultural attraction is the **Sammlung Rosengart** (Map p119; ☑041 220 16 60; www.rosengart.ch; Pilatusstrasse 10; adult/child Sfr18/10; ☉10am-6pm), occupying a graceful neoclassical pile in the heart of town. It showcases the outstanding stash of Angela Rosengart, a Swiss art dealer and close friend of Picasso. Alongside works by the great Spanish master are paintings and sketches by Klee, Cézanne, Renoir, Chagall, Kandinsky, Miró, Matisse, Modigliani and Monet, among others. Complementing this

and distribution of chocolate, from Ghana to Switzerland and beyond.

The museum is 10 minutes from the city centre – take bus 6, 8 or 24, or an S3 train to the Verkehrshaus stop, or, better yet, take a boat opposite the train station and disembark at Verkehrshaus-Lido.

Lion Monument

By far the most touching of the 19th-century sights that lured so many British to Lucerne is the **Lion Monument** (Löwendenkmal; Denkmalstrasse). Lukas Ahorn carved this 10m-long sculpture of a dying lion into the rock face in 1820 to commemorate Swiss soldiers who died defending King Louis XVI during the French Revolution. Mark Twain once called it the 'saddest and most moving piece of rock in the world'. For Narnia fans, it often evokes Aslan at the stone table.

Gletschergarten

Next door to the Lion Monument, the **Gletschergarten** (Glacier Garden; ☎041 410 43 40; www.gletschergarten.ch; Denkmalstrasse 4; adult/child Sfr15/8; ☉9am-6pm Apr-Oct, 10am-5pm Nov-Mar; 🚼) houses a strip of rock bearing the scars (including huge potholes) inflicted on it by the glacier that slid over it some 20 million years ago. Kids of all ages and devotees of kitsch will love getting lost in the mirror maze inspired by Spain's Alhambra Palace.

Kultur und Kongresszentrum

French architect Jean Nouvel's waterfront arts and **convention centre** (KKL; ☎041 226 79 50; www.kkl-luzern.ch; Europaplatz; guided tour adult/child Sfr15/9; ☉ticket counter 9am-6.30pm Mon-Fri, 10am-4pm Sat) is a postmodern jaw-dropper in an otherwise historic city. Inside, the narrow concert hall, partly

Lion Monument

built below the lake's surface, is surrounded by a reverberation chamber and has an adjustable suspended ceiling, creating near-perfect acoustics. Countless accolades showered upon the hall have raised the profile of the **Lucerne Festival** (☏041 226 44 00; www.lucernefestival.ch), increasingly a highlight on the global music calendar. Check the website for opening hours.

Museggmauer

For a bird's-eye view over Lucerne's rooftops to the glittering lake and mountains

---

⚜ Don't Miss

Lucerne's world-class music festival is divided into three separate 'seasons': Easter, summer and 'at the Piano' (in November). Concerts take place all around town.

WALKINGMAP/SHUTTERSTOCK ©

beyond, wander along the top of the old city walls that date back to 1386. A walkway is open between the **Schirmerturm** (Map p119), where you enter, and the **Wachturm** (Map p119), from where you have to retrace your steps. You can also ascend and descend the **Zytturm** (Map p119) or **Männliturm** (Map p119) FREE; the latter is further west and not connected to the ramparts walkway.

Strandbad Lido

Perfect for a splash or sunbathe is this **lakefront beach** (☏041 370 38 06; www.lido-luzern.ch; Lidostrasse 6a; adult/child Sfr7/4; ⏰9am-8pm Jun-Aug, 10am-7pm May & Sep) with a playground, volleyball court and heated outdoor pool near Camping Lido. Alternatively, swim for free on the lake's opposite shore in Seepark, off Alpenquai.

Bourbaki Panorama

Edouard Castres' painstakingly detailed 1100-sq-metre **circular painting** (☏041 412 30 30; www.bourbakipanorama.ch; Löwenplatz 11; adult/child Sfr12/7; ⏰9am-6pm Apr-Oct, 10am-5pm Nov-Mar) depicting the internment of French troops in Switzerland after the Franco–Prussian War of 1870–71 is accompanied by a moving narrative (with written English translation).

Historisches Museum

Lucerne's **history museum** (History Museum; Map p119; ☏041 228 54 24; www.historischesmuseum.lu.ch; Pfistergasse 24; adult/child Sfr10/5; ⏰10am-5pm Tue-Sun) is cleverly organised into a series of attention-grabbing themed sections, each interpreted in German or English with the help of a barcode-reading audioguide.

★ Top Tip

SNG (Map p119; ☏041 368 08 08; www.sng.ch; Alpenquai 11; pedalo/motorboat/pontoon boat per hr from Sfr30/60/90) ⚓ rents out boats and offers reasonably priced 60-minute lake cruises (adult/child Sfr19/10).

Lake Lucerne

This gorgeous lake at the very heart of Switzerland offers up a tapestry of green hillsides, shimmering cobalt waters, majestic peaks, and tucked-away lakeside resorts, all accessible by boat.

Great For...

☑ Don't Miss

Climbing Mt Pilatus aboard the world's steepest cog railway, with gradients up to 48%.

Mt Pilatus

Rearing above Lucerne from the southwest, and accessed by the world's steepest cog railway, Mt Pilatus (www.pilatus.ch) makes an unforgettable, scenic day excursion. The mountain rose to fame in the 19th-century when Wagner waxed lyrical about its Alpine vistas and Queen Victoria trotted up here on horseback. Legend has it that this 2132m peak was named after Pontius Pilate, whose corpse was thrown into a lake on its summit and whose restless ghost has haunted its heights ever since. It's more likely that the moniker derives from the Latin word *pileatus*, meaning 'cloud covered' – as the mountain frequently is.

Stanserhorn

Looming above the lake, 1898m Stanserhorn (www.stanserhorn.ch) boasts

Weggis

❶ Need to Know

SGV's scenic **cruises** (Map p119; www.lakelucerne.ch) are ideal for navigating the lake – and free for Swiss Pass holders.

✕ Take a Break

Savour snacks and jaw-dropping vistas on the Rigi Kulm Hotel's outdoor terrace atop Mt Rigi.

★ Top Tip

Lake Lucerne's mesmerising light and landscapes figure prominently in Turner paintings such as *The Bay of Uri from Brunnen* (1841).

360-degree vistas of Lake Lucerne, Mt Titlis and Mt Pilatus and other surrounding mountains. Getting to the summit is half the fun. It involves a vintage 1893 funicular followed by a state-of-the-art double-decker cable car with an open upper deck. Up top, 'Stanserhorn Rangers' point out what is going on, including marmot-viewing and a geo-trail.

Mt Rigi

Turner couldn't quite make up his mind about how he preferred 1797m Rigi (www.rigi.ch), so in 1842 the genius painted the mountain in three different lights to reflect its changing moods. On a clear day, there are impressive views to a jagged spine of peaks including Mt Titlis and the Jungfrau giants. To the north and west, you overlook Arth-Goldau and Zugersee, which curves around until it almost joins Küssnacht and an arm of Lake Lucerne. Sunrises and sunsets viewed from Rigi's summit are the stuff of bucket lists.

Weggis

Sheltered from cold northerlies by Mt Rigi, Weggis enjoys a mild climate, sprouting a few palm and fig trees by the lakefront. With many lakeside hotels and resorts, Weggis makes an excellent place to stay, but most visitors come through while on a day excursion to Mt Rigi from Lucerne.

Brunnen

Tucked into the folds of mountains, where Lake Lucerne and Lake Uri meet at right angles, Brunnen enjoys mesmerising views south and west. As the local *föhn* wind rushes down from the mountains, it creates perfect conditions for sailing, paragliding, windsurfing and kitesurfing. When the wind is up, brightly coloured sails come out. And don't forget the folkloric hot air of the weekly alpenhorn concerts in summer.

Engelberg & Mt Titlis

Framed by the glacial bulk of Mt Titlis – Central Switzerland's highest peak – Engelberg boasts impeccable off-piste credentials, along with idyllic scenery that has featured in many a Bollywood movie.

Great For...

☑ Don't Miss

Posing for photos with your head poking through the cheesy Bollywood cutouts atop Mt Titlis.

Mt Titlis

With a name that makes English speakers titter, **Titlis** (www.titlis.ch) is Central Switzerland's tallest mountain, has its only glacier and is reached by the world's first revolving **cable car** (www.titlis.ch/en/tickets/cable-car-ride; adult/child return Sfr89/44.50; ⊙8.30am-5pm), completed in 1992. However, that's the last leg of a breathtaking three-stage journey. First, you glide up to Trübsee (1800m) via Gerschnialp (1300m; don't get off at Gerschnialp if you're continuing to the top). Next, another gondola at Trübsee whisks you up to Stand (2450m), where you board the revolving Rotair for the final head-spinning journey over the dazzling **Titlis Glacier**. As you twirl above the deeply crevassed ice, peaks rise like shark fins ahead, while tarn-speckled pastures, cliffs and waterfalls lie behind.

❶ Need to Know

Hourly Engelberg Express trains run from Lucerne to Engelberg (Sfr9.20, 45 minutes).

✕ Take a Break

Enjoy incongruously good Indian food at Spice Bazaar (p122) in the heart of town.

★ Top Tip

Many hotels and other tourist services shut down between the busy summer and ski seasons.

A glacial blast of air hits you at Titlis station (3020m). Inside is a kind of high-altitude theme park, with a marvellously kitsch ice cave, where you can watch neon lights make the sculpted ice tunnels sparkle. There's also an overpriced restaurant and a nostalgic photo studio on the 4th floor, which specialises in snaps of Bollywood stars in dirndls. Strike a pose with a giant Toblerone or an alpenhorn against a backdrop of fake snowy mountains (from Sfr35).

The genuine oohs and ahhs come when you step out onto the terrace, where the panorama of glacier-capped peaks stretches to Eiger, Mönch and Jungfrau in the Bernese Oberland. For even more thrilling views, step onto the adjacent **Cliff Walk** (www.titlis.ch/en/glacier/cliff-walk; ☺9.15am-4.45pm) FREE, a 100m-long, 1m-wide, cable-supported swinging walkway that qualified as Europe's highest suspension bridge when opened in 2012. More ambitious hikers can tackle the 45-minute climb to Titlis' 3239m summit (wear sturdy shoes).

For winter sports thrills even in midsummer, take the **Ice Flyer chairlift** (return adult/child Sfr12/6; ☺9.30am-4.30pm) down to the **Glacier Park** (www.titlis.ch/en/glacier/glacier-park; ☺9.30am-4.30pm) FREE, where there are free snow tubes, scooters and sledges to test out. The nearby freestyle park has a half-pipe and good summer snowboarding.

You can return to Engleberg via cable car or, in fine weather, you can walk some sections. Between Stand and Trübsee, the Geologischer Wanderweg is open from July to September; it takes about two hours up and 1½ hours down. From Trübsee up to Jochpass (2207m) takes about 1½ hours, and down to Engelberg takes around the same time.

If you're hiking, cable car destinations from Engelberg include Gerschnialp (one-way/return Sfr8/12), Trübsee (Sfr21/30), Jochpass (Sfr31/44) and Stand (Sfr36/51).

Reductions on all fares, including to Titlis, are 50% for Swiss, Eurail and InterRail pass holders.

The last ascent by cable car is at 3.40pm, last descent at 4.50pm; it closes for maintenance for two weeks in early November.

Skiing Engelberg

Snowboarders catch big air on Titlis, Engstlenalp and the half-pipe at Jochpass, while novice and intermediate skiers slide over to family-friendly Brunni and Gerschnialp for baby blues and cruisy reds. The real thrills for powder hounds, however, lie off-piste. Backcountry legends include Laub, Steinberg and the biggest leg-burner of all, Galtiberg, running from Klein Titlis to the valley 2000m below. A one-day ski pass costs Sfr62.

There's a **Ski & Snowboard School** (041 639 54 54; www.skischule-engelberg. ch; Klosterstrasse 3; 8am-5.30pm) inside the tourist office, and places to hire ski and snowboard gear (from about Sfr50 per day) throughout town. **Ski Lodge Engelberg** (041 637 35 00; www. skilodgeengelberg.com; Erlenweg 36) is another great source of information, or stop by Dani's **Okay Ski Shop** (041 637 07 77; www.okay-shop.com; Hotel Bellevue, Bahnhofplatz), where hardcore riders hang out and exchange tips.

Engelberg is a regular stop on the FIS ski-jumping circuit. In December, the town hosts the **FIS Ski Jumping World Cup** (www.weltcup-engelberg.ch), which draws athletes from all over the world.

Skiing, Engelberg slopes

Hiking, Cycling & Adventure Sports

There are some 360km of marked hiking trails in and around Engelberg. For gentle ambles and gorgeous scenery, head for Brunni on the opposite side of the valley. The **Brunni cable car** (www.brunni.ch; cable car one way/return Sfr18/30, incl chairlift Sfr26/42) goes up to Ristis at 1600m, where a chairlift takes you to the Swiss Alpine Club's refurbished **Brunni Hütte** (☑041

> ✕ **Don't Miss**
>
> Watch the cheesemakers at work and sample dairy delights at Engelberg's state-of-the-art cheesemaking operation, Show Cheese Dairy (www.schaukaeserei-engelberg.ch), located on the grounds of Engelberg Monastery.

STEFANO EMBER/SHUTTERSTOCK ©

637 37 32; www.berghuette.ch; dm adult/child Sfr26/14, incl breakfast & dinner Sfr65/41). From here you can watch a magnificent sunset before spending the night.

More strenuous hikes include the trek over the Surenenpass (2291m) to Attinghausen, where you can catch a bus to Altdorf and the southern end of Lake Uri, and the climb over Jochpass (2210m) to Meiringen via Engstlenalp. Pick up a map and check on snow conditions before attempting these more demanding treks.

In town, you can rent a mountain bike or join a two-wheeled adventure at **Bike 'n' Roll** (☑041 638 02 55; www.bikenroll.ch; Dorfstrasse 31; city/hardtail/full-suspension bike per day Sfr25/30/40; ☺8.30am-noon & 2-6.30pm Mon-Sat), which also rents out climbing gear (per day Sfr20) for tackling Engelberg's five *vie ferrate*. Further afield, the Stans-based outfit **Outventure** (☑041 611 14 41; www.outventure.ch; Mühlebachstrasse 5, Stans; ☺noon-6pm Mon-Fri, 10am-6pm Sat & Sun) offers bungee jumping (Sfr169), tandem paragliding (from Sfr150), guided *via ferrata* tours (Sfr145) and more.

Engelberg Monastery

The Engelberg valley was once ecclesiastically governed and the Benedictine abbey was the seat of power. Now the resident monks teach instead of rule, but their **12th-century home** (Kloster Engelberg; ☑041 639 61 19; www.kloster-engelberg.ch; church admission free, tours adult/child Sfr8/free; ☺1hr tour 10am & 4pm Wed-Sat) has kept its grandeur. Rebuilt after a devastating fire in 1729, it contains rooms decorated with incredibly detailed wood inlays, and a baroque monastery church. A 4pm tour is available from mid-June to early October regardless of group size; at other times, a four-person minimum may apply.

> ★ **Top Tip**
>
> In winter, après-ski rules. There's lots going on and drinking is the name of the game. Once the snow disappears, things quieten down considerably.

Walking Tour: Bürgenstock Felsenweg

This panoramic walk follows the Bürgenstock, a high limestone ridge above Lake Lucerne.

Start Bürgenstock
End Ennetbürgen
Distance 7.5km
Duration 2 to 2½ hours

2 Continue east along the cliff face through a series of short tunnels blasted into vertical rock walls.

Kehrsiten

Schwandwald

Schiltgrat

START **1**

Hammetschwand
▲(1128m)

2

3

Mt Bürgenstock ▲
(1128m)

3 Follow the signposted Waldstätterweg along the wooded ridge to **Chänzili**.

1 From Kehrsiten-Bürgenstock ferry port, take the funicular up to **Bürgenstock** and walk east through Bürgenstock Hotels resort.

Engelberger Aa

Classic Photo
Dramatic views of Lake Lucerne framed by rocky overhangs along the cliff-hugging trail.

Lake Lucerne

4 Zigzag steeply down through forest and intermittent exposed rock faces to **Mattgrat**.

5 Plunge back into forest, bearing left at a signposted fork and descending to the historic **St Jost Kapelle**.

Unter Nas

6 Descend through pastureland and along the lightly forested lakeside to meet a sealed street at **Ennetbürgen**.

Take a Break...
Gasthaus Obermatt (www. gasthaus-obermatt.ch) offers Swiss comfort food near the trail's end.

Buochs

7 Continue straight past the ferry dock to Ennetbürgen's village centre.

Niederdorf

Lucerne

🟢 ACTIVITIES

Next Bike   Cycling

(Map p119; ☎041 508 08 00; www.nextbike.ch; Lucerne Bahnhof; bikes per hour/day Sfr2/20) This outfit offers bike rental at the train station; use the app or call the number, provide credit card details and receive a numbered code to open a combination lock. There are several scenic routes along the lakefront, including the easygoing 16km pedal to Winkel via Kastanienbaum.

SkyGlide   Paragliding

(☎041 620 20 22; www.skyglide.ch; paragliding from Sfr170) This well-regarded tandem paragliding outfit will send you soaring over Lake Lucerne. Lots of locations to choose from.

⊗ EATING

Jazzkantine   Cafe $

(Map p119; ☎041 410 73 73; www.jazzkantine.com; Grabenstrasse 8; pasta from Sfr16, sandwiches from Sfr7; ⊙9am-12.30am Mon-Sat) With its long bar, sturdy wooden tables and chalkboard menus in the back of the Old Town, this arty haunt serves tasty Italian dishes and good coffee. Regular jazz workshops and gigs take place downstairs.

KKL World Café   International $

(Map p119; ☎041 226 71 00; www.kkl-luzern.ch/en/cuisine; Europaplatz 1; mains from Sfr17; ⊙9am-8pm) Salads and sandwiches fill the display cases at the KKL's slick bistro-cum-cafeteria; there are also wok dishes at lunch and dinner.

Wirtshaus Galliker   Swiss $$

(Map p119; ☎041 240 10 02; Schützenstrasse 1; mains from Sfr21; ⊙11.30am-2pm & 6-8.30pm Tue-Sat) Passionately run by the Galliker family for over four generations, this old-style, wood-panelled tavern attracts a lively bunch of regulars. Motherly waitresses dish up Lucerne soul food – rösti, *Chögalipaschtetli* (veal pastry pie) and the like – that is batten-the-hatches filling.

Brasserie Bodu   French $$

(Map p119; ☎041 410 01 77; www.brasseriebodu.ch; Kornmarkt 5; mains from Sfr22; ⊙9am-midnight Mon-Sat, from 11am Sun) Banquettes, wood panelling and elbow-to-elbow tables create a warm ambience at this classic French-style bistro, where diners huddle around bottles of Bordeaux and bowls of bouillabaisse (a fish stew) or succulent sirloin steaks.

Grottino 1313   Italian $$$

(☎041 610 13 13; www.grottino1313.ch; Industriestrasse 7; lunch menus from Sfr20, dinner menu Sfr64; ⊙11.30am-2pm Mon-Fri, 6-11.30pm daily) Offering a welcome escape from Lucerne's tourist throngs, this relaxed yet stylish eatery south of the train station serves 'surprise' menus featuring starters like chestnut soup with figs, creative pasta dishes, meats cooked over an open fire and scrumptious desserts. The herb-fringed front patio is lovely on a summer afternoon, while the candlelit interior exudes sheer cosiness on a chilly evening.

Bam Bou
by Thomas   Mediterranean $$$

(Map p119; ☎041 226 86 86 10; www.bambou-luzern.ch; Sempacherstrasse 14; lunch mains from Sfr23; ⊙11.30am-2pm & 6-10pm Tue-Sat) This below-street-level restaurant at **the Hotel** has undergone a transformation and is now run by award-winning chefs Corinna and Ralf Thomas, specialising in excellent French-Mediterranean cuisine.

Schiffrestaurant
Wilhelm Tell   Swiss $$$

(Map p119; ☎041 410 23 30; https://schiffrestaurant.ch; Landungsbrücke 9; 3-course menu Sfr54; ⊙11am-midnight Tue-Sat, to 11pm Sun) The old paddle steamer *Wilhelm Tell* has been around for nearly 110 years, but doesn't leave its dock these days. Its now a lovely floating restaurant and bar. Come for lunch or dinner in its restaurant, or simply sit out on the deck and enjoy the surroundings with a coffee, cocktail or beer. This family-run business has an enthusiastic crew.

Lucerne

Lucerne

◉ Sights
1 Historisches Museum A2
2 Kapellbrücke C2
3 Männliturm A1
4 Sammlung Rosengart C3
5 Schirmerturm B1
6 Spreuerbrücke A2
7 Wachturm B1
8 Zytturm B1

⊕ Activities, Courses & Tours
9 Next Bike D3
10 SNG C1

⊗ Eating
11 Bam Bou by Thomas C3
12 Brasserie Bodu B2
13 Jazzkantine B1
14 KKL World Café D2
15 Schiffrestaurant Wilhelm Tell D1
16 Wirtshaus Galliker A2

⊖ Drinking & Nightlife
17 Luz Seebistro C2
18 Rathaus Bräuerei B2

⊗ Entertainment
19 Stadtkeller B2

⊖ DRINKING & NIGHTLIFE

Luz Seebistro _Cafe_

(Map p119; ☎041 367 68 72; www.luzseebistro.
ch; ⊗7.30am-12.30am) On the lakefront just
opposite the train station, this fin-de-siècle
boathouse makes an atmospheric spot for
drinks at sunset or a coffee break any time
of day. It also serves reasonably priced
snacks (from Sfr7).

Rathaus Bräuerei _Brewery_

(Map p119; ☎041 410 61 11; www.rathaus
brauerei.ch; Unter der Egg 2; ⊗11.30am-midnight
Mon-Sat, to 11pm Sun) Sip home-brewed
beer under the vaulted arches of this
buzzy tavern near Kapellbrücke, or nab a
pavement table and watch the river flow.
You know this place is good as it's positively
brimming with locals.

Fasnacht Fever

Next time someone grumbles about the Swiss being so irritatingly orderly and well behaved, send them to Lucerne for **Fasnacht** (Carnival) in February – they'll never use those tired clichés again. More boisterous than in Basel or Bern, Lucerne's six-day pre-Lenten bash is stark raving bonkers. The fun kicks off on 'Dirty Thursday' with the character Fritschi greeting the crowds from the town hall and a cannon signalling that hedonistic misrule can begin. Warty witches, leering ogres, jangling jesters, it doesn't matter which costume or mask you choose – dress up, drink and dance, it's tradition! Guggenmusik bands (literally) rock the bridges, acrobats and actors perform, and parades fill the streets with colour, chaos and ear-splitting music in the build-up to the Shrove Tuesday Monstercorso Parade.

Fasnacht masks and costumes
DMITRY CHULOV/SHUTTERSTOCK ©

😵 ENTERTAINMENT

Stadtkeller   Traditional Music
(Map p119; 📞041 410 47 33; www.swissfolklore show.com; Sternenplatz 3; ☺shows lunch 12.15pm, dinner 8pm) Alpenhorns, cowbells, flag throwing, yodelling – name the Swiss cliché and you'll find it at this tourist-oriented club with regular lunch and dinner folklore shows. While it's more than a tad touristy, it's also pretty good fun.

ℹ️ INFORMATION

Tourist Office (Map p119; 📞041 227 17 17; www. luzern.com; Zentralstrasse 5; ☺8.30am-7pm Mon-Fri, 9am-7pm Sat, 9am-5pm Sun May-Oct, shorter hours Nov-Apr) Reached from Zentralstrasse or platform 3 of the Hauptbahnhof.

ℹ️ GETTING THERE & AWAY

Frequent trains connect Lucerne to Interlaken Ost (Sfr33, 1¾ hours), Bern (Sfr40, one to 1½ hours), Lugano (Sfr61, two hours) and Zürich (Sfr26, 45 minutes to one hour).

The A2 freeway connecting Basel and Lugano passes by Lucerne, while the A14/A4 provides the road link to Zürich.

Lake Lucerne boat trips depart from the quays around Bahnhofplatz and Europaplatz.

ℹ️ GETTING AROUND

If you don't have a Swiss Travel Pass (which is valid on lake journeys), consider purchasing the regional **Tell-Pass** (www.tell-pass.ch; adult per 2/3/4/5/10 days Sfr180/210/230/240/300, child up to 10 days Chf30). Sold at Lucerne tourist office and all boat stations, it provides unlimited travel region-wide on trains, boats, buses, cable cars and mountain railways for two to 10 days.

Weggis

Weggis (9km east of Lucerne) enjoys a mild climate, sheltered by the nearby mountains. It's hard to believe this genteel lakeside resort with small-town friendliness was the birthplace of the rebellious 'Moderner Bund' art movement, the forerunner of Dada.

Grape   American $$
(📞041 392 07 07; www.thegrape.ch; Seestrasse 60; pizza/mains from Sfr19/26; ☺10am-2pm & 6pm-midnight Mon, Tue & Thu, to midnight Fri-Sun) Weggis' California dreamer is this hip haunt with a menu that skips from wood-fired pizza to modern burger combos to steaks and sugary desserts. (Toblerone parfait with cherries and almonds, anyone?)

ℹ️ INFORMATION

Tourist Office (📞041 227 18 00; www.wvrt.ch; Seestrasse 5; ⏰8.30am-6pm Mon-Fri, 9am-4pm Sat & Sun) Next to Weggis' boat dock.

ℹ️ GETTING THERE & AWAY

Lucerne is a 40-minute boat ride or 19km drive from Weggis. A cable car runs from Weggis up to Rigi Kaltbad (one way/return Sfr30/48, 10 minutes), halfway up Mt Rigi.

Brunnen

Brunnen offers magnificent views both south and west. Most of the action is central, around the ferry quay and on, or just off, Bahnhofstrasse, which leads inland from the quay.

⊙ SIGHTS

Swiss Knife
Valley Museum   Museum

(📞041 820 60 10; www.swissknifevalley.ch; Bahnhofstrasse 3; ⏰10am-6.30pm Mon-Fri, to 5pm Sat & Sun; 👶) **FREE** This teensy museum

displays historical knives from prehistoric, Roman and medieval times, including folding precursors to the Victorinox classic. Touch-screen films in four languages chart the history of knives in general and Victorinox specifically. But the real highlight is the 'build-your-own-knife' section: for Sfr30 staff will help you construct your own souvenir Victorinox (ages six and over, reserve in advance).

🍴 EATING

Gasthaus Ochsen   European $$

(📞041 820 11 59; www.hotelochsen.ch; Bahnhofstrasse 18; mains Sfr19.50-41; ⏰8am-11pm Mon-Sat, to 10pm Sun May-Sep, shorter hours Oct-Apr) Photos of celebrity Swiss patrons line the walls at Brunnen's oldest haunt, which specialises in *Poulet im Chörbli* (chicken in a basket). There's a great little *apéro* bar under the same ownership just across the way, and decent rooms above the restaurant (single/double Sfr90/160). It's all very appealing.

Gasthaus Ochsen

Weisses Rössli
Swiss $$

(041 825 13 00; www.weisses-roessli-brunnen.ch; Bahnhofstrasse 8; mains from Sfr22; ⊙11am-2pm & 6-9.30pm) Friendly service, hearty Swiss staples accompanied by fresh vegetables, and a front terrace with nice views of Brunnen's main street backed by the lake make this an agreeable spot for lunch or dinner. Weisses Rössli is also a hotel.

DRINKING & NIGHTLIFE

Elvira's Trübli
Wine Bar

(041 820 10 11; Olympstrasse 6; ⊙4pm-midnight Tue-Sat) Affable owner Elvira stocks an impressive array of vintages at this popular wine bar, tucked down a side street just in from the waterfront.

INFORMATION

Tourist Office (041 825 00 40; www.brunnentourismus.ch; Bahnhofstrasse 15; ⊙8.30am-6pm Mon-Fri, 9am-1pm Sat Jun-Sep, 8.30am-noon & 1.30-5.30pm Mon-Fri Oct-May) Near the waterfront, a five-minute walk from the train station.

On Mt Titlis (p112)

GETTING THERE & AWAY

The most pleasant way to reach Brunnen is by boat from Lucerne (Sfr39, two hours). The train (Sfr17.60, 45 to 50 minutes) is cheaper and quicker, although a change in Arth-Goldau is sometimes necessary. There are also road connections from Lucerne, Zug and Flüelen. If you have a vehicle, the drive around the lake from Lucerne (39km) is spectacular.

Engelberg

Engelberg (literally 'Angel Mountain') attracts two kinds of pilgrims: those seeking spiritual enlightenment in its Benedictine monastery and those worshipping the virgin powder on its divine slopes.

EATING

Spice Bazaar
Indian $

(041 639 70 70; www.central-engelberg.ch; Dorfstrasse 48; mains from Sfr18; ⊙11.30am-11pm) This Indian restaurant at the Hotel Central gets rave reviews from both visitors and locals, serving up all sorts of favourites, such as Badami Chicken (Sfr29.50),

Tandoori Mix Grill (Sfr40) and Swiss–Indian fusion such as Spice of Life Fondue (Sfr24; minimum two people).

Brasserie
Konrad   Modern European $$

(☑041 637 35 00; www.skilodgeengelberg.com; Erlenweg 36; mains from Sfr29; ☺5.30-11pm; ⧉) At Ski Lodge Engelberg's on-site restaurant, Chef Jonas Bolling conjures up extraordinarily good New Nordic cuisine that's pretty as a picture and perfect for refuelling after a tough day on the slopes (the three-course skier's menu is a steal at Sfr59). If you're not a hotel guest, be sure to reserve a table in the high season.

Alpenclub   Swiss $$

(☑041 637 12 43; www.alpenclub.ch; Dorfstrasse 5; pizza from Sfr16, mains from Sfr28; ☺5.30-10pm Mon-Fri, from 11.30am Sat & Sun) This low-ceilinged, candlelit tavern creaks under the weight of its 200-year history at the Alpenclub hotel complex. Feast away on fondue, pizza, Italian staples or the house speciality: sizzling beef tenderloin with garlic, onion and herb sauce.

Restaurant-Steakhouse
Bierlialp   Swiss $$

(☑041 637 17 17; www.restaurant-bierlialp.ch; Dorfstrasse 21; pizza/pasta/meat mains from Sfr15/22/35; ☺6-11pm) Specialising in meat, pasta and pizza. Start at the salad buffet (Sfr12.50) then move on. The pizzas and pastas are good, but if you're a meat eater with a fat wallet, go for the Irish Black Angus Beef (Sfr52). There's a dessert buffet to top it all off.

🍷 DRINKING & NIGHTLIFE

Yucatan   Bar

(☑041 637 13 24; www.bellevue-terminus.ch; Bahnhofplatz; ☺3pm-midnight) Engelberg's après-ski heavyweight is this lively joint opposite the train station. Mega-burgers, fajitas, quesadillas, Thai curries and caipirinhas fuel parties with DJs, bands and jiving on the bar.

Lake Lucerne Region Visitors Card

If you're staying overnight in Lucerne, be sure to ask for your free **Lake Lucerne Region Visitors Card** (Vierwaldstättersee Gästekarte; www.luzern.com/en/festivals-events/visitors-card). Stamped by your hotel, the card entitles you to discounts on various museums, sporting facilities, cable cars and lake cruises in Lucerne and the surrounding area.

Engelberg
DENIS LININE/SHUTTERSTOCK ©

ℹ️ INFORMATION

Tourist Office (☑041 639 77 77; www.engelberg.ch; Klosterstrasse 3; ☺8am-5.30pm Mon-Sat year-round, plus Sun Dec-Easter) A five-minute walk from the train station, this tourist office can help with hotel reservations.

ℹ️ GETTING THERE & AWAY

Engelberg is the southern terminus of the Engelberg Express train, which runs hourly to/from Lucerne (Sfr9.20, 45 minutes). Day-trippers should check the Mt Titlis excursion tickets available from the Lucerne tourist office (p120).

A road off the A2 freeway near Stans leads to Engelberg, 35km by road from Lucerne.

From late April to October, a free shuttle bus leaves Engelberg's train station roughly every half hour between 8am and 5pm for all the village's major hotels and attractions. In winter, free ski buses follow multiple routes to and from the slopes.

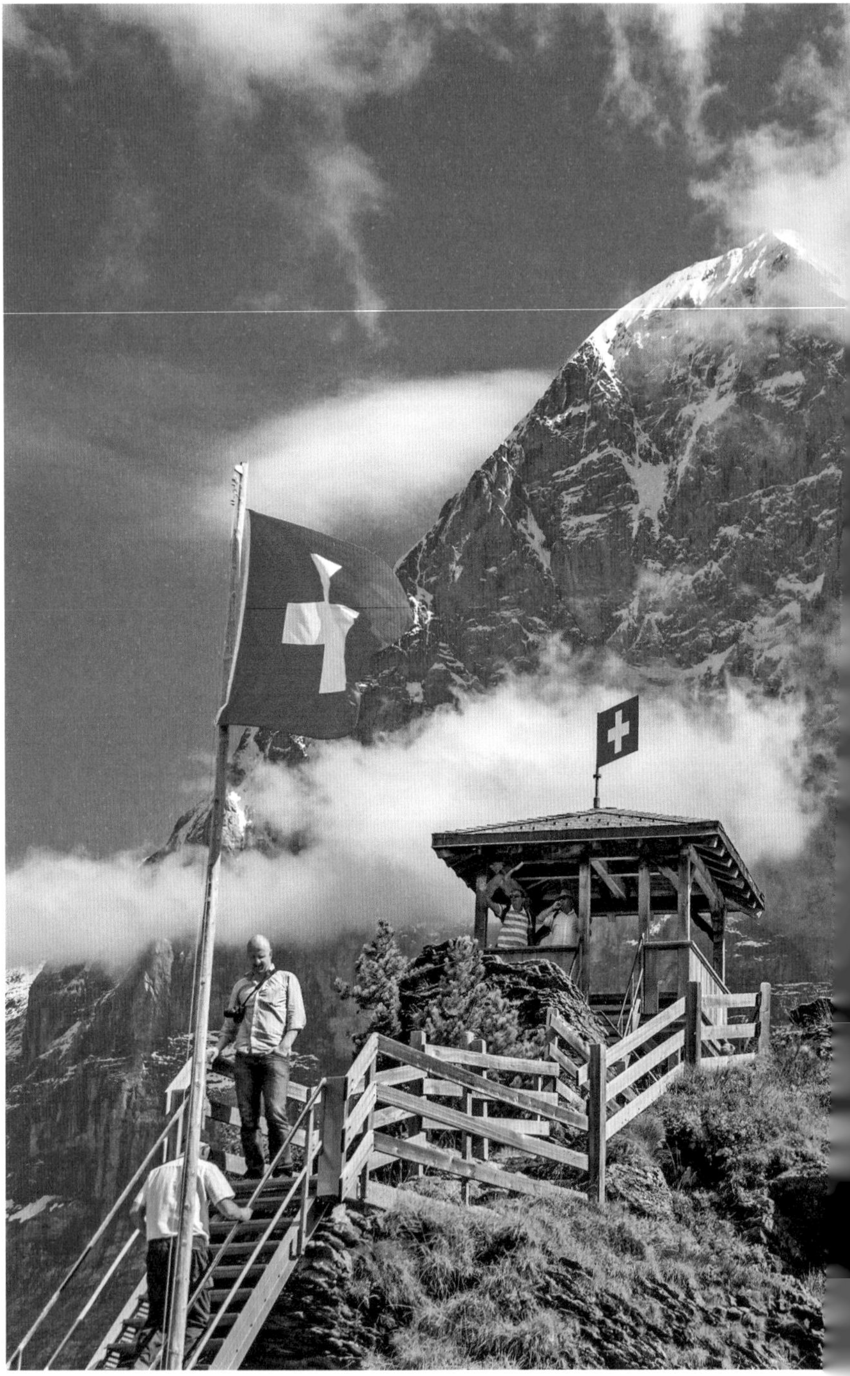

BERNESE OBERLAND

Bernese Oberland at a Glance...

Whether you're hiking below Eiger's fearsome north face, carving powder on a crisp Mürren morning, or gawping at the misty Staubbach Falls, the Swiss Alps don't get more in-your-face beautiful than this. Watched over by Mönch (Monk), Jungfrau (Virgin) and Eiger (Ogre), the Bernese Oberland sends spirits soaring to heaven.

Mark Twain wrote that no opiate compared to walking here, and the region's cinematic good looks have served as a backdrop for the exploits of Sherlock Holmes and 007. Yet photographers struggle to do the region justice, as evidenced by tutting tourists searching in vain for a postcard to match their memories.

Two Days in the Bernese Oberland

Begin your journey by soaking up the belle époque splendor of **Interlaken** (p136), then climbing by train, funicular or cable car to take in the Alpine views from **Harder Kulm** (p137), **Heimwefluh** (p137) and **Schynige Platte** (p136). On day two, take the classic train journey to **Jungfraujoch** (3454m; p128) for full-on views of the spectacular **Aletsch Glacier** (p129) and the region's three iconic peaks: Mönch, Jungfrau and Eiger.

Four Days in the Bernese Oberland

On days three and four, delve deeper into the Bernese Oberland's two most magnificent valleys. From Interlaken it's an easy train trip south to gorgeous glacier-carved **Lauterbrunnen** (p145), home to cliff faces, waterfalls and the car-free resorts of **Wengen** (p133) and **Mürren** (p133), or southeast to **Grindelwald** (p132), where some of the region's prettiest hikes climb into stunning green high country.

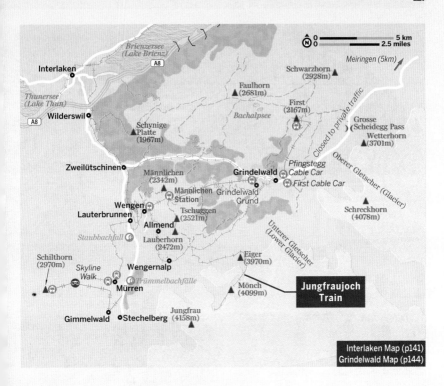

Interlaken Map (p141)
Grindelwald Map (p144)

Arriving in the Bernese Oberland

Car or Train Interlaken, the gateway to the Bernese Oberland, is easily accessible by road and rail from major Swiss cities, including Geneva, Zürich, Bern, Basel and Lucerne.

Air Bern is the closest airport (51km), followed by Zürich (133km), Basel (156km) and Geneva (225km).

Sleeping

The Bernese Oberland takes the expression 'room with a view' to another level, with stylish boutique hotels, snug B&Bs and timber chalets with altitude and broad mountain views. Interlaken catapults you back to the grace of another era in belle époque grand hotels. Prices skyrocket during the high winter season.

Jungfraujoch Train

The train ride up to Jungfraujoch (3454m) is one of Switzerland's classic experiences, and the icy wilderness of swirling glaciers and 4000m turrets that unfolds up top is staggeringly beautiful.

Great For...

☑ Don't Miss

The unexpectedly fine glacier views from stops within the tunnel at Eigerwand and Eismeer.

The Ride

The **train journey** (www.jungfrau.ch; return Interlaken Ost–Jungfraujoch Sfr210.80, Kleine Scheidegg–Jungfraujoch Sfr128; ⊗trains 8am-6.43pm May-Sep, shorter hours rest of year) from Kleine Scheidegg to Jungfraujoch, Europe's highest station, is one of the peak experiences of any trip to Switzerland. Following an audacious route right through the heart of the Eiger, the railway was completed in 1912 and today carries more than two million people a year through some of Europe's most phenomenal high-Alpine scenery.

The tunnel leading to the summit is an astonishing feat of engineering that took 3000 men 16 years to drill. Within the tunnel, passengers are allowed to disembark at Eigerwand and Eismeer, where

❶ Need to Know

Visit www.jungfrau.ch or call 📞033 828 79 31 for up-to-date weather conditions at the summit.

✖ Take a Break

Refuel at the mountaintop's self-service cafeteria, Indian buffet, Swiss-German restaurant or Lindt chocolate shop.

> ### ★ Top Tip
> A Good Morning Ticket, valid on the morning's first two trains, offers substantial savings.

panoramic windows offer tantalising glimpses across rivers of crevassed ice.

The Summit

Within the sci-fi Sphinx meteorological station at the summit, where trains disgorge passengers, you'll find ice sculptures, restaurants, indoor viewpoints and a souvenir shop where you can purchase your very own chunk of Eiger to grace the mantelpiece. Outside, you're immediately greeted by breathtaking vistas of rippling peaks that stretch as far as Germany's Black Forest on cloudless days.

Good weather is essential to make the most of the summit experience; check www.jungfrau.ch or call 📞033 828 79 31 for current conditions. Don't forget to take warm clothing, sturdy shoes, sunglasses and sunscreen, as there's snow and glare up here all year.

Aletsch Glacier

Jungfraujoch commands a phenomenal view of the largest glacier in the Alps: the 23km Aletsch Glacier, which powers its way through peaks hovering around the 4000m mark. One of the world's natural marvels, this mesmerising glacier is the icing on the cake of the Swiss Alps Jungfrau-Aletsch Unesco World Heritage Site. Its ice is glacial blue and 900m thick at its deepest point. From late June to early October, Grindelwald Sports (p143) offers two-day hikes across the glacier, led by experienced mountain guides.

Ice Palace

Tunnels of ice polished as smooth as cut glass lead through the so-called **Ice Palace** (www.jungfrau.ch; ⊗open during railway operating times; 👬) at Jungfraujoch, which offers a frosty reception at -3°C. Mountain guides wielding saws and pickaxes carved the chambers out of solid ice in the 1930s. Now they are adorned with frozen sculptures of bears, ibexes and eagles.

Snow Fun Park

It's thrilling just to walk around and savour the views from the summit, but if you're in the mood for something a little more adventurous, you can zip across the frozen plateau on a flying fox (adult/child Sfr20/15), dash downhill on a sled or tube (Sfr15/10), or enjoy a bit of tame skiing or boarding (Sfr35/25) at the **Snow Fun Park** (☉11am-5pm; 🐾). A day pass covering all activities costs Sfr45/25.

Mönchsjochhütte

At **Mönchsjochhütte** (📞033 971 34 72; www.moenchsjoch.ch; dm Sfr28, incl half-board Sfr64; ☉late Mar–mid-Oct), 3650m up into the mountains, hardcore rock climbers share a dinner table and dorm while psyching themselves up to tackle Eiger or Mönch. If you're spending a few hours at the summit, you can walk over and get a taste of the excitement yourself: from the Jungfraujoch train station, cross the Aletsch Glacier along the prepared path (about one hour).

Planning Your Journey

Trains from Interlaken Ost follow two different routes to Jungfraujoch: one via Lauterbrunnen, Wengen and Kleine Scheidegg; the other via Grindelwald and Kleine Scheidegg. Either way, the journey time is 2¼ to 2½ hours each way and the return

★ **Top Tip**

Swiss Travel Pass holders travel free as far as Grindelwald or Wengen, and receive a 25% discount on the remainder of the journey to Jungfraujoch summit.

fare is Sfr210.80. The last train back from Jungfraujoch leaves at 6.43pm in summer and 4.43pm in winter.

Note that the ordinary return ticket to Jungfraujoch is valid for one month, and you're allowed to break your journey at various stops along the way, so a single ticket can form the backbone of an extended exploration of the region. For example, from Interlaken Ost, you could venture as far as Grindelwald and stop for a few days' hiking, before moving on to Kleine Scheidegg, Jungfraujoch, Wengen and Lauterbrunnen.

From early May to late October you can qualify for a discounted Good Morning Ticket (Sfr145) by taking one of the first two trains from Interlaken Ost (6.35am or 7.05am) and boarding a return train from the summit no later than 1.13pm.

Getting these early trains is easier if your starting place is deeper in the region. For example, if you sleep overnight at Kleine Scheidegg, you'll qualify for a Good Morning discount (Sfr95 return instead of Sfr128) on either of the first two trains leaving Kleine Scheidegg for Jungfraujoch (8am and 8.30am).

Mönchsjochhütte

Skiing the Jungfrau Region

Whether you want to slalom wide, sunny slopes below the Eiger or ski the breathtakingly sheer 16km Inferno run from Schilthorn to Lauterbrunnen, the region has a piste that suits.

Great For...

☑ Don't Miss

Wengen's legendary Lauberhornrennen ski race in mid-January, where pros zip by at 160km/h.

Ski Passes

Grindelwald, Männlichen, Mürren and Wengen have access to 214km of prepared runs and 44 ski lifts. Go for a day pass for either Grindelwald-Wengen or Mürren-Schilthorn (adult/child Sfr63/32), or a seven-day pass (Sfr309/155). A region pass costs only slightly more (adult per day/week Sfr72/384), but moving between ski areas by train can be slow and crowded.

Grindelwald

From **Kleine Scheidegg** or **Männlichen** there are long, easy runs back to Grindelwald, with the Eiger towering above. For a crowd-free swoosh, check out Grindelwald's 15.5km of well-groomed **cross-country skiing trails** or slip on snowshoes to pad through the winter wonderland in quiet exhilaration on six different trails.

Kleine Scheidegg

ⓘ Need to Know

Jungfrau-area slopes are generally open between mid-November and mid-December, closing around mid-April.

✕ Take a Break

Warm up with an après-ski glühwein (mulled wine) at the Tanne Bar (p147) in Wengen.

> ★ **Top Tip**
>
> The comprehensive Jungfrau region lift ticket (Sfr396) grants seven days' unlimited skiing on 206km of slopes.

4.30pm Sep, to 4pm Oct, noon-3.45pm mid Jan–mid-Apr), a flying fox that swings between First and Schreckfeld at breathtaking speeds of up to 84km/h.

First

Reached by cable car from Grindelwald, and stretching from Oberjoch at 2486m clear down to the village, First has 60km of well-groomed pistes – mostly wide and meandering intermediate reds, with some challenging black runs mixed in. The south-facing slopes have interesting skiing through meadows and forests. Freestylers should check out the kickers and rails at **Bärgelegg**, or have a go on the superpipe at **Schreckfeld** station.

In winter you can stomp through the deep powder on trail 50 to **Faulhorn**. The 2½-hour walk takes in the frozen Bachalpsee and the Jungfrau range in all its wintry glory. Faulhorn is also the starting point for Europe's longest **toboggan run** (⊘Dec-Apr) `FREE`.

Ramp up the thrill factor on the **First Flyer** (adult/child Sfr29/22, incl cable car Sfr74/45; ⊘10am-5.30pm late Jun & Aug, to

Mürren

In winter Mürren has 53km of prepared ski runs, mostly designed for intermediates. The village's **Swiss Ski School** (☎033 855 12 47; www.swiss-snowsports-muerren.ch; Haus Finel, Inder Gruben; ⊘9am-12.30pm & 1.30-5pm) offers private and group ski and snowboarding lessons, including tuition for children. In late January, don't miss Mürren's venerable **Inferno Run** (www.inferno-muerren.ch; ⊘Jan), a death-defying downhill ski race.

Wengen

At the world-famous **Lauberhornrennen** ski race (www.lauberhorn.ch; ⊘mid-Jan), mere mortals can pound powder by taking the cable car to Männlichen or train to Allmend, Wengernalp or Kleine Scheidegg. Skiing is mostly cruisy blues and reds, though experts can brave exhilarating black runs at Lauberhorn and the aptly named 'Oh God'.

Hiking in the Bernese Oberland

There are hundreds of kilometres of trails in the Bernese Oberland, suitable for every level of skill and fortitude. All grant access to some of the world's most stunning alpine scenery.

Great For...

☑ Don't Miss

The free loaner hiking poles offered at the start of the track to 297m-high Staubbachfall.

Grindelwald to Wengen

One of the region's most stunning day hikes is the 15km trek from Grindelwald Grund to Wengen via Kleine Scheidegg, which heads up through wildflower-freckled meadows to skirt below the Eiger's north face and reach Kleine Scheidegg, granting arresting views of the 'Big Three': Eiger (3970m), Mönch (4107m) and Jungfrau (4158m). Allow around 5½ to six hours.

Eiger Trail

This spectacular 6km trail (two hours) runs from Eigergletscher to Alpiglen, affording close-ups of the Eiger's fearsome north face. To reach Eigergletscher, take the undemanding one-hour trail from Kleine Scheidegg.

Panoramaweg

From Wengen and Grindelwald, cable cars soar up to Männlichen (2230m), where

Hiking trail between Männlichen and Kleine Scheidegg

CHEN MIN CHUN/SHUTTERSTOCK ©

ℹ Need to Know

The best months for walking in the region are from June to September.

✕ Take a Break

Refuel with rösti and sugar-dusted *Öpfelchüechli* (apple fritters) at **Restaurant Brandegg** (🖉033 853 10 57; www.brandegg.ch; mains Sfr18-30; ⊙9am-6pm Sun-Thu, to 9pm Fri & Sat late May-late Oct; 🖶) on the Kleine Scheidegg trail.

★ Top Tip

Trains and cable cars parallel many walking routes, so you can ride up and hike back down.

---

sensational views unfold deep into the glaciated heart of the region. If you only have time for one hike from Männlichen, make it the spirit-soaring Panoramaweg to Kleine Scheidegg, taking in wildflower-cloaked pastures, a veritable orchestra of chiming cowbells and peerless views of the Eiger, Mönch, Jungfrau and the pearl-white pyramid of Silberhorn (3695m). The easy trail skirts the base of Tschuggen and knife-edge Lauberhorn to reach Rotstöckli and Kleine Scheidegg in 1½ hours.

Felixweg

Little ones in tow? Keep them amused on the 1½-hour Felixweg from Männlichen to Holenstein. Kids can get the low-down on Alpine flora and fauna, spot marmots from the watchtower and ride the flying fox. There are two scenic barbecue areas en route. The trail is not (yet) suitable for buggies.

Stechelberg to Lauterbrunnen

The magnificent Lauterbrunnen valley is home to 72 waterfalls, including the 297m-high Staubbachfall (p145), whose ethereal beauty inspired both Goethe and Lord Byron to pen poems. The 6.7km walk from Stechelberg to Lauterbrunnen affords a glimpse of some of the valley's most impressive falls, highlighted by the bang-crash spectacle of the glacier-fed Trümmelbachfälle. Inside the mountain, up to 20,000L of water per second corkscrews through ravines and potholes shaped by the swirling waters. The 10 falls drain from 24 sq km of Alpine glaciers and snow deposits.

Grütschalp to Mürren

Ride the cable car up from Lauterbrunnen to Grütschalp, then follow the trail along the railway tracks. The walk to Mürren takes about an hour and is mostly level. There are unbeatable views, alpine woods and babbling glacier-fed streams.

Interlaken Outdoors

Switzerland is the world's second-biggest adventure-sports centre and Interlaken is its busiest hub. Add in some exceptionally scenic funicular and cogwheel rail journeys, and it's obvious why outdoorsy travellers love Interlaken.

Great For...

☑ **Don't Miss**

Testing your climbing skills on the 70 routes, rated from 4a to 8a, at Interlaken's K44.

Adventure Sports

Almost every heart-quickening pursuit you can think of is offered around Interlaken. You can white-water raft on the Lütschine, Simme and Saane rivers, canyon the Saxetet, Grimsel or Chli Schliere gorges, and canyon jump at the Gletscherschlucht near Grindelwald. If that doesn't grab you, there's paragliding, glacier bungee jumping, skydiving, ice climbing, hydrospeeding and, phew, much more. Operators can arrange most sports from May to September. Advance bookings are essential.

Schynige Platte

The must-do day trip from Interlaken is the Schynige Platte plateau (1967m), which provides a natural balcony on the

St Beatus Caves

PURWANTO LIM/SHUTTERSTOCK ©

❶ Need to Know

Interlaken has two train stations. If headed for the Jungfrau region, you'll leave from Interlaken Ost.

✕ Take a Break

After you've been rafting, canyoning or ice climbing all day, one of the 50 beers at Hüsi Bierhaus (p142) will hit the spot.

★ Top Tip

For an insider's perspective on Interlaken, check out the free walking tours offered at www.interlakenfreetour.com.

Lake Bridge) jutting out above the valley. The wildlife park near the valley station is home to Alpine critters, including marmots and ibex.

Heimwehfluh

A nostalgic funicular trundles up to family-friendly **Heimwehfluh** (www.heimwehfluh.ch; funicular adult/child return Sfr16/8, toboggan Sfr9/7; ☺10am-5pm Apr-late Oct; 🚌) for long views across Interlaken. Kids love the bob run down the hill – lay off the brakes to pick up speed.

St Beatus Caves

Sculpted over millennia, the **St Beatus Caves** (www.beatushoehlen.ch; adult/child Sfr18/10; ☺9.45am-5pm late Mar-late Oct) are great for a wander through caverns of dramatically lit stalagmites, stalactites and underground lakes. They are a half-hour boat or bus ride from Interlaken West.

Bernese Alps and lakes Thun and Brienz, glinting far below. A relic from a bygone era of slow travel, the cogwheel summit train allows the views to unfold little by little. At the top, a botanical garden thick with colour and fragrance awaits. Hiking trails teeter along the ridge and through meadows chiming with cowbells. Paragliders launch themselves from the plateau in summer.

Harder Kulm

For far-reaching views to the 4000m giants, take the eight-minute funicular ride to 1322m **Harder Kulm** (Map p141; www.jungfrau.ch/harderkulm; adult/child Sfr16/8). Many hiking paths begin here, and the vertigo-free can enjoy the panorama from the Zweiseensteg (Two

Walking Tour: Faulhornweg

This high-level route is one of Switzerland's finest, with long views to Thunersee, Brienzersee, Eiger, Mönch and Jungfrau.

Start Schynige Platte
End Bachalpsee
Distance 15km
Duration 5 hours

Iseltwald °
(566m)

Brienzersee (Lake Brienz)

3 The way dips and rises before coming to **Egg**, a boulder-strewn pass at 2067m.

▲ Roteflue
(2295m)

Sägistal   *Sägistalsee*

2 Head around scree slopes on the western flank of canyon-like **Loucherhorn** (2230m) to cross a low grassy crest.

③   Indri ▲
            Sägissa
            (2265m)   ④
                        Männdlenen
                        (2344m)

②

Inner Iselten

Oberberghorn ▲
(2069m)

①

Schilt
(1813m)

START

Alpengarten ◉   Schynige
                  Platte

▲ Bira
(2456m)

Winteregg

Take a Break...
Berghotel Faulhorn (☎033 853 27 13; www.berghotel-faulhorn.ch; ☉Jun-Oct) is the Alps' oldest, highest hotel.

1 Walk northeast over rolling pastures past the Alpine hut of Oberberg to **Louchera** (2020m).

° Zweilütschinen

Classic Photo
The panorama from Faulhorn, stretching to the Black Forest in Germany and Vosges in France.

5 Traverse a broad ledge between stratified cliffs to Winteregg ridge, then climb left to **Faulhorn summit** (2681m).

7 Descend the well-trodden path through cow-grazed pastures to the gondola-lift station at **First** (2167m).

4 Head northeastward into the Sägistal, then swing around talus-choked Bonera gully to **Berghaus Männdlenen** (2344m).

6 Watch for marmots while descending to Gassenboden (2553m), then drop eastward to the petrol-blue **Bachalpsee** (2265m).

Bonera (Hühnertal)

Faulhorn (2681m)

Lookout

Hagelseewli

Milibach

Uf Spitzen (2381m)

First FINISH

Burg (2207m)

Blüössalp

Grindelwald

TAKE A BREAK XANTOLUS/SHUTTERSTOCK ©, 5 BURGEN/SHUTTERSTOCK ©, 6 ILKOV KALININ/SHUTTERSTOCK ©

❄ Schilthorn

On a clear day, nothing compares to the 360-degree, 200-peak panorama from the top of 2970m Schilthorn, where vistas extend all the way from Titlis to Mont Blanc to the German Black Forest.

Scenes from the James Bond movie *On Her Majesty's Secret Service* were shot here in 1968–69. Learn about stunt skiing and other aspects of the film's production at the interactive **Bond World 007** (www.schilthorn.ch; Schilthorn; free with cable-car ticket; ⊙8am-6pm) up top, or enjoy lunch at the revolving mountaintop restaurant, **Piz Gloria** (☑033 856 21 50; www.schilthorn.ch; Höheweg 2; mains Sfr21-45; ⊙8am-5pm).

En route from Mürren to Schilthorn, you'll change cable cars at Birg station (2677m), where you can contemplate more spine-tingling views from the sun terrace and eyrie-like **Skyline Walk** (www.schilthorn.ch; Birg; ⛷) viewpoint, or test your nerves on the aptly named **Thrill Walk** (www.schilthorn.ch; Birg), a sequence of see-through plexiglass platforms anchored to the cliff face.

From Interlaken the round-trip involves a train from Interlaken Ost to Lauterbrunnen, a cable car to Grütschalp, another train to Mürren and pair of cable cars to Schilthorn via Birg. For the return, retrace your route from Schilthorn to Mürren, then, for different views, take a cable car to Stechelberg, bus 141 to Lauterbrunnen and a train back to Interlaken.

Piz Gloria
SAHACHATZ/SHUTTERSTOCK ©

Interlaken

◎ SIGHTS

Bernatone Alphornbau   Workshop
(☑079 840 38 10; www.bernatone.ch; Im Holz, Habkern; ⊙10am-noon & 1.30-5pm Mon-Fri; ⛷)
It doesn't get more Swiss than the alpenhorn, that fabulous-looking instrument often played by bearded Alpine men with ruddy cheeks and a good set of lungs at summer folk festivals. Call ahead and you can visit the workshop of master alpenhorn maker Heinz Tschiemer. A genuine alpenhorn, which takes around 60 days to make, will set you back around Sfr3000 but smaller instruments are also available for purchase. From Interlaken West, take bus 106 to Haberkern (18 minutes).

⊕ SHOPPING

Swiss Mountain Market   Food & Drinks
(Map p141; www.mountain-market.ch; Höheweg 133; ⊙10am-noon & 2-6.30pm Mon-Fri, 10am-4pm Sat) Amid Interlaken's ocean of tourist kitsch, this store stands out with its terrific selection of regional products from the Bernese Oberland. Take home local craft beer, cheese, Alpine herbal teas and cosmetics, goat-butter creams and chocolate from nearby Ballenberg.

Vertical Sport   Sports & Outdoors
(Map p141; http://verticalsport.ch; Jungfrausstrasse 44; ⊙9am-noon & 1.30-6pm Mon-Fri, 9am-4pm Sat) Located at the K44 climbing hall, this store sells and rents out top-quality climbing gear and is run by expert mountaineers who can give sound advice.

⊗ EATING

The Verandah   Swiss $$
(Map p141; ☑033 822 75 75; Höheweg 139, Hotel Royal-St Georges; mains Sfr21-38; ⊙6-10pm)
This restaurant at Hotel Royal-St Georges

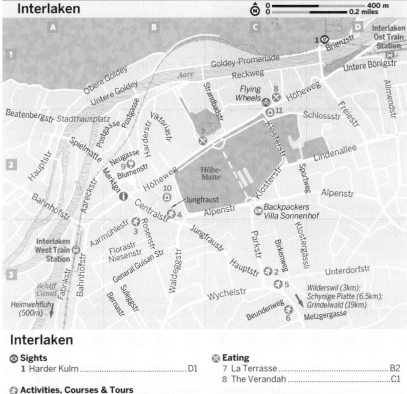

Interlaken

◉ Sights
1 Harder Kulm D1

◎ Activities, Courses & Tours
2 Alpinraft C3
3 Hang Gliding Interlaken B3
4 K44 .... B2
5 Outdoor Interlaken C3
6 Skydive Switzerland – Scenic Air C3

⊗ Eating
7 La Terrasse B2
8 The Verandah C1

◎ Drinking & Nightlife
9 Hüsi Bierhaus B2

◎ Shopping
10 Funky Chocolate Club B2
11 Swiss Mountain Market............................. C2
    Vertical Sport....................................(see 4)

is a winning combination of old-school elegance and contemporary style, with its stucco trimmings and slick bistro seating. The menu has riffs on Swiss food, with well-prepared classics such as fondue and rösti, grilled fish and meats.

La Terrasse   French $$$
(Map p141; ☎033 828 28 28; www.victoria-jungfrau.ch; Höheweg 41; mains Sfr38-65; ⊗7-10pm Tue-Sat) Housed in Interlaken's plushest belle époque hotel, La Terrasse is a class act, with a season-driven menu and a sumptuous setting redolent of a French orangery. The cuisine plays up French-Swiss flavours, so expect starters such as asparagus cappuccino with wild garlic and vanilla, followed by bouillabaisse with caviar or guinea fowl with summer truffle and thyme potatoes.

🍴 Funky Chocolate Club

'Chocolate today, broccoli tomorrow' is the strapline of this fun venture. Run by two passionate chocoholics, Tatiana and Vladimir, the **Funky Chocolate Club** (Map p141; ☏078 606 35 48; https://funkychocolateclub.com; Jungfraustrasse 35; ⏱10am-6.30pm; ⓦ) promises you will get 'chocolate wasted'. It delivers with a shop brimming with fair-trade and organic chocolate (vegan, dairy, nut and gluten-free varieties available). You'll also find chocolate fondue, hot chocolate, even pro tools for chocolatiers.

To get messy with chocolate yourself and stir up your own creations, hook into one of its workshops (adult/child Sfr65/59) at 11am, 2pm, 4pm and 6pm Wednesday to Sunday. There's also an excellent shop where you can stock up on niche-brand Swiss chocolate and gorge on strawberries with chocolate fondue (Sfr8.90).

Hazlenut chocolate
ROMAN BABAKIN/SHUTTERSTOCK ©

🍷 DRINKING & NIGHTLIFE
Hüsi Bierhaus   Pub

(Map p141; www.huesi-interlaken.ch; Postgasse 3; ⏱1.30pm-12.30am Mon-Thu, to 1.30am Fri, 11.30am-1.30am Sat, 11.30am-12.30am Sun) Some 50 different craft beers from around the world – Trappist brews to Swiss IPAs – keep the punters happy at Hüsi's. It also rolls out tasty pub grub (Sfr17.50

to Sfr33.50) from schnitzel to beer-laced bratwurst. Cover band Uptown Lights play Saturday nights.

ℹ INFORMATION
Tourist Office (Map p141; ☏033 826 53 00; www.interlakentourism.ch; Marktgasse 1; ⏱8am-7pm Mon-Fri, to 5pm Sat, 10am-4pm Sun Jul & Aug, shorter hours Sep-Jun) Interlaken's well-stocked, well-staffed tourist office also provides hotel booking services.

ℹ GETTING THERE & AWAY
Interlaken has two train stations: Interlaken West and Interlaken Ost; each has bike hire, money-changing facilities and an adjacent ferry landing stage for boats headed for Lake Thun and Lake Brienz.

Trains to Lucerne (Sfr32, 1¾ to two hours), Brig (Sfr45, one to 1¾ hours, via Spiez) and Montreux (Sfr71, 2¼ to 2¾ hours, via Spiez/Visp or Bern/Lausanne) depart frequently from Interlaken Ost train station.

The A8 motorway heads northeast to Lucerne and the A6 northwest to Bern, but the only way south for vehicles without a big detour round the mountains is to take the car-carrying train from Kandersteg, south of Spiez.

Should you wish to hire a car in Interlaken for trips further into Switzerland, big-name rental companies, including **Hertz** (☏033 822 61 72; www.hertz.ch; Hauptstrasse 4), are reasonably central.

ℹ GETTING AROUND
You can easily get around Interlaken on foot, but taxis and buses are found at each train station. Alternatively, pick up road bikes, tandems, all-terrain bikes and e-bikes at **Flying Wheels** (Map p141; ☏033 557 88 38; www.flyingwheels.ch; Höheweg 133) or other rental agencies around town.

Grindelwald

◎ SIGHTS

Gletscherschlucht Gorge

(Glacier Gorge; www.grindelwaldsports.ch; adult/
child Sfr19/10; ⊙9.30am-6pm Sat-Thu, to 10pm
Fri) Turbulent waters carve a path through
this craggy glacier gorge. A footpath
weaves through tunnels hacked into cliffs
veined with pink and green marble. It's
justifiably a popular spot for canyon and
bungee-jumping expeditions. The gorge is
a half-hour walk south from Grindelwald or
take bus 2 from the train station.

✪ ACTIVITIES

Paragliding Jungfrau Paragliding

(☐079 779 90 00; www.paragliding-jungfrau.ch)
Call ahead to organise your jump from
First (from Sfr180) at a height of 2150m.
Longer flights (Sfr280) are also available
if you want to maximise your airtime.
Meeting points are provided at the time of
booking.

Sportzentrum
Grindelwald Health & Fitness

(Map p144; www.sportzentrum-grindelwald.ch;
Dorfstrasse 110) If the weather turns gloomy,
Grindelwald's sport centre shelters a
swimming pool, mini spa, bouldering and
climbing halls, an ice rink and an indoor
rope park. See the website for opening
times and prices. A guest card yields substantial discounts.

Grindelwald
Sports Adventure Sports

(Map p144; ☐033 854 12 80; www.grindelwald
sports.ch; Dorfstrasse 103; ⊙8.30am-7pm)
Opposite the tourist office, this outfit
arranges mountain climbing, ski and snowboard instruction and the heart-stopping
canyon swing and bungee in the Gletscherschlucht. It also houses a cosy cafe and
sells walking guides.

Free Interlaken
Walking Tour

Want to see Interlaken like a local?
Guides show visitors their home turf on
fun and insightful two-hour guided walking tours, which begin at 6pm every day
from April to September, and at 11am on
Mondays, Wednesdays and Saturdays
from October to March. The meeting
point is **Backpackers Villa Sonnenhof**
(Map p141; ☐033 826 71 71; www.villa.ch;
Alpenstrasse 16; dm Sfr40-47, d Sfr110-148;
🅿🛜). The tour is free, but tips are, of
course, appreciated. For more details,
consult www.interlakenfreetour.com.

Lake Thun, Interlaken
LAPON PINTA/SHUTTERSTOCK ©

⊗ EATING

Cafe 3692 Cafe $

(Map p144; ☐033 853 16 54; www.cafe3692.
ch; Terrassenweg 61; snacks & light meals
Sfr7-25; ⊙8.30am-6pm Sun-Tue, to midnight
Fri & Sat) Run by dream duo Myriam and
Bruno, Cafe 3692 is a delight. Bruno
is a talented carpenter and has let his
imagination run riot – a gnarled apple tree
is an eye-catching artwork, a mine-cart
trolley cleverly transforms into a grill, and
the ceiling is a wave of woodwork. Garden
herbs and Grindelwald-sourced ingredients
are knocked up into tasty specials.

The Alpine teas are superb, as are Heidi's
delectable pastries and pralines. The mine
cart is wheeled out for barbecues every
Friday and Saturday night in summer. Puz-
zled about the name? It refers to the local
summit of Wetterhorn (3692m).

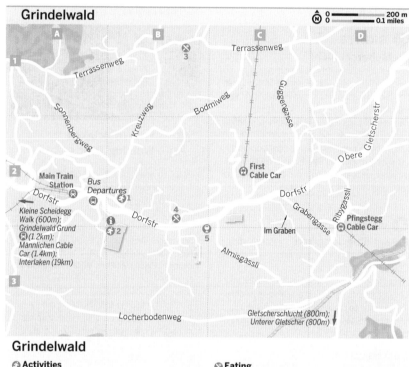

Grindelwald

Memory   Swiss **$$**
(Map p144; ☎033 854 31 31; Dorfstrasse 133;
mains Sfr17-36; ⊙9am-11.30pm) Always
packed, the Eiger Hotel's unpretentious
restaurant rolls out tasty Swiss grub such
as rösti, raclette and fondue, as well as –
titter ye not – 'horny' chicken with a spicy
'Christian' sauce. Try to bag a table on the
street-facing terrace.

⊖ DRINKING & NIGHTLIFE

Avocado Bar   Bar
(Map p144; Dorfstrasse 158; ⊙3pm-12.30am;
🛜) This is a young 'n' fun place to kick
back on a leather pouffe with a post-ski

schnapps or people-watch on the terrace in
summer. There's occasional live music on
Wednesdays.

❶ INFORMATION

Tourist Office (Map p144; ☎033 854 12 12;
www.grindelwald.ch; Dorfstrasse 110; ⊙8am-
6pm Mon-Fri, 9am-6pm Sat & Sun; 🛜) The
tourist office in the Sportzentrum hands out
brochures and hiking maps, and has a free inter-
net terminal and wi-fi. There's an accommoda-
tion board outside or you can ask staff to book
rooms for you.

Staubbachfall

ℹ️ GETTING THERE & AWAY

Grindelwald is off the A8 from Interlaken. A smaller road continues from the village over the Grosse Scheidegg Pass (1960m). It's closed to private traffic, but from mid-June to early October **postal buses** (Map p144) travel this scenic route to Meiringen (Sfr54, 2¼ hours) roughly hourly from 8am to 5pm. Cable cars haul you up to the mountains above Grindelwald, including **First** (www.jungfrau.ch; return adult/child Sfr66/33; ⏱8.30am-5pm, to 4.15pm in winter), **Männlichen** (www.maennlichen.ch; adult/child Sfr30/15; ⏱8.15am-5pm) and **Pfingstegg** (www.pfingstegg. ch; one way/return Sfr12.60/18.80; ⏱8am-7pm, to 5.30pm in low season, closed Nov-Apr).

Lauterbrunnen

◎ SIGHTS

Staubbachfall   Waterfall
(Staubbach Falls; ⏱8am-8pm Jun-Oct) Especially in the early morning light, you can see how the vaporous, 297m-high Staubbach Falls captivated prominent writers with its threads of spray floating down the cliffs.

What appears to be ultra-fine mist from a distance, however, becomes a torrent when you walk behind the falls. Be prepared to get wet. Wear sturdy shoes for the short but steep uphill walk.

⊕ ACTIVITIES

Doris Hike   Hiking
(📞033 855 42 40; www.doris-hike.ch) Doris' informative guided hikes include glacier, waterfall and high-Alpine options. Call ahead for times and prices.

✖️ EATING

Airtime   Cafe $

(📞033 855 15 15; www.airtime.ch; snacks & light meals Sfr6-15.50; ⏱9am-6pm; 📶) Inspired by their travels in New Zealand, Daniela and Beni have set up this funky cafe, book exchange, laundry service and extreme-sports agency. Munch home-roasted granola, sandwiches, pies and homemade cakes (including a gluten-free chocolate one) as you use the free wi-fi or browse a novel. You can book adrenaline-fuelled pursuits such as ice climbing, canyoning and bungee jumping here.

Hotel Oberland   Swiss $$

(☑033 855 12 41; pizza Sfr16-24.50, mains Sfr22-40; ⊙11.30am-9pm) The street-facing terrace at this traditional haunt is always humming. On the menu are Swiss and international favourites from fondue to pizza, vegetable curry and hybrid dishes such as Indian-style rösti. There are plenty of veggie picks, too.

ℹ️ INFORMATION

Tourist Office (☑033 856 85 68; www.lauterbrunnen.swiss; Stutzli 460; ⊙8.30am-noon & 2-6.30pm Jun-Sep, shorter hours rest of year) Opposite the train station.

ℹ️ GETTING THERE & AWAY

Regular trains make the short hop from Interlaken (Sfr7.60, 21 minutes). Situated in the valley of the same name, Lauterbrunnen is a major jumping-off point for reaching Alpine resorts such as Wengen (Sfr6.80, 14 minutes) by train and Mürren (Sfr11.40, 23 minutes) by cable car/train.

If you're travelling to the car-free resorts of Wengen or Mürren, there's a multistorey **car park** (☑033 828 74 00; www.jungfraubahn.ch; per day/week Sfr14/84) by the station, but it's advisable to book ahead. There is also an open-air car park by the Stechelberg cable-car station, charging Sfr10 for a day.

Wengen

🍴 EATING

Restaurant Bären   Swiss $$

(☑033 855 14 19; mains Sfr30-53; ⊙8am-1.30pm & 5-11.30pm Mon-Fri, 5-11.30pm Sat & Sun; 🖋) Mixing tradition with creative flair, this excellent restaurant (attached to the hotel of the same name) prides itself on using regionally raised meats, home-grown herbs, vegetables and edible flowers and locally hunted game. Dishes range from perfectly cooked veal with strawberry risotto to vegetarian *Spätzli* (egg noodles) with stewed mushrooms. Wild cards include chestnut mousse and wasabi-pumpkin-seed parfait for dessert.

Allmendhubel funicular track, Mürren

Restaurant 1903   Swiss $$$

(☑033 855 34 22; www.hotel-schoenegg.ch; mains Sfr35-58; ⏱6.30-10pm, closed May & mid-Oct–mid-Dec) At Hotel Schönegg, chef Sylvain Stefanazzi Ogi serves seasonally inspired dishes such as oxtail ravioli with bone marrow and Swiss chard and perch fillets with black gnocchi and Champagne sauce. The pine-clad, candlelit dining room is wonderfully cosy in winter and the leafy mountain-facing terrace is perfect for summertime dining.

🍷 DRINKING & NIGHTLIFE

Tanne Bar   Bar

(⏱4pm-late) A popular hangout for Swiss and Scandi skiers, this snug, wood-panelled bar on Wengen's main drag cranks it up during the ski season with après-ski glühwein and cocktails as the night wears on.

ℹ️ INFORMATION

Tourist Office (☑033 856 85 85; www.wengen. ch; ⏱9am-6pm, to 9pm Jul & Aug, closed Sat & Sun Nov, Mar & Apr; 🛜) Next to the Männlichen cable car.

ℹ️ GETTING THERE & AWAY

Old-fashioned trains curl up the mountain twice hourly to Wengen from Lauterbrunnen (Sfr6.80, 14 minutes).

Mürren

➕ ACTIVITIES

Klettersteig   Via Ferrata

(☑033 856 86 86; www.klettersteig-muerren.ch; ⏱mid-Jun–Oct) Mürren's 2.2km Klettersteig is one of the region's most mesmerising *vie ferrate* (iron ways), affording head-spinning views of the Jungfrau giants as it teeters across the sheer cliff faces to Gimmelwald. With its ladders, cables, suspension bridge and arresting views of Eiger north face, it's breathtaking in every sense of the word.

Hire equipment (Sfr28 per day) from **Intersport** (☑033 855 23 55; www.

staegersport.ch/muerren; Chalet Enzian; ⏱9am-noon & 1-6pm), opposite the Klettersteig entrance in Mürren's centre.

Allmendhubel   Mountain

In summer the Allmendhubel **funicular** (www.schilthorn.ch; return adult/child Sfr14/7; ⏱every 20min 9am-5pm; 🚼) takes you above Mürren to a panoramic restaurant and the Skyline Chill relaxation area where funky wave-shaped loungers grant wraparound mountain views. Kids love the giant butterflies, marmot burrows and alpine flowers at the adventure playground.

North Face Trail   Hiking

From the top station of the Allmendhubel funicular, you can set out on many walks, including the spectacular North Face Trail (1½ hours), via Schiltalp to the west, leading through wildflower-strewn meadows with big views to the glaciers and waterfalls of the Lauterbrunnen Valley and the monstrous Eiger north face – bring binoculars to spy intrepid climbers.

🍴 EATING

Restaurant La Grotte   Swiss $$

(☑033 855 18 26; Hotel Blumental; mains Sfr15-45; ⏱11am-2pm & 5-9pm) Brimming with cowbells, cauldrons and Alpine props, this kitsch-meets-rustic mock cave of a restaurant is touristy but fun. Fondues and flambés are good bets.

ℹ️ INFORMATION

Tourist Office (☑033 856 86 86; www. mymuerren.ch; ⏱8.30am-noon & 1-5.15pm; 🛜) The tourist office in the sports centre has a free room-booking service, as well as a wide array of maps and leaflets.

ℹ️ GETTING THERE & AWAY

The quickest and easiest way to reach Mürren from Lauterbrunnen is to take the cable car to Grutschalp (four minutes) then transfer to a Mürren-bound train (14 minutes, total one-way fare Sfr11.40).

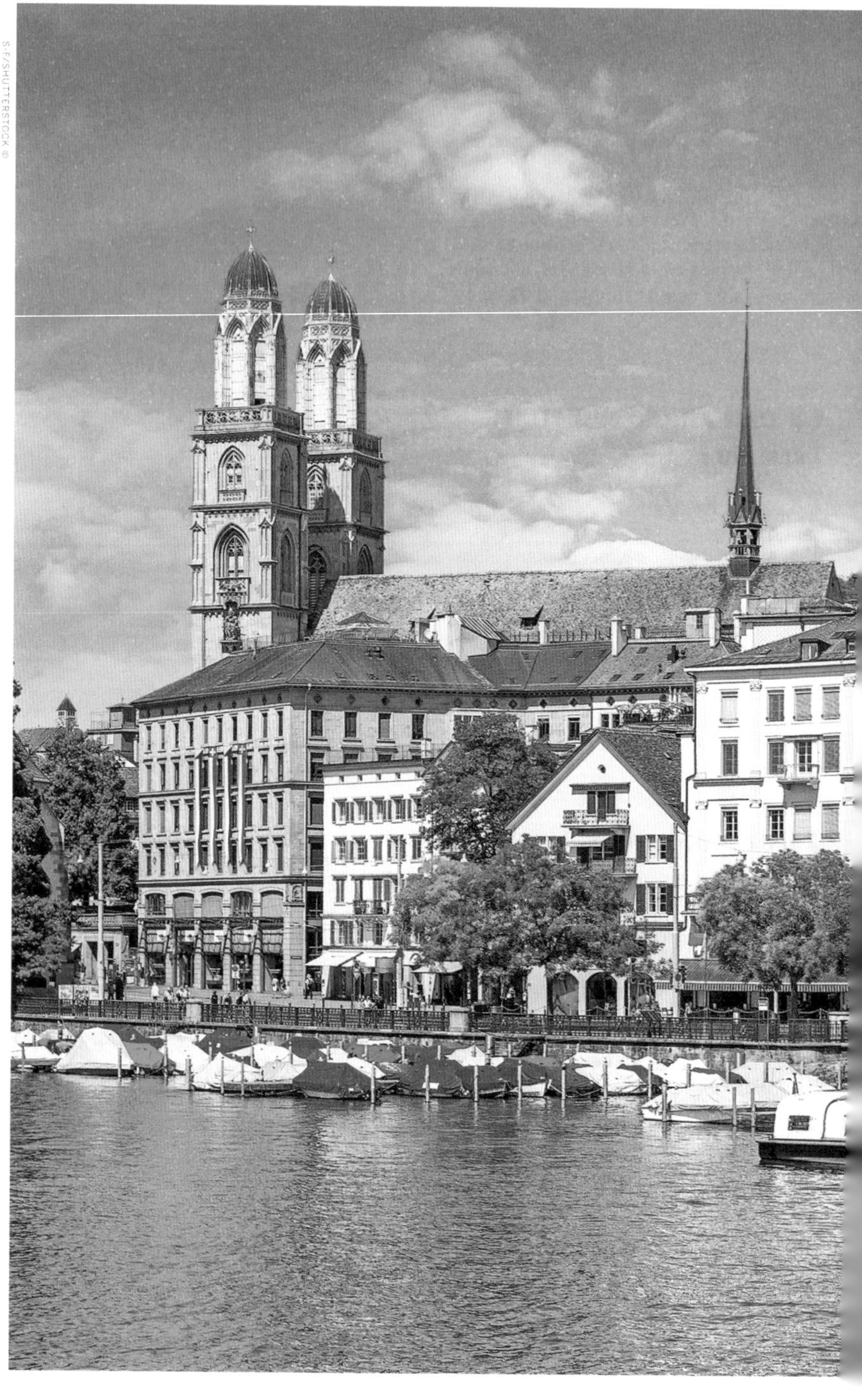

S-F/SHUTTERSTOCK ©

ZÜRICH

In This Chapter

Zürich at a Glance...

Culturally vibrant and attractively set at the meeting of river and lake, Zürich is one of the world's most liveable cities. Switzerland's largest and wealthiest metropolis has emerged as one of central Europe's hippest destinations, with an artsy, postindustrial edge best epitomised by its exuberant summer Street Parade.

Much of the historic centre, with its winding lanes and tall church steeples, is intact. Yet Zürich has also embraced contemporary trends, converting old factories into cultural centres, restaurants and creative living spaces, such as in Züri-West, epicentre of the city's nightlife.

Two Days in Zürich

Klck off with hot chocolate at **Café Sprüngli** (p152), then explore downtown Zürich on foot, admiring the views from hilltop **Lindenhof** (p167), window-shopping in swankiy Bahnhofstrasse and funky Niederdorf, and admiring Chagall's luminescent stained-glass in the **Fraumünster** (p165). On day two, hit top museums such as **Kunsthaus** (p165), **Schweizerisches Landesmuseum** (p165) and the new **FIFA World Football Museum** (p166).

Four Days in Zürich

On day three, discover Zürich's gorgeous lake and riverfront with a swim at **Seebad Utoquai** (p166), **Letten** (p167), **Männerbad** (p168) or **Frauenbad** (p168). Then wander through Züri-West's converted industrial spaces, including **Im Viadukt** (p155) and **Freitag** (p154), and drink alfresco at **Frau Gerolds Garten** (p170). On day four, take a side trip to **Schaffhausen** (p158), **Rheinfall** (p156), or **St Gallen** (p162).

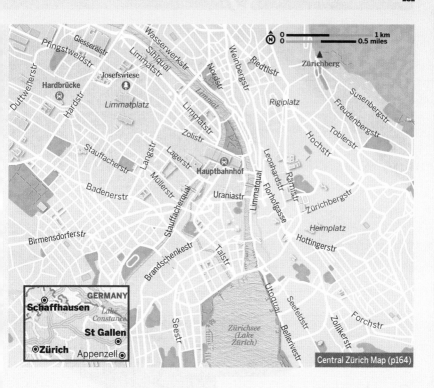

Central Zürich Map (p164)

Arriving in Zürich

Zürich Airport Up to nine SBB (www.sbb.ch) trains run hourly to Hauptbahnhof from 5am to midnight; taxis cost around Sfr60 to the centre.

Hauptbahnhof Zürich's centrally located train station offers efficient, frequent connections to cities throughout Switzerland, including Lucerne (Sfr26, 50 minutes), Bern (Sfr51, one hour), Basel (Sfr34, one hour), Geneva (Sfr89, 2¾ hours) and Lugano (Sfr66, 2¼ hours).

Sleeping

High prices and top-of-the-line amenities generally go hand in hand in Zürich's business-oriented accommodation scene. A few cheaper places can be found in outlying neighbourhoods. Many hotels offer lower prices on weekends, but note that finding a room on the weekend of the August Street Parade is tough and prices skyrocket. Prices can also head north during major trade fairs (including those in Basel).

Gastronomic Zürich

Zürich's lucky denizens can choose from an astounding 2000-plus eateries. Traditional cuisine is very rich, as epitomised by the city's signature Zürcher Geschnetzeltes (veal in creamy mushroom and white-wine sauce).

Great For...

☑ **Don't Miss**

The divine hot chocolate at Café Sprüngli, topped with a decadent dollop of whipped cream.

Café Sprüngli

Sit down for cakes, ice cream, light lunch and exquisite coffee drinks at **Café Sprüngli** (☑044 224 46 46; www.spruengli.ch; Bahnhofstrasse 21; sweets Sfr8-16; ☺7.30am-6.30pm Mon-Fri, 8am-6pm Sat), an epicentre of sweet Switzerland. Whatever you do, don't miss the heavenly chocolate shop next door, where you can buy delectable pralines and truffles, plus the house speciality – rainbow-bright Luxemburgerli macaroons.

Haus Hiltl

Established in 1898, the world's oldest vegetarian restaurant, **Hiltl** (☑044 227 70 00; www.hiltl.ch; Sihlstrasse 28; per 100g Sfr4.90, mains Sfr25-35; ☺6am-midnight Mon-Sat, 8am-midnight Sun; ✈), proffers an astounding buffet of meatless delights, from Indian and Thai curries to Mediterranean grilled veggies, plus

Macarons, Café Sprüngli

ⓘ Need to Know

Lunchtime is roughly noon to 2.30pm; dinner runs from 6pm to as late as 11pm or midnight.

✕ Take a Break

Hide away poolside at Rimini Bar (p170) or embrace the touristy beer garden vibe at Bauschänzli (p169).

> ### ★ Top Tip
> Service is included in restaurant bills, but locals often round up the total for good service.

Sfr36-76; ⊙noon-midnight) is a brasserie-style establishment with white tablecloths, dark wood and an Old World feel. Impeccably mannered waiters move discreetly below Chagall, Miró, Matisse and Picasso originals, serving a daily-changing menu that regularly crosses international borders.

salads and desserts. Sit in the informal cafe or the spiffier adjoining restaurant. Good-value takeaway service is also available.

Didi's Frieden

With its unique blend of familiarity and refinement, **Didi's Frieden** (☎044 253 18 10; www.didisfrieden.ch; Stampfenbachstrasse 32; 4-/5-course menu Sfr98/108; ⊙11am-2.30pm & 5pm-midnight Mon-Fri, 6pm-midnight Sat) features among Zürich's top tables. The look is understated elegance with white tablecloths and wine-glass chandeliers. Service is discreet yet attentive, while menus sing of the seasons in dishes like venison ravioli with dark chocolate and shallot jus.

Kronenhalle

A haunt of city movers and shakers in suits, the **Crown Hall** (☎044 262 99 00; www.kronenhalle.ch; Rämistrasse 4; mains

Zeughauskeller

Tuck into the heartiest of Swiss fare under the heavy oak beams at this sprawling, atmospheric 15th-century beer hall. **Zeughauskeller** (☎044 220 15 15; www.zeughauskeller.ch; Bahnhofstrasse 28a; lunch specials Sfr21.50, mains Sfr19-37; ⊙11.30am-11pm) has ample sidewalk seating, and its multilingual menu goes to town with a dozen varieties of sausage and other Swiss faves like pork roast with lashings of sauerkraut. Vegetarian options are also available.

Raclette Stube

For the quintessential Swiss cheese experiences – fondue and raclette – pop by warm and welcoming **Raclette Stube** (☎044 251 41 30; www.raclette-stube.ch; Zähringerstrasse 16; fondue Sfr29-32, raclette Sfr40; ⊙6-11pm).

Zürich Shopping

Zürich is a shopper's dream. For top-of-the-line fashion and high-end boutiques, head for Bahnhofstrasse. Elsewhere, fun and funky shops are sprinkled throughout Niederdorf and the converted industrial spaces of Züri-West.

Great For...

☑ Don't Miss

The gritty urban views from the top of the shipping container 'skyscraper' at Freitag.

Freitag

The Freitag brothers recycle colourful truck tarps into unique bags. Their **outlet** (☎043 366 95 20; www.freitag.ch; Geroldstrasse 17; ☺10.30am-7pm Mon-Fri, 10am-6pm Sat) is pure whimsy – a pile of shipping containers that's been dubbed Kreis 5's first skyscraper. Climb to the rooftop terrace for spectacular city views.

Max Chocolatier

Of all Zürich's tempting chocolatiers, **Max** (www.maxchocolatier.com; Schlüsselgasse 12; ☺10.30am-7pm Tue-Fri, 10am-5.30pm Sat) has the edge. This chic Old Town boutique has a fabulous array of beautifully packaged bars, truffles and pralines, made with 100% natural Swiss ingredients. Keep an eye out for seasonal one-offs such as Alpine hay, cassis and violets, or elderflower. Check the website for details of tasting workshops.

Freitag

ⓘ Need to Know

Almost every shop in Switzerland closes on Sundays – even in Zürich!

✕ Take a Break

Briefly detour from your shopping reverie for a drink and a bite at Frau Gerolds Garten (p170).

★ Top Tip

Saturday is prime time for fleamarket shopping at Flohmarkt Kanzlei (p168) and Bürkliplatz (p167).

Im Viadukt

In a city enamoured with reinvention and repurposing, **Im Viadukt** (www.im-viadukt.ch; Viaduktstrasse; ⊘10am-8pm Mon-Thu, 8am-8pm Fri & Sat) stands proud. Once a down-at-heel storage facility under stone railway bridges, it's recently been reborn into a humming complex of locally owned shops (clothes, furniture etc), restaurants, cafes and artisan food markets. Stroll the viaduct's three-block length between Limmatstrasse and Gerold-strasse and see what catches your eye.

Uhren Atelier Rindermarkt

In a land famous for its watches, there are bound to be a few used ones, and that's precisely the focus at this hole-in-the-wall **shop** (⊘044 262 60 90; www.uhrenatelier.ch; Rindermarkt 21; ⊘11am-5.30pm Mon-Wed, to 6pm Thu & Fri, to 4pm Sat). Owners Anton Beal and Theodor Wachtel stock a dazzling array

of vintage timepieces, along with multiple brands of new watches. A repair service is also available.

Landolt-Arbenz

In business since 1882, distinguished old stationery shop **Landolt-Arbenz** (⊘043 443 77 10; www.landolt-arbenz.ch; Bahnhofstrasse 65; ⊘10am-7pm Mon-Fri, to 6pm Sat) displays a mind-boggling collection of fine pens, inks and art supplies across its two floors.

Andrea Hinnen

Brilliant colours and bold patterns distinguish the work of Swiss-born, New York–trained clothing designer **Andrea Hinnen** (⊘044 240 02 12; www.andreahinnen.com; Rotwandstrasse 53; ⊘noon-7pm Tue-Fri, to 5pm Sat). Chat with the artist while browsing her intimate boutique.

Tiger Fink

Parents and travellers searching for a perfect baby gift will love the colourful selection of kids' clothing, books and toys at Zürich original **Tiger Fink** (⊘044 261 79 11; www.tiger-fink.ch; Kreuzstrasse 36; ⊘11am-6.30pm Mon, 9.30am-6.30pm Tue-Fri, 9.30am-5pm Sat).

Rheinfall

Ensnared in wispy spray, at 23m high, 150m wide and with water falling at 700 cu meters per second, the thunderous Rheinfall might not compete with Niagara's size, but Europe's largest waterfall is stunning nonetheless.

Formed by tectonic shifts during the last ice age 15,000 years ago, the **Rheinfall** (Rhine Falls; www.rheinfall.ch) is a real crash-bang spectacle, raging at a speed of around 700 cu metres per second as it spills into a basin in a series of swirling cascades, billowing plumes of spray and white water. Europe's biggest plain waterfall is best seen on the trail that wends down from medieval Schloss Laufen or on one of the boats that cross to the rock that rises above it. Trails thread up and along its shore, with viewpoints providing abundant photo ops.

Boat Tours: Rhyfall Mändli

During summer, **ferries** (www.maendli.ch; adult/child return Sfr10/5) flit in and out of the water at the bottom of the Rheinfall cascade. The best is the round trip that stops at the tall rock in the middle of the falls,

Great For...

☑ **Don't Miss**

The 360-degree falls view from the viewing platform atop a rock in mid-river.

ℹ **Need to Know**

The Rheinfall is best visited in warm weather, when boat tours are operating.

✕ **Take a Break**

Enjoy a scenic lunch with front-row views of the falls at Schlössli Worth.

★ **Top Tip**

Consider carrying a lightweight rain jacket to ward off spray from the falls.

windows affording magical views of the falls, strikingly illuminated after dark. Market-fresh cuisine such as venison carpaccio with rocket or baked trout with basil butter is paired with fine local wines.

Adventure Park

For an above-the-treetops perspective of the Rheinfall, visit **Adventure Park** (www.ap-rheinfall.ch; Nohlstrasse; adult/child Sfr40/26; ☉10am-7pm Apr-Oct; 🚣), one of Switzerland's biggest rope parks, with routes graded according to difficulty.

Getting to the Falls

Frequent trains run from Zürich to Schloss Laufen am Rheinfall (from Sfr17.20, 50 minutes), with a change in Schaffhausen or Winterthur. From Schloss Laufen am Rheinfall station, you'll need to climb the hill to the castle. By car, you'll pull up in the car park behind the castle.

Neuhausen am Rheinfall is 4km southwest of Schaffhausen. Buses 1 and 6 run every 10 minutes between the two towns (Sfr4.80, 15 minutes). Upon arrival in Neuhausen, bear right towards Schlössli Worth or left across the combined train and pedestrian bridge to Schloss Laufen.

from where you can climb to the top and watch the water rush all around you.

Schloss Laufen am Rheinfall

Looking proudly back on 1000 years of history, the medieval **Schloss Laufen** (www. schlosslaufen.ch; adult/child Sfr5/3; ☉8am-7pm Jun-Aug, shorter hours rest of year) offers a close-quarters view of the Rheinfall cascade. Buy a ticket at its souvenir shop to walk or take the panoramic lift down to the Känzeli viewing platform, where you can appreciate the falls' full impact.

Dining by the Falls

Schlössli Worth (☎052 672 24 21; www. schloessliwoerth.ch; Rheinfallquai 30; mains Sfr42-68; ☉11.30am-11.30pm), on the north bank of the Rheinfall, harbours a lounge-style restaurant with floor-to-ceiling

A Day in Schaffhausen

Ornate frescos and oriel windows grace the pastel-coloured houses of Schaffhausen's pedestrianised Old Town on the banks of the Rhine. Only 40 minutes from Zürich, it makes a delightful day trip.

Great for...

☑ Don't Miss

The *vinothek* at Schaffhausen's tourist office, where you can buy locally produced wines.

Schaffhausen is the kind of quaint medieval town more readily associated with Germany – no coincidence, given its proximity to the border. Presiding above town on a vineyard-streaked hill is one of Schaffhausen defining landmark, the circular 16th-century Munot fortress.

Allerheiligen Münster

Completed in 1103, Schaffhausen's **Allerheiligen Münster** (All Saints' Cathedral; Münsterplatz; ⏰10am-noon & 2-5pm Tue-Sun, cloister 7.30am-8pm Mon-Fri, 9am-8pm Sat & Sun) is a rare, largely intact specimen of the Romanesque style in Switzerland. It opens to a beautifully simple cloister. The herb garden has been lovingly tended since the Middle Ages and is a tranquil spot for contemplation. Walk through the cloister to reach the **Museum zu Allerheiligen** (www.

View of Munot from the Rhine

TRABANTOS/SHUTTERSTOCK ©

❶ Need to Know

The **Tourist Office** (www.schaffhauserland. ch; Herrenacker 15) hands out brochures and stocks cycling maps and guides.

✕ Take a Break

Tuck into modern interpretations of traditional fare at Wirtschaft zum Frieden (p161).

★ Top Tip

Schaffhausen has the dubious honour of being the only Swiss city bombed (mistakenly) in WWII.

allerheiligen.ch; Klosterstrasse 16; adult/child Sfr12/free; ⏱11am-5pm Tue-Sun).

Munot

Steps lead up through terraced vineyards to this fine specimen of a 16th-century **fortress** (⏱8am-8pm May-Sep, 9am-5pm Oct-Apr) **FREE**. The unusual circular battlements were built with forced labour following the Reformation and conceal an atmospheric vaulted casemate. Climb the spiral staircase for views over a patchwork of rooftops and spires to the Rhine and wooded hills fringing the city.

Vorstadt

Schaffhausen is often nicknamed the Erkerstadt because of its 171 *Erker*, once a status symbol of rich merchants. Some of the most impressive line up along Vorstadt, including the 17th-century **Zum Goldenen**

Ochsen (Vorstadt 17), whose frescoed facade displays an eponymous golden ox. The frescos of the 16th-century **Zum Grossen Käfig** (Vorstadt 45) present an extraordinarily colourful tale of the parading of Turkish sultan Bajazet in a cage by the triumphant Mongol leader Tamerlane.

A block east, eye-catching **Haus zum Ritter** (Vordergasse 65), built in 1492, boasts a detailed Renaissance-style fresco depicting a knight.

Fronwagplatz

At the very heart of the Altstadt lies this square, flanked by ornate facades. The 16th-century **Mohrenbrunnen** (Moor's Fountain) marks the northern end of the old marketplace, while at the southern end stands the **Metzgerbrunnen** (Butcher's Fountain), a William Tell–type figure and a large clock tower. Facing the latter is the late-baroque **Herrenstube** (Fronwagplatz 3), built in 1748, which was once the drinking hole of quaffing nobles.

Herrenacker

Framed by pastel-coloured houses with steep tiled roofs, this is one of Schaffhausen's prettiest squares. In August it's an atmospheric backdrop for music fest **Stars in Town** (www.starsintown.ch; ⊘Aug).

Altstadt Walks

On Saturdays in warm weather, 1¼-hour **walking tours** (adult/child Sfr14/10; ⊘2pm Sat May–mid-Oct) of the Old Town kick off at the tourist office. The well-informed guides speak German, English and French.

Rhybadi

If you're itching to leap into the Rhine, do it at this rickety 19th-century wooden **bathhouse** (www.rhybadi.ch; Rheinuferstrasse; adult/child Sfr4/2; ⊘8am-9pm Sun-Thu, to 10.30pm Fri & Sat May-Sep). There are diving boards and old-fashioned changing rooms reminiscent of an era when 'proper' folk bathed fully clothed.

Untersee und Rhein

The 45km **boat trip** (☑052 634 08 88; www.urh.ch; Freier Platz; one way to Stein am Rhein/Konstanz Sfr26/50; ⊘Apr-Oct) from Schaffhausen to Konstanz via Stein am Rhein and Reichenau takes in one of the Rhine's more beautiful stretches. The journey takes 3¾ hours downstream to Schaffhausen and 4¾ hours the other way.

Eating in Schaffhausen
Suppenglück

Doing what it says on the tin, this **hole-in-the-wall cafe** (☑079 254 56 26; http://suppenglueck.ch; Webergasse 46; soups & salads Sfr8.50-11.50; ⊘11am-2pm Mon-Fri)

Stein am Rhein

ladles out wholesome homemade soups – from spicy Thai-style numbers to goulash and cream of asparagus – best mopped up with wood-fired bread. It also does excellent salads, smoothies and organic lemonade.

D'Chuchi

Petite and cosy, with exposed brick, soft lighting and banquette seating, **D'Chuchi** (☏052 620 05 28; www.dchuchi.ch; Brunnengasse 3; mains Sfr28-44; ☺11.30am-2pm & 6-11.30pm Wed-Fri, 6-11.30pm Tue & Sat) has just a handful of tables – so book ahead.

🍷 **Wine Harvest Festival**
Visiting in October? Don't miss Trottenfest (www.trottenfest.ch; ☺mid-Oct), when vintners throw open their doors for tastings in Osterfingen, 16km west of Schaffhausen.

TRABANTOS/SHUTTERSTOCK ®

The chef prides himself on using regional, seasonal ingredients, and there's a succinct but well-edited menu with dishes such as pikeperch with wild-garlic risotto and black salsify or flat-iron steak with parsley root.

Gasthaus zum Adler

Home to famous local painter Tobias Stimmer in the 16th century, the **Adler** (☏052 625 55 15; www.gasthaus-adler.ch; Vorstadt 69; mains Sfr24.50-44.50; ☺8.30am-11pm Tue-Sat, 9am-10pm Sun; 🐾) has been doing a roaring trade as an inn for the past three centuries. The menu keeps things traditional and regional, with a nod to seasonal produce (mushrooms, asparagus, game and the like). Vegetarians are well catered for.

Wirtschaft Zum Frieden

Locals have been eating, drinking and making merry at this wood-panelled **inn** (www.wirtschaft-frieden.ch; Herrenacker 11; mains Sfr35-50; ☺11am-2.30pm & 5-11.30pm Tue-Fri, 10am-2.30pm & 5-11.30pm Sat; 🐾) since 1445. It's still an incredibly cosy choice today, with a tiled oven, cheek-by-jowl tables and old black-and-white photos. Come in for regional fare with a Med-style twist, such as tartar of Aargau water buffalo with pecorino mash or lemon ravioli with wild-garlic pesto. There's always a handful of veggie picks, too.

Getting to Schaffhausen

Direct trains run half-hourly to Schaffhausen from Zürich (Sfr23.20, 40 minutes).

By road, Schaffhausen is off the A4 motorway, which sweeps north to the German border and south to Winterthur, where it meets the A1 to Zürich.

★ **Did You Know?**
Schaffhausen has more bay windows than any other Swiss town.

St Gallen

One of northern Switzerland's most cultured towns, St Gallen is well worth the one-hour pilgrimage from Zürich. Its trophy site is its sublime rococo library, part of the venerable Unesco–listed Abbey District.

Great for...

☑ Don't Miss

Stadtlounge, a zany art installation covering Schreinerstrasse in red rubber, 400m west of the library.

Stiftsbibliothek

St Gallen's abbey **library** (www.stibi.ch; Klosterhof 6d; adult/child Sfr12/9, audioguide Sfr5; ⊙10am-5pm) is one of the world's oldest, and it's Switzerland's finest example of rococo architecture. Along with the rest of the Benedictine monastery, founded by St Gall in 612, the library forms a Unesco World Heritage Site. Filled with priceless leather-bound books and manuscripts painstakingly handwritten and illustrated by monks during the Middle Ages, it's a lavish confection of frescos, stucco, cherubs and parquetry. Multilingual audioguides are available, as are felt slippers, to protect the floor.

Only 30,000 of the collection's 170,000 volumes are in the library at any one time, arranged into special exhibitions. Of the library's 2100 precious manuscripts – some are works of art and remarkably

Interior of St Gallen's Dom (Cathedral)

G215/SHUTTERSTOCK ©

❶ Need to Know

There are regular trains to St Gallen from Zürich (Sfr31, 65 minutes via Winterthur). By car, the main link is the A1 motorway, which runs from Zürich and Winterthur to the Austrian border.

✕ Take a Break

Enjoy a traditional Swiss lunch at Bäumli wine tavern.

★ Top Tip

Visitors swoosh through the library in loaned felt slippers, required to protect the parquet floors.

well preserved – just a handful are on display. The oldest manuscript, dating to 760, was penned by monk Winithar, who complained about not having sufficient parchment. Other curiosities include a magnificent 16th-century globe, replete with naturalistic detail, and an Egyptian mummy.

The vaulted cellar houses the Lapidarium, which showcases a collection of Carolingian, Ottonian and Gothic sculpture from the former church on the site. There's also some interesting background, albeit mostly in German, about the art of illustration.

Dom

St Gallen's twin-towered, mid-18th-century **cathedral** (Klosterhof; ◷9am-6pm Mon, Tue, Thu & Fri, 10am-6pm Wed, 9am-4pm Sat, noon-5.30pm Sun) is only slightly less ornate than

the world-famous Stiftsbibliothek nearby. The cathedral features dark and stormy frescos and mint-green stucco embellishments. The cupola shows a vision of paradise with the Holy Trinity at the centre. Oddly, entry is via two modest doors on the north flank – there is no door in the main facade, which is actually the cathedral's apse. Concerts (www.dommusik-sg.ch) are held here; it is closed during services.

Bäumli

Creaking with 500 years of personality, this late-medieval **wine tavern** (☎071 222 11 74; www.weinstube-baeumli.ch; Schmiedgasse 18; mains Sfr25-47; ◷11am-2pm & 5-11pm Tue-Fri, 11am-11pm Sat) houses a wood-panelled, candlelit restaurant that showcases all the typical *Erststock-Beizli* (1st-floor tavern) specialities, such as bratwurst with fried onions, lamb cutlets, Wiener schnitzel, cordon bleu (pork schnitzel stuffed with ham and cheese) and *Geschnetzeltes* (sliced pork or veal).

Central Zürich

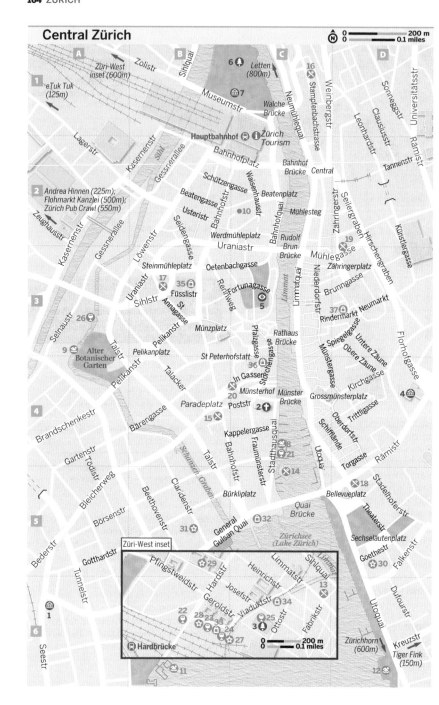

Züri-West inset (600m)

Zolistr
Sihlquai
6 Letten (800m)
16
Stampfenbachstrasse
Weinbergstr
Sonneggstr
Universitätsstr

eTuk Tuk (125m)
Museumstr
7
Walche Brücke
Neumühlequai
Leonhardstr
Clausiusstr
Ramistr

Lagerstr
Kasernenstr
Gessnerallee
Sihl
Hauptbahnhof
Zürich Tourism
Bahnhofplatz
Bahnhof Brücke Central
Tannenstr

Andrea Hinnen (225m); Flohmarkt Kanzlei (500m); Zürich Pub Crawl (550m)
Zeughausstr
Kasernenstr
Gessnerallee
Löwenstr
Seidengasse
Usteristr
Schützengasse
Beatengasse
Waisenhausstr
Bahnhofstr
10
Beatengasse
Beatenplatz
Bahnhofquai
Mühlesteg
Seilergraben
Zähringerstr
Hirschengraben
Künstlergasse

Werdmühleplatz
Uraniastr
Rudolf Brun Brücke
Mühlegasse
19
Zähringerplatz
Oetenbachgasse

Steinmühleplatz
Uraniastr
17
35
Füsslistr
Sihlstr
St Annagasse
Rennweg
Fortunagasse
5
Limmat
Limmatquai
Niederdorfstr
Brunngasse
Rindermarkt
37
Neumarkt
Florhofgasse

Selnaustr
26
Münzplatz
Talstr
Pelikanstr
Pelikanstr
9 Alter Botanischer Garten
Pelikanplatz
Talacker
St Peterhofstatt
Pfalzgasse
36
In Gassen
Strehlgasse
Rathaus Brücke
Spiegelgasse
Münstergasse
Untere Zäune
Obere Zäune

20
Münsterhof
Paradeplatz
Poststr
15
2
Münster Brücke
Grossmünsterplatz
4
Kirchgasse
Trittligasse
Ramistr

Brandschenkestr
Gartenstr
Trödlistr
Bleicherweg
Börsenstr
Bärengasse
Talstr
Claridenstr
Beethovenstr
Kappelergasse
Bahnhofstr
Fraumünsterstr
Stadthausquai
8
21
14
Uetoquai
Schifflände
Oberdorfstr
Torgasse
18
Bellevueplatz
Stadelhoferstr
Theaterstr

Bürkliplatz
Schanzen Graben
Quai Brücke
Quai
Zürichsee (Lake Zürich)
Sechseläutenplatz
Goethestr
30
Falkenstr

Bederstr
Gotthardstr
Tunnelstr
Seestr
31
General Gulisan Quai
32
Limmat
Sihlquai
Uetoquai
Dufourstr

Züri-West inset
Pfingstweidstr
Hardstr
29
Heinrichstr
Josefstr
Geroldstr
Viaduktstr
Limmatstr
13
34
22
28 23 35
3
24
27
25
Ottostr
Fabrikstr
Hardbrücke
11
0   200 m
0   0.1 miles
Zürichhorn (600m)
Kreuzstr
Tiger Fink (150m)
12

N
0   200 m
0   0.1 miles

Central Zürich

◎ SIGHTS

The city spreads around the northwest end of Zürichsee (Lake Zürich), from where the Limmat River runs further north still, splitting the city in two. The majority of Zürich's big-hitters cluster in and around the medieval centre, but the edgy Züri-West neighbourhood also has some terrific galleries. Best explored on foot, the narrow streets of the Niederdorf quarter on the river's east bank are crammed with restaurants, bars, shops and sights.

Fraumünster   Church
(Map p164; www.fraumuenster.ch/en; Münsterhof; Sfr5 incl audioguide; ⊙10am-6pm Mar-Oct, to 5pm Nov-Feb; ⛴6, 7, 10, 11, 14 to Paradeplatz) This 13th-century church is renowned for its stunning stained-glass windows, designed by the Russian-Jewish master Marc Chagall (1887–1985), who executed the series of five windows in the choir stalls in 1971 and the rose window in the southern transept in 1978. The rose window in the northern transept was created by Augusto

Giacometti in 1945. Admission includes a multilingual audioguide.

Kunsthaus   Museum
(Map p164; ☎044 253 84 84; www.kunsthaus.ch; Heimplatz 1; adult/child Sfr16/free, Wed free; ⊙10am-8pm Wed & Thu, to 6pm Tue & Fri-Sun; ⛴5, 8, 9, 10 to Kunsthaus) Zürich's impressive fine-arts gallery boasts a rich collection of largely European art. It stretches from the Middle Ages through a mix of Old Masters to Alberto Giacometti stick figures, Monet and van Gogh masterpieces, Rodin sculptures, and other 19th- and 20th-century art. Swiss Rail and Museum Passes don't provide free admission but the **ZürichCard** (www.zuerichcard.ch; adult/child 24hr Sfr24/16, 72hr Sfr48/32) does.

Schweizerisches
Landesmuseum   Museum
(Swiss National Museum; Map p164; ☎058 466 65 11; www.nationalmuseum.ch/e/zuerich; Museumstrasse 2; adult/child Sfr10/free; ⊙10am-5pm Tue, Wed & Fri-Sun, to 7pm Thu; ⛴Zürich Hauptbahnhof, ᚏZürich Hauptbahnhof)

Foosball table, FIFA World Football Museum

Inside a purpose-built cross between a mansion and a castle sprawls this eclectic and imaginatively presented museum. The permanent collection offers an extensive romp through Swiss history, with exhibits ranging from elaborately carved and painted sleds to domestic and religious artefacts, via a series of reconstructed historical rooms spanning six centuries. In August 2016 the museum celebrated a major expansion with the opening of its new archaeology section in a brand-new wing.

FIFA World Football Museum Museum

(Map p164; www.fifamuseum.com; Seestrasse 27; adult/child Sfr24; ◷10am-7pm Tue-Sat, 9am-6pm Sun; 🚊2, 5, 6, 7, 8, 11, 13, 14, 17 to Bahnhof Enge, ⊠Bahnhof Enge) Fans of the game won't want to miss out on this museum, opened in 2017, which races you through the history of FIFA (Fédération Internationale de Football Association) and the World Cup in a series of hands-on displays. Highlights include the original World Cup Trophy and a giant pinball machine where you can put your own skills to the test. The museum is southwest of the centre.

🏃 ACTIVITIES

Zürich comes into its own in summer, when the parks lining the lake are overrun with bathers, sunseekers, in-line skaters, footballers, lovers, picnickers, party animals and preeners. Police even patrol on rollerblades!

From May to mid-September, official swimming areas known as *Badis* (usually wooden piers with a pavilion) open around the lake and up the Limmat River. There are also plenty of free, unofficial places to take a dip.

Seebad Utoquai Swimming

(Map p164; ☎044 251 61 51; www.bad-utoquai. ch; Utoquai 49; adult/child Sfr8/4; ◷7am-8pm mid-May–late Sep; 🚊2, 4, 10, 11, 14, 15 to Kreuzstrasse) Just north of leafy Zürichhorn park, 400m south of Bellevueplatz, this is the most popular bathing pavilion on the Zürichsee's eastern shore.

Seebad Enge
Swimming

(Map p164; ☎044 201 38 89; www.seebadenge.
ch; Mythenquai 9, 700m southwest of Bürkliplatz;
swimming/sauna Sfr8/29; ☺9am-7pm May &
Sep, to 8pm Jun-Aug; sauna 11am-11pm Mon-Sat,
10am-10pm Sun late Sep-early May; ☐2, 5, 10,
11 to Rentenanstalt) At this happening bath,
the bar stays open until midnight when the
weather is good. Other offerings include
massage, yoga, stand-up paddleboarding
and a winter sauna (women only on Mondays, mixed rest of week). No children.

Letten
Swimming

(☎044 362 92 00; Lettensteg 10; ☐3, 4, 6, 10,
11, 13, 15, 17 to Limmatplatz) FREE North of the
train station on the eastern bank of the
Limmat (just south of Kornhausbrücke),
this is where Züri-West trendsetters swim,
dive off bridges, skateboard, play volleyball,
or just drink at the riverside bars and chat
on the grass and concrete steps.

TOURS

eTuk Tuk
Driving

(☎044 514 33 44; www.etuktuk.ch; Lagerstrasse
107; ☺9am-7pm) These ecofriendly tuk-tuk
tours are a novel way to take a spin around
Zürich. Clued-up guides run 40-minute
'Heart of Zürich' tours (Sfr29), taking in the
Old Town and Niederdorf, hour-long tours
of the city centre (Sfr36), a 90-minute tour
of Zürich and its surrounds (Sfr45), plus
wacky 90-minute chocolate fondue tours
(Sfr154), including fruit, marshmallows,
chocolate and dessert wine. Check ahead
where the tours begin.

SHOPPING

Bürkliplatz Flea Market
Market

(Map p164; www.buerkli-flohmarkt.ch; Bürkliplatz;
☺7am-5pm Sat May-Oct; ☐2, 4, 5, 8, 9, 10, 11, 14,
15 to Bürkliplatz) Rummage to your heart's
content for everything from secondhand
jewellery, records, clothes and ceramics
to rare antiques at the city's leading flea
market.

Top Parks for a Picnic

For a city of its size, Zürich has an amazing wealth of green spaces. When the
weather's good, pack a picnic – or grab
a takeaway box from Hiltl (p152) – and
head for one of these peaceful city spots.

Lindenhof (Map p164; ☐4, 6, 7, 10, 11, 13,
14, 15, 17 to Rennweg) Spectacular views
across the Limmat to the Grossmünster
from a tree-shaded hilltop park, smack
in the heart of the Aldstadt (Old Town).
Watch the *boules* players while you eat.

Platzspitz (Map p164; ☐Zürich Hauptbahnhof, ☐Zürich Hauptbahnhof) A green point
of land where the Limmat and Sihl rivers
come together, just north of the train
station and Landesmuseum. James
Joyce was fond of this spot and included
references to both rivers in *Finnegans
Wake*.

Josefswiese (Map p164; ☒; ☐3, 4, 6 to
Schiffbau) An atmospheric Kreis 5 park
in the shadow of a towering smokestack
and railway viaduct, this family-friendly
place has grassy expanses and a fountain for splashing in, along with drinks
and snacks for sale at the adjacent **Kiosk
Josefswiese** (Map p164; www.josefswiese.
ch; ☺10am-6pm Mar-May & Sep-Oct,
9am-10pm Jun-Aug; ☒; ☐3, 4, 6 to Schiffbau).

Zürichhorn (☐2, 4, 10, 14, 15 to Fröhlich-
strasse) This long and leafy lakeside park
spreads down the eastern shore of the
Zürichsee, south of the Opernhaus, with
the Seebad Utoquai close at hand for an
after-lunch dip.

Lindenhof

 Zürich's Hip Waterside Bars

The **Frauenbad** (Map p164; ☑044 211 95 92; Stadthausquai; adult/child Sfr8/4; ☺9am-7.30pm mid-May–mid-Sep; 🚊2, 5, 8, 9, 10, 11, 14, 15 to Bürkliplatz) and **Männerbad** (Map p164; ☑044 211 95 94; Badweg 10; ☺11am-7pm Sun-Thu, to 6.30pm Fri mid-May–mid-Sep; 🚊2, 8, 9, 13, 14, 17 to Sihlstrasse) FREE public baths are open only to women and men respectively during the day, but both sexes are allowed in their trendy bars at night.

At the former, up to 150 men are allowed into the **Barfussbar** (Barefoot Bar; Map p164; ☑044 251 33 31; www.barfussbar.ch; Stadthausquai; ☺8pm-midnight Wed, Thu & Sun mid-May–mid-Sep; 🚊2, 5, 8, 9, 10, 11, 14, 15 to Bürkliplatz). Leave your shoes at the entrance – and drink while you dip your feet in the water! Open-air dance nights feature everything from disco to tango. At the Männerbad, women are welcome any night of the week at its Rimini Bar (p170).

Frauenbad
MARKUS KELLER/GETTY IMAGES ©

Flohmarkt Kanzlei   Market

(www.flohmarktkanzlei.ch; Kanzleistrasse 56; ☺8am-4pm Sat; 🚊8 to Helvetiaplatz) Sort the treasures from the tat at the biggest flea market in Switzerland. Flohmarkt Kanzlei has some 300 stands selling everything from designer vintage clothes to vinyl, porcelain and rare collectables. Snack stands stave off hunger.

ENTERTAINMENT

To see what's on, pick up a copy of *Züritipp* (www.zueritipp.ch), which comes out on Thursdays with the *TagesAnzeiger* newspaper. Also look for the bimonthly *Zürich Guide* (www.inyourpocket.com/Switzerland/Zurich).

Rote Fabrik   Live Music

(☑music 044 485 58 68, theatre 044 485 58 28; www.rotefabrik.ch; Seestrasse 395; 🚊161, 165) With a fabulous lakeside location, this multi-faceted performing-arts centre stages rock, jazz and hip-hop concerts, original-language films, theatre and dance performances. There's also a bar and a restaurant. Take bus 161 or 165 from Bürkliplatz.

Bogen F   Live Music

(Map p164; ☑043 204 18 90; www.bogenf.ch; Viaduktstrasse 97; ☺cafe from 3pm Thu & Fri, 11am Sat; performance times vary; S Hardbrücke) This vibrant performance space, attached to its eponymous cafe in Kreis 5's Viadukt complex, brings in indie bands from all over the world (recent performers hail from as far away as the US, Canada, Sweden, South Africa and Japan).

Helsinki   Live Music

(Map p164; www.helsinkiklub.ch; Geroldstrasse 35; ☺8pm-1.30pm Thu, 8am-4pm Fri & Sat, 8pm-2am Sun; S Hardbrücke) A leftover hut from the area's industrial days, the Helsinki attracts people of all tastes and ages for its low-lit, relaxed band scene. On Sundays, catch house band Hollander Trio from Hell (country, rockabilly, rock, blues, even polka!); other nights, the eclectic mix ranges from soul and funk to hip-hop and tango. From Hauptbahnhof, take any train to Hardbrücke.

Moods   Live Music

(Map p164; ☑044 276 80 00; www.moods.ch; Schiffbaustrasse 6; ☺7.30pm-late Mon-Sat, from 6pm Sun; 🚊3, 4, 6 to Schiffbau) Though this is one of Zürich's top jazz spots, other musical genres including funk, hip-hop, swing, Latin and world music also grab the occasional spot on its busy calendar.

Opernhaus
Opera

(Map p164; ☑044 268 66 66; www.opernhaus. ch; Falkenstrasse 1; 🎭; 🚋2, 4, 10, 11, 14, 15 to Opernhaus) Behind an opulent neoclassical facade, the city's premier opera house enjoys a worldwide reputation and stages top-drawer concerts, opera and ballet productions. There's also a terrific line-up of opera for children.

Tonhalle
Classical Music

(Map p164; ☑044 206 34 34; www.tonhalle -orchester.ch; Claridenstrasse 7; 🚋2, 4, 5, 8, 9, 10, 11, 14, 15 to Bürkliplatz) An opulent venue used by Zürich's orchestra and chamber orchestra.

❌ EATING

Bauschänzli
Cafeteria $

(Map p164; ☑044 212 49 19; www.bausch aenzli.ch; Stadthausquai 2; mains Sfr13-22; ⏱11am-11pm Apr-Sep; 🚋2, 4, 5, 8, 9, 10, 11, 14, 15 to Bürkliplatz) Location is the big draw at this beer garden/cafeteria-style eatery

built atop 17th-century fortifications that jut into the middle of the Limmat river. Watch swans, boats and passers-by as you nosh on bratwurst, fried perch, Wiener schnitzel and chips, and sip from cold mugs of beer. From early October to early November, it hosts Zürich's month-long version of Oktoberfest.

Alpenrose
Swiss $$

(Map p164; ☑044 431 11 66; www. restaurantalpenrose.ch; Fabrikstrasse 12; lunch set menus Sfr23-27, dinner mains Sfr24-38; ⏱9am-11.30pm Tue-Fri, from 5pm Sat & Sun; 🚋3, 4, 6, 10, 11, 13, 15, 17 to Quellenstrasse) With its tall, stencilled windows, warm wood panelling and stucco ceiling orna-mentation, the Alpenrose exudes cosy Old World charm, and the cuisine here lives up to the promise. Hearty Swiss classics, such as herb-stuffed trout with home-made *Spätzli* (egg noodles) and buttered carrots are exquisitely prepared and presented, accompanied by a good wine list and a nice selection of desserts.

Opernhaus

🍸 DRINKING & NIGHTLIFE

Options abound across town, but the bulk of the more animated drinking dens are in Züri-West, especially along Langstrasse in Kreis 4 and Hardstrasse in Kreis 5. **Pub Crawl Zurich** (Map p164; www.pubcrawlzurich. com; Beatengasse 11; Sfr19; 🚇 Zürich Hauptbahnhof, 🚇 Zürich Hauptbahnhof) and **Zurich Pub Crawl** (📞079 774 55 87; www.zuerichpubcrawl. ch; Sfr20; 🕘9pm-late Fri & Sat) both offer regular Saturday night bar-hopping tours.

When heading out to a club, generally dress well and expect to pay Sfr15 to Sfr30 admission. Be aware that men can only enter some clubs if they are 21 or older (ID will be requested). Otherwise, the cut-off age in most places is 18 for both sexes.

Zürich's civic-minded public transport agency ZVV (for details, see www.zvv.ch) operates a special nighttime train and bus network in the wee hours of Saturday and Sunday mornings, to help revellers get home safely. There's a Sfr5 surcharge for use of the service.

Frau Gerolds Garten — Bar

(Map p164; www.fraugerold.ch; Geroldstrasse 23/23a; 🕘bar-restaurant 11am-midnight Mon-Sat, noon-10pm Sun Apr-Sep, 6pm-midnight Mon-Sat Oct-Mar, market & shops 11am-7pm Mon-Fri, to 6pm Sat year-round; 🚴; 🚆Hardbrücke) Hmm, where to start? The wine bar? The margarita bar? The gin bar? Whichever poison you choose, this wildly popular focal point of Zürich's summer drinking scene is pure unadulterated fun and one of the best grown-up playgrounds in Europe. Strewn with shipping containers, illuminated with multicoloured fairy lights and sandwiched between cheery flower beds and a screeching railyard, its outdoor seating options range from picnic tables to pillow-strewn terraces and a 2nd-floor sundeck. In winter, the restaurant moves indoors to a funky pavilion and great fondue warms the soul.

Rimini Bar — Bar

(Map p164; www.rimini.ch; Badweg 10; 🕘7.15pm-midnight Sun-Thu, 6.45pm-midnight Fri, 2pm-midnight Sat Apr-Oct; 🚌2, 6, 7, 8, 9, 13, 17, 19 to Bahnhof Selnau) Secluded behind a fence along the Sihl River, this bar at the

Frau Gerolds Garten

TRAVELSTOCK44/ALAMY ©

Männerbad public baths is one of Zürich's most inviting open-air drinking spots. Its vast wood deck is adorned with red-orange party lights, picnic tables and throw cushions for lounging, accompanied by the sound of water from the adjacent pools. Open in good weather only.

Hive Club   Club
(Map p164; ☎044 271 12 10; www.hiveclub.ch; Geroldstrasse 5; cover Sfr35; ☺11pm-4am Thu, to 7am Fri, to 9am Sat; ⑤Hardbrücke) Electronic music creates the buzz at this artsy, alternative club adjacent to Frau Gerolds Garten in Kreis 5. Enter through an alley strung with multicoloured umbrellas, giant animal heads, mushrooms and watering cans. Big-name DJs keep things going into the wee hours three nights a week.

Clouds   Bar
(Map p164; http://clouds.ch; Prime Tower, Maagplatz 5; ☺4pm-midnight Tue-Thu, to 2am Fri & Sat; ⑤Hardbrücke) Zürich seems unfathomably tiny from the heights of this backlit, glass-fronted lounge bar on the 35th floor of the Prime Tower in the happening 5th district. Pick out city landmarks, the lake and Uetliberg over signature gin and tonics, antipasti and cocktails. The 'Martini in C' is a blend of Clouds' own gin, ginger liqueur, dry orange curacao and vermouth.

ℹ INFORMATION

Zürich Tourism (Map p164; ☎044 215 40 00, hotel reservations 044 215 40 40; www.zuerich.com; Hauptbahnhof; ☺8am-8.30pm Mon-Sat, 8.30am to 6.30pm Sun May-Oct, 8.30am-7pm Mon-Sat, 9am-6pm Sun Nov-Apr) Book tours and reserve rooms at this very helpful tourist office in Zürich's main station.

ℹ GETTING THERE & AWAY

Air Zürich Airport (ZRH; ☎043 816 22 11; www.zurich-airport.com) is 9km north of the centre, with flights to most European capitals as well as some in Africa, Asia and North America. Several trains an hour connect Zürich's airport with the Hauptbahnhof between around 5am and midnight (Sfr6.80, 10 to 13 minutes). A taxi to the centre costs around Sfr60.

Car & Motorcycle The A3 approaches Zürich from the south along the southern shore of Zürichsee. The A1 is the fastest route from Bern and Basel. It proceeds northeast to Winterthur.

Train Direct trains run frequently to Stuttgart (Sfr63, four hours), Munich (Sfr96, four to 4¼ hours), Innsbruck (Sfr76, 3½ hours) and other international destinations. There are regular direct departures to most major Swiss destinations, such as Lucerne (Sfr26, 45 to 50 minutes), Bern (Sfr51, one to 1½ hours) and Basel (Sfr34, 55 minutes to 1¼ hours).

ℹ GETTING AROUND

Bus Extensive routes. Regular services run daily from 5.30am to shortly past midnight.

S-Bahn Surburban trains covering the wider Zürich area – handy for reaching the outskirts.

Tram The quickest and most efficient way of getting from A to B in the city centre.

Boat Lake and river cruises offer great city views.

Bicycle Zürich is a cycle-friendly city, with free and inexpensive bike-hire schemes making cycling an enticing way of getting around.

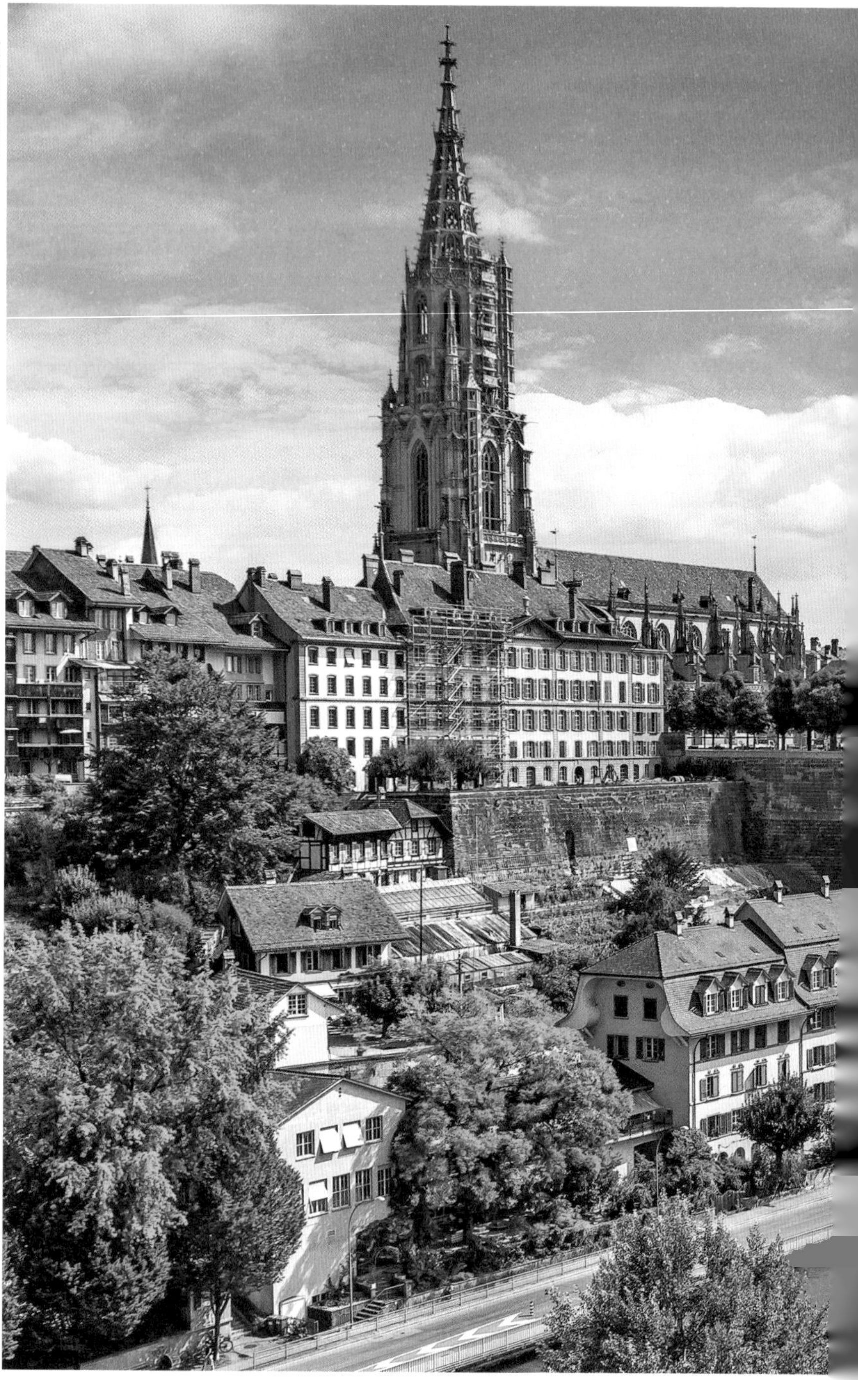

BERN

Bern at a Glance...

Wandering through Bern's picture-postcard, Unesco World Heritage–listed Old Town, with its provincial, laid-back air, it's hard to believe that this charming little city is the capital of Switzerland. From the surrounding hills, you're presented with an equally captivating picture of red roofs arrayed on a spit of land within a bend of the Aare River.

Bern seduces and surprises at every turn. Its museums are excellent, its street life dynamic and its locals happy to switch from their famously lilting dialect to textbook French, High German or English – which all goes to show that there's more to Bern than bureaucracy.

One Day in Bern

Stroll along Bern's arcaded Old Town streets, stopping to watch the elaborate twirling figures on the 13th-century **Zytglogge** (p176) clock tower, admiring the 16th-century fountains, and tracing the history of everyone's favourite wild-haired genius at **Einstein-Haus Bern** (p177). After lunch at **Kornhauskeller** (p186), hop aboard bus 12 and dive into the work of Switzerland's most famous artist at Renzo Piano's modernist **Zentrum Paul Klee** (p183).

Two Days in Bern

Explore the wealth of attractions just outside Bern's city centre. Several fine museums are clustered just south of the Aare River near Helvetiaplatz, including the **Historisches Museum Bern** (p183), **Neue Museum für Kommunikation** (p183), **Naturhistorisches Museum** (p184) and **Schweizerisches Alpines Museum** (p184). For a break, head down to **Terrasse & Casa** (p185), a pair of restaurants in a beautiful mid-river setting.

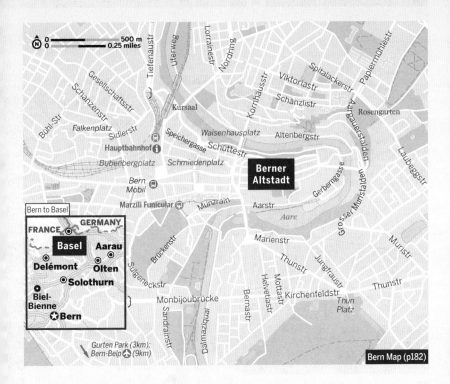

Bern to Basel

FRANCE | GERMANY

Basel | Aarau

Delémont | Olten

Biel-Bienne | Solothurn

☆ Bern

Gurten Park (3km);
Bern-Belp (9km)

Bern Map (p182)

Arriving in Bern

Air Tiny Bern-Belp Airport (www.flughafenbern.ch), 9km southeast of the centre, offers direct flights to London and other European cities with Bern-based SkyWork (www.flyskywork.com) and other budget airlines.

Train Trains run at least hourly to Geneva (Sfr51, 1¾ hours), Basel (Sfr41, 55 minutes), Interlaken Ost (Sfr29, 55 minutes) and Zürich (Sfr51, 55 minutes to 1½ hours).

Sleeping

Accommodation in Bern runs the gamut, from rural campgrounds, quaint country inns and B&Bs to good-value business hotels and a handful of high-end boutique offerings to boot. Staying in the city centre puts you close to the train station and allows daily contact with the Old Town's dynamic street life.

Berner Altstadt

Bern's flag-festooned, cobbled centre, rebuilt in grey-green sandstone after a devastating 1405 fire, is an aesthetic delight, with covered arcades, cellar shops, and fantastical folk figures frolicking on 16th-century fountains.

Great For...

☑ Don't Miss

Riding the Marzili Funicular (p185) down to the banks of the rushing Aare River.

Historic Sights

Zytglogge   Tower

(Marktgasse) Bern's most famous Old Town sight, this ornate clock tower once formed part of the city's western gate (1191–1256). Crowds congregate to watch its revolving figures twirl at four minutes before the hour, after which the chimes begin. From May to October tours enter the tower; contact the tourist office (p187) for details. The clock tower supposedly helped Albert Einstein hone his special theory of relativity, developed while working as a patent clerk in Bern.

Münster   Cathedral

(www.bernermuenster.ch; Münsterplatz 1; tower adult/child Sfr5/2; ⊙10am-5pm Mon-Sat, 11.30am-5pm Sun Apr–mid-Oct, noon-4pm Mon-Fri, 10am-5pm Sat, 11.30am-4pm Sun mid-Oct–Mar) Bern's 15th-century Gothic cathedral boasts Switzerland's loftiest spire (100m);

ℹ Need to Know

Bern is especially charming in summer, when restaurants and cafes spill onto every sidewalk.

✕ Take a Break

The frescoed cellars of Bern's historic Kornhauskeller (p186) make for a classy Old Town lunch break.

> ### ★ Top Tip
> To witness the twirling bears on Bern's whimsical Zytglogge, arrive five minutes before the hour.

Einstein-Haus Bern   Museum

(☏031 312 00 91; www.einstein-bern.ch; Kramgasse 49; adult/student Sfr6/4.50; ⏰10am-5pm Mon-Sat mid-Feb–Mar, 10am-5pm daily Apr–mid-Dec) Housed in the humble apartment that Einstein shared with his young family while working at the Bern patent office, this small museum includes a 20-minute biographical film telling Einstein's life story. Displays trace the development of Einstein's general equation $E=mc^2$ and the sometimes poignant trajectory of his family life.

Bundeshaus   Historic Building

(☏031 322 85 22; www.parliament.ch; Bundesplatz) **FREE** Home of the Swiss Federal Assembly, the Florentine-style Bundeshaus (1902) contains statues of the nation's founding fathers, a stained-glass dome and a 214-bulb chandelier. When parliament is in recess, there are 45-minute tours (in English at 2pm every other Saturday; reserve ahead). During parliamentary sessions, bring ID to watch from the public gallery. The Bundesplatz features a fountain with 26 jets, representing every Swiss canton; it's the perfect summertime playground for kids.

climb the 344-step spiral staircase for vertiginous views. Coming down, stop by the Upper Bells (1356), rung at 11am, noon and 3pm daily, and the three 10-tonne Lower Bells (Switzerland's largest). Don't miss the main portal's Last Judgement, which portrays Bern's mayor going to heaven, while his Zürich counterpart is shown into hell. Afterwards wander through the adjacent Münsterplattform, a bijou clifftop park with a sunny pavilion cafe.

Kindlifresserbrunnen   Fountain

(Kornhausplatz) Bern is home to 11 decorative 16th-century fountains depicting historic and folkloric characters. The most famous is Kindlifresserbrunnen (Ogre Fountain), which depicts a giant snacking on children. The other fountains are located along Marktgasse, as it becomes Kramgasse and Gerechtigkeitsgasse.

Day Trip to Basel

Only an hour's train ride from Bern, the sophisticated city of Basel is beloved by art and architecture buffs, who visit for its wealth of galleries, museums and iconic buildings.

Great For...

☑ Don't Miss

The Tinguely Brunnen (p180), Jean Tinguely's wacky water-spewing fountain, centrally located in Theaterplatz.

Basel's Art & Culture

Fondation Beyeler

An astounding private-turned-public collection, **Fondation Beyeler** (☏061 645 97 00; www.fondationbeyeler.ch; Baselstrasse 101, Riehen; adult/under 25yr Sfr25/free; ☉10am-6pm Thu-Tue, to 8pm Wed; ℗) was assembled by former art dealers Hildy and Ernst Beyeler and is housed in a long, low, light-filled, open-plan building designed by Italian architect Renzo Piano. The varied exhibits juxtapose 19th- and 20th-century works by Picasso and Rothko with sculptures by Miró and Max Ernst and tribal figures from Oceania as well as regular visiting exhibitions.

Vitra Campus

Showcasing the works of the adjoining, eponymous, high-end furniture manufacturer, **Vitra Campus** (☏+49 7621 702 3500;

Fondation Beyeler

❶ Need to Know

Trains run half-hourly between Bern and Basel (Sfr41, 55 minutes) from 5.30am to midnight.

✕ Take a Break

Relax between museum visits in the beer garden at Herzog & de Meuron–designed Volkshaus Basel (p181).

★ Top Tip

Basel Tourismus organises two-hour English-language city walking tours (adult/child from Sfr18/9).

🖉061 206 62 62; www.kunstmuseumbasel.ch; St Alban-Graben 16; adult/student/child Sfr16/8/free; ⊙10am-6pm Tue, Wed & Fri-Sun, to 8pm Thu; P) reopened in mid-2016 after updates to the existing galleries (Hauptbau) and construction of a new modernist wing (Neubau). It houses the world's largest collection of Holbeins and a substantial collection of Renaissance and impressionist works among its thousands of pieces. The entrance price includes admission to the permanent collection – surcharges are applicable for visiting exhibits. Guided tours (from Sfr5) are available.

Museum Jean Tinguely

Built by leading Ticino architect Mario Botta, the **Museum Jean Tinguely** (🖉061 681 93 20; www.tinguely.ch; Paul Sacher-Anlage 2; adult/student/child Sfr18/12/free; ⊙11am-6pm Tue-Sun; P) showcases the mischievous and downright bizarre artistic concoctions of sculptor-turned-mad-scientist Jean Tinguely. Buttons next to some of Tinguely's 'kinetic' sculptures allow visitors to set them in motion. It's great fun to watch them shake and twirl, with springs, feathers and wheels

www.vitra.com/en-hu/campus; Charles-Eames-Strasse 1, Weil am Rhein; Vitra Campus adult/child €17/15, Design Museum only €11/9, 1-/2-hr tours €7/14; ⊙10am-6pm) comprises the dazzling Vitra Design Museum (of Guggenheim Bilbao architect Frank Gehry fame), the Vitra Haus and new-in-2016 Vitra Schaudepot (both by Herzog & De Meuron) and an ever-expanding bevy of installations by cutting-edge architects and designers, including Carsten Höller's whimsical, corkscrewing 30m-high Vitra Slide. Visiting is a must for serious lovers of architecture and design. Save your pennies and suitcase space for ubercool souvenirs.

Kunstmuseum Basel

Housing the most comprehensive collection of public art in Switzerland, the superb **Kunstmuseum Basel** (Museum of Fine Arts;

radiating at every angle, or to hear the haunting musical sounds produced by the gigantic Méta-Harmonies on the upper floor.

Tinguely Brunnen

With its riot of wacky machines spewing and shooting forth water, this zany fountain in Theaterplatz offers a taste of the mad-cap moving sculptures to be found in the Museum Jean Tinguely.

Spielzeug Welten Museum Basel

Adults and kids alike love this fascinating and lovingly curated fantasy land. **Spielzeug Welten Museum Basel** (Toy Worlds Museum; ☑061 225 95 95; www.spielzeug -welten-museum-basel.ch; Steinenvorstadt 1; adult/child Sfr7/5; ☺10am-6pm; ℗⦿) claims the world's biggest collection of teddy bears and a slew of extraordinarily detailed

doll houses among its 6000 objects displayed over four floors.

Schweizerisches Museum für Papier, Schrift und Druck

Set in an old paper mill astride a medieval canal and complete with a functioning waterwheel, this **paper museum** (Swiss Museum of Paper, Script & Print; ☑061 225 90 90; www.papiermuseum.ch; St Alban-Tal 37; adult/child Sfr15/9; ☺11am-5pm Tue-Fri & Sun, 1-5pm Sat) evokes centuries past, when a dozen mills operated nearby. This one produced paper for centuries and the museum explores that story.

Eating & Drinking

Markthalle

Around the corner from Basel SBB station you'll find this large indoor market and **food**

Tinguely Brunnen

hall (www.markthalle-basel.ch; Steinentorberg 20; dishes Sfr10-25; ⏰8am-7pm Mon, to midnight Tue-Sat, 10am-5pm Sun; 🅿🚇), which is a popular spot for a cheap lunch on the go. Vendors are always changing and feature Swiss specialities and world flavours.

Volkshaus Basel
Stylish Herzog & de Meuron–designed venue **Volkshaus Basel** (📞061 690 93 10; www.volkshaus-basel.ch/en; Rebgasse 12-14; mains Sfr28-60; ⏰restaurant noon-2pm & 6-10pm Mon-Sat, bar 10am-midnight Mon-Wed, to 1am Thu-Sat) is part resto-bar, part gallery and

> ### ⚡ Don't Miss
> The excellent 5km Rehberger-Weg walking path links the Fondation Beyeler and Vitra Campus galleries, featuring 24 colourful and unique public-art installations en route.

part performance space. For relaxed dining, head for the atmospheric beer garden in a cobblestone courtyard decorated with columns, vine-clad walls and light-draped rows of trees. The menu ranges from brasserie classics (steak frites) to more innovative offerings (house-pickled wild salmon with mustard, dill and beetroot).

Restaurant Stucki
Under the tutelage of chef Tanja Grandits, long-lauded **Restaurant Stucki** (📞061 361 82 22; www.tanjagrandits.ch; Bruderholzallee 42; ⏰3-/4-course lunch Sfr75/92, 8-/12-course aroma menu Sfr190/240; 🅿🚇) remains one of Basel's finest – dining here is an absolute treat. The signature Aroma Menu, featuring the likes of juniper honey mountain lamb and buttermilk mousse with caramel puffed rice and melon, is so beautifully presented that you'll feel guilty taking a knife to your plate. But you must.

Restaurant Schlüsselzunft
Housed in a 15th-century guild house that had a neo-Renaissance remake early in the 20th century, elegant **Restaurant Schlüss-elzunft** (📞061 261 20 46; www.schluesselzunft. ch; Freie Strasse 25; mains Sfr34-56; ⏰9am-11.30pm Mon-Sat, 11am-10pm Sun, closed Sun Jun-Aug) has an internal courtyard with sweeping staircase. The menu offers innovative flavour combinations such as veal in massaman curry sauce with fruit spring rolls.

Das Viertel
East from the SBB Bahnhof along the railway tracks, rooftop **Das Viertel** (📞061 331 04 00; www.dasviertel.ch; Münchensteiner-strasse 81; ⏰terrace bar 6pm-midnight Mon-Sat, from 10am Sun, club 11pm-3am Fri & Sat) draws crowds to its sun-drenched terrace. On weekends it morphs into a club, hosting international DJs into the wee hours.

★ Entertainment
For comprehensive entertainment listings, check out www.basellive.ch (in German).

Bern

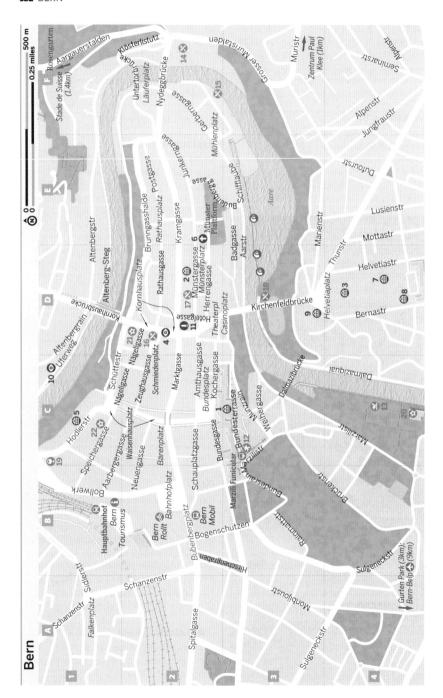

Stade de Suisse
(1.4km)

Rosengarten

Aargauerstalden

Klösterlistutz

Untertorbrücke

Läuferplatz

Nydeggbrücke

Gerberngasse

Mühlenplatz

Junkerngasse

Postgasse

Rathausplatz

Brunngasshalde

Kornhausplatz

Altenbergstr

Altenberg-Steg

Altenbergrain

Uferweg

Kornhausbrücke

Schüttestr

Nägeligasse

Zeughausgasse

Nägeligasse

Nägeligasse

Schmiedenplatz

Rathausgasse

Münstergasse

Münsterplatz

Herrengasse

Kramgasse

Badgasse

Aarstr

Münster
Plattform

Bundesterrasse

Schifflaube

Aare

Kirchenfeldbrücke

Theaterpl

Casinoplatz

Hotelgasse

Marktgasse

Amthausgasse

Bundesplatz

Kochergasse

Schauplatzgasse

Bundesgasse

Münzrain

Weihergasse

Zillistr

Marzili Funicular

Bundesrain

Marzilistr

Brückenstr

Rainmattstr

Bärenplatz

Bärenplatz

Waisenhausplatz

Aarbergergasse

Neuengasse

Speichergasse

Hodlerstr

Bollwerk

Hauptbahnhof

Bern
Tourismus

Bern
Rollt

Bern
Mobil

Bahnhofplatz

Bubenbergplatz

Bogenschützen

Hirschengraben

Schanzenstr

Schanzenstr

Falkenplatz

Sidlerstr

Spitalgasse

Monbijoustr

Sulgeneckstr

Sulgeneckstr

Grosser Muristalden

Muristr

Zentrum Paul
Klee (1km)

Alpenstr

Seminarstr

Alpenstr

Jungfraustr

Dufourstr

Lusienstr

Mottastr

Marienstr

Helvetiastr

Helvetiaplatz

Thunstr

Bernastr

Dalmazibrücke

Dalmaziquai

Marzilistr

Brückenstr

Gurten Park (3km);
Bern-Belp (9km)

500 m
0.25 miles

Bern

◉ SIGHTS

Zentrum Paul Klee   Museum

(📞031 359 01 01; www.zpk.org; Monument im Fruchtland 3; adult/child Sfr20/7; ⊙10am-5pm Tue-Sun) Bern's answer to the Guggenheim, Renzo Piano's architecturally bold, 150m-long wave-like edifice houses an exhibition space that showcases rotating works from Paul Klee's prodigious and often playful career. Interactive computer displays and audioguides help interpret the Swiss-born artist's work. Next door, the fun-packed **Kindermuseum Creaviva** (📞031 359 01 61; www.creaviva-zpk.org; Monument im Fruchtland 3; ⊙10am-5pm Tue-Sun; 🚸) FREE lets kids experiment with hands-on art exhibits or create original artwork with the atelier's materials during the weekend **Five Franc Studio** (www.creaviva-zpk.org/5-franc-studio; Zentrum Paul Klee; Sfr5; ⊙10am-4.30pm Sat & Sun; 🚸). Bus 12 runs from Bubenbergplatz direct to the museum.

Museum für Kommunikation   Museum

(Museum of Communication; Map p182; 📞031 357 55 55; www.mfk.ch; Helvetiastrasse 16; adult/child Sfr15/5; ⊙10am-5pm Tue-Sun) Fresh from extensive renovation and expansion, Bern's (New) Museum of Communication opened its doors in August 2017. Occupying almost 2000 sq metres of exhibition space,

it has cutting-edge interactive stations that explore the hows and whys of human communications with a focus on the role technology plays in our interactions with each other. Expect engaging, hands-on, high-tech interactive exhibits complemented by the museum's fabulous original collection of retro phones and computers.

Kunstmuseum   Museum

(Museum of Fine Arts; Map p182; 📞031 328 09 44; www.kunstmuseumbern.ch; Hodlerstrasse 8-12; adult/child Sfr7/free; ⊙10am-5pm Wed-Sun, to 9pm Tue) Bern's Museum of Fine Arts houses Switzerland's oldest permanent collection, ranging from an exquisite early Renaissance *Madonna and Child* by Fra Angelico to 19th- and 20th-century works by the likes of Hodler, Monet and Picasso.

Historisches Museum Bern   Museum

(Bern Historical Museum; Map p182; 📞031 350 77 11; www.bhm.ch; Helvetiaplatz 5; adult/child Sfr13/4, incl Einstein-Haus Bern Sfr18/8; ⊙10am-5pm Tue-Sun) Tapestries, diptychs and other treasures vividly illustrate Bernese history from the Stone Age to the 20th century in this marvellous castle-like edifice, the best of several museums surrounding Helvetiaplatz. The highlight for many is the 2nd floor, devoted to a superb permanent exhibition on Einstein.

Naturhistorisches Museum
Museum

(Map p182; 🕿031 350 71 11; www.nmbe. ch; Bernastrasse 15; adult/child Sfr8/free; ⏰2-5pm Mon, 9am-5pm Tue-Fri, 10am-5pm Sat & Sun) The Natural History Museum near Helvetiaplatz features the famous moth-eaten and taxidermied remains of Barry, a 19th-century St Bernard rescue dog. Its best-loved exhibit traces the history of St Bernard dogs in the Swiss Alps and recounts some of Barry's legendary (ie not necessarily factual!) accomplishments.

Schweizerisches Alpines Museum
Museum

(Map p182; 🕿031 350 04 40; www.alpines museum.ch; Helvetiaplatz 4; adult/child Sfr14/6; ⏰10am-5pm Tue-Sun) The Swiss Alpine Museum hosts special exhibitions; its permanent collections of relief maps and Alpine mountaineering exhibits are kept under wraps.

University Botanical Garden
Gardens

(Map p182; 🕿031 631 49 45; www.botanischer garten.ch; Altenbergrain 21; ⏰8am-5.30pm Mar-Sep, to 5pm Oct-Feb) **FREE** A flight of steps leads from the northern end of Lorrainebrücke to the University Botanical Garden, a riverside garden with plenty of green specimens to admire and a couple of greenhouses.

Gurten Park
Park

(🕿031 961 23 23; www.gurtenpark.ch; Gurten; Gurten funicular one way/return adult Sfr6/10.50, child Sfr3/5.50) A great outdoorsy escape only 3km south of town, this small peak boasts a couple of restaurants, a miniature railway, cycling trails, a summer circus, winter sledge runs, an adventure playground and more. Enjoy fine views as you hike down the mountain (about one hour), following the clearly marked paths. To get there, take tram 9 towards Wabern, alight at Gurtenbahn and ride the **Gurten funicular** (⏰7am-11.30pm Mon-Sat, to 8pm Sun) to the top.

Marzili Funicular

ROMAN BABAKIN/SHUTTERSTOCK ©

ACTIVITIES

Marzili Pools   Swimming

(Map p182; www.aaremarzili.ch; ☺8.30am-8pm Jun-Aug, to 7pm May & Sep) **FREE** In summer this open-air 25m swimming pool beside the Aare River is the perfect place to get a tan and kick back with locals among the expansive lawns, foosball tables and sunbathing racks.

Marzili Funicular   Cable Car

(Drahtseilbahn Marzili; Map p182; www. marzilibahn.ch; one way Sfr1.40; ☺6.15am-9pm) Descends from behind the parliament building to the riverside Marzili quarter.

EATING

Terrasse & Casa   Swiss $$

(Map p182; ☏031 350 50 01; www. schwellenmaetteli.ch; Dalmaziquai 11; mains Sfr20-64; ☺Terrasse 9am-12.30am Mon-Sat, 10am-11.30pm Sun, Casa noon-2.30pm & 6-11.30pm Mon-Fri, 6-11.30pm Sat, noon-11pm Sun) Dubbed 'Bern's Riviera', this twinset of eateries enjoys a blissful Aare-side setting. Terrasse is a glass shoebox with wooden decking over the water, sunloungers over-looking a weir (illuminated at night) and comfy sofa seating, perfect for lingering over Sunday brunch, a drink, or midweek two-course lunch specials (Sfr25). Next door, Casa serves Italian delicacies in a cosy, country-style house.

Altes Tramdepot   Swiss $$

(Map p182; ☏031 368 14 15; www.altes tramdepot.ch; Grosser Muristalden 6, Am Bären-graben; mains Sfr18-46; ☺11am-12.30am Mon-Fri, from 10am Sat & Sun) At this cavernous microbrewery, Swiss specialities compete against wok-cooked stir-fries for your affection, and the microbrews go down a treat – sample three different varieties for Sfr10.90, four for Sfr14.60, or five for Sfr18.20.

Cinématte Restaurant   Swiss $$

(Map p182; ☏031 312 21 22; www.cinematte.ch; Wasserwerkgasse 7; mains Sfr31-47; ☺6-9pm Thu-Mon) This chic eatery with a delightful

Bern's Markets

Market traders take over Bern on the fourth Monday in November during the legendary **Zibelemärit** (Onion Market; ☺Nov), a riot of 600-odd market stalls selling delicately woven onion plaits, wreaths, ropes, pies and sculptures alongside other tasty regional produce. Folklore says the market dates back to the great fire of 1405 when farmers from Fribourg canton helped the Bernese recover – they were allowed to sell their produce in Bern as a reward.

In reality the market probably began as part of Martinmas, the medieval festi-val celebrating winter's start. Whatever the tale the onion market is a fabulous excuse for pure, often-crazy revelry as street performers surge forth in the carnival atmosphere and people walk around throwing confetti and hitting each other on the head with squeaky plastic hammers.

Bern retains its festive feel well into December, when the **Berner Weihnachtsmarkt** (Christmas Markets; Waisenhausplatz & Münsterplatz; ☺Dec) – Christmas markets in Waisenhausplatz and Münsterplatz – offer beautiful handmade goods and the chance to warm your cockles over a glühwein (hot mulled wine) or two.

Onion plaits

🍽 Holey-Moley: AOC Emmentaler Cheese

Named for its birthplace in the Emme River valley, Switzerland's incomparable Emmentaler cheese has a proud history dating to the Middle Ages. Copycat cheesemakers around the world have expropriated the Emmental name, but only authentic Emmentaler Switzerland AOC conforms to the original production technique, using raw milk from grass-fed cows, cellar-ripened in giant wheels for at least 120 days.

Emmentaler's famous holes, known as 'eyes', result from the release of carbon-dioxide bubbles by bacteria during the ageing process. Once seen as an imperfection, they're now worn with pride: the larger the holes, the longer the cheese has matured, and the more pronounced its flavour.

See the process and sample the goodness for yourself at **Emmentaler Schaukäserei** (Emmental Open Cheese Dairy; 📞034 435 16 11; www.showdairy.ch; Schaukäsereistrasse 6, Affoltern; ⏰9am-6.30pm Apr-Oct, to 5pm Nov-Mar) **FREE** in Affoltern, 35km northeast of Bern.

Emmentaler cheese
HAYATI KAYHAN/SHUTTERSTOCK ©

wooden deck overlooking the Aare serves an ever-changing menu of Swiss specialities.

Metzgerstübli   European $$

(Map p182; 📞031 311 00 45; www.metzgerstübli. ch; Münstergasse 60; 3-course dinner Sfr85, mains Sfr15-49; ⏰10am-11pm Tue-Fri, 7am-noon & 5-11.30pm Sat & Sun) This homely

restaurant in the Old Town has convivial staff serving a well-executed menu of standard European fare: meat, fish, pasta. Dinner set menus are great value for money.

Kornhauskeller   Mediterranean $$$

(Map p182; 📞031 327 72 72; www.bindella.ch; Kornhausplatz 18; mains Sfr24-58; ⏰11.45am-2.30pm & 6pm-12.30am) Fine dining takes place beneath vaulted frescoed arches at Bern's ornate former granary, now a stunning cellar restaurant serving Mediterranean cuisine. Beautiful people sip cocktails alongside historic stained-glass windows on the mezzanine while, in its neighbouring cafe, punters lunch in the sun on the busy pavement terrace.

🍸 DRINKING & NIGHTLIFE

Kapitel Bollwerk   Bar

(Map p182; 📞031 311 60 90; www.kapitel.ch; Bollwerk 41; ⏰11am-11.30pm Tue & Wed, to 3.30am Thu, to 5am Fri, 4pm-6am Sat) Starting as a restaurant where businesspeople come for light, healthy lunches, this award-winning venue morphs by evening into a bar recognised around town for its savvy bartenders and unparalleled choice of cocktails. Come 11pm it transforms again into one of Bern's hippest clubs, with international DJs spinning electronic music.

⭐ ENTERTAINMENT

Dampfzentrale   Cultural Centre

(Map p182; 📞031 310 05 40; www.dampfzentrale. ch; Marzilistrasse 47; ⏰club 11pm-late Sat, other events variable hours) Host to an action-packed Saturday-night club, this industrial brick riverside building also stages concerts, festivals and contemporary dance; check the website for details.

Turnhalle   Performing Arts

(Map p182; 📞031 311 15 51; www.turnhalle.ch; Speichergasse 4; ⏰cafeteria 11.45am-2pm Mon-Fri, bar-cafe 9am-12.30am Mon-Wed, to 2am Thu, to 3.30am Fri & Sat) Part bar, part nightspot,

Kornhauskeller

part community arts centre that hosts frequent evening performances, Turnhalle also serves an excellent-value weekday lunch (dishes Sfr6 to Sfr8). The cafeteria-style offerings include mains (with one daily veggie option), salads, vegetables and desserts. Choose up to six items, then grab a seat on the spacious sunny patio out front.

Konzerttheater
Bern   Performing Arts
(Map p182; 031 329 51 11; www.konzert theaterbern.ch; Kornhausplatz 20) Built in 1903, Bern's neoclassical theatre stages opera, dance, classical music and plays (in German). Check the website for the latest programming.

INFORMATION

Bern Tourismus (Map p182; 031 328 12 12; www.bern.com; Bahnhoftplatz 10a; 9am-7pm Mon-Sat, to 6pm Sun) On the street-level floor of the train station. City tours, free hotel bookings and internet access.

GETTING AROUND

Bern Mobil (Map p182; www.bernmobil.ch; tickets 30min/1hr/day Sfr2.60/4.60/13) operates an excellent bus and tram network. Tickets are available from machines at all stops. Local hotel guests receive a Bern Ticket, offering free use of public transport throughout the city. The ticket covers all Bern Mobil services – including the Marzili and Gurten funiculars – within zones 100 and 101 (city centre and immediate surroundings). It does not cover Moonliner buses or services beyond zones 100 and 101.

Airport Bus Bern 334 (www.bernmobil.ch) links Bern-Belp airport with Belp train station, where frequent S-Bahn trains connect into Bern. Single tickets covering the entire 30-minute journey (adult/child Sfr7/3.70) can be purchased at machines or on board.

Borrow a free bike from **Bern Rollt** (Map p182; 031 318 93 50; www.bernrollt.ch; Milchgässli; 1st 4hr free, per additional hour Sfr1; 8am-9.30pm), adjacent to the train station. You'll need ID and Sfr20 as a deposit. Bern is also rolling out the **PubliBike** (www.publibike.ch/en) bike-sharing scheme. Pick up a 'DayBike' card from the offices of Bern Tourismus.

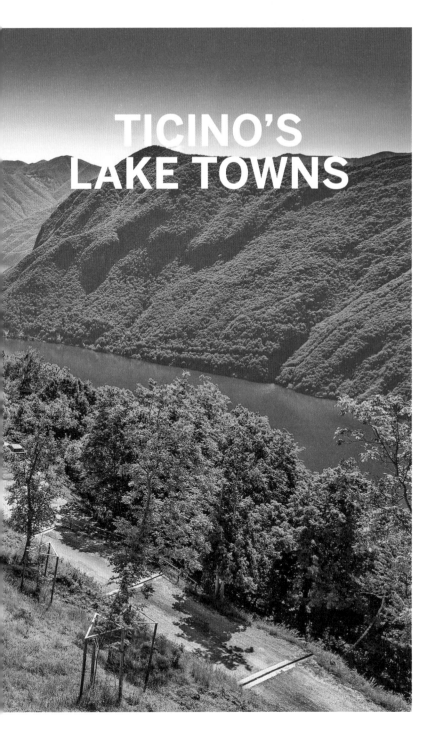

TICINO'S
LAKE TOWNS

Ticino's Lake Towns at a Glance...

The summer air is rich and hot in Ticino. Vespas scoot along palm-fringed promenades. A baroque campanile chimes. Kids play in piazzas flanked by pastel-coloured mansions. Italian weather, Italian style – not to mention the gelato, pasta, architecture and language. The Alps are every bit as magnificent here, but you can admire them while sipping a full-bodied merlot at a pavement cafe, enjoying a hearty lunch at a chestnut-shaded grotto (rustic Ticino-style inn or restaurant), or floating in the mirror-like lakes of Lugano and Locarno. Ticino tempers its classic Alpine looks with Italian good living.

Two Days in Ticino Lake Towns

Start with a leisurely stroll through Lugano's lakefront **Parco Ciani** (p195), a longer walk along the **Sentiero di Gandria** (p195) or a boat cruise around Lago di Lugano. After lunch at **Le Bucce di Gandria** (p204), spend the afternoon exploring Lugano's museums and churches, or ascend by funicular to **Monte Brè** (p196) or **Monte San Salvatore** (p196) for fabulous views. Dedicate day two to discovering Bellinzona's picturesque trio of castles.

Four Days in Ticino Lake Towns

On day three, bask in the balmy glow of Locarno's lakefront, ogling the camellias in **Parco delle Camelie** (p197) and pausing under the palms in **Parco Muralto** (p197). Later, climb high above Lake Maggiore, stopping first at **Santuario della Madonna del Sasso** (p197) before continuing to **Cimetta** (p197) to hike and watch the paragliders. On day four, explore a remote valley or two in the neighbouring Alps.

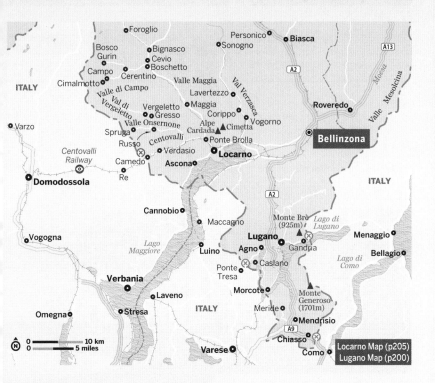

Arriving in Ticino

Milan Malpensa Airport Regular buses run from Italy's northernmost airport to Lugano (Sfr25, 70 minutes) and Bellinzona (Sfr40, two hours).

Zürich Airport The Gotthard Base Tunnel has improved rail travel times to Bellinzona (Sfr64, two hours).

Train Regular connections to Lugano and Bellinzona from Zurich, Lucerne and other Swiss cities.

Sleeping

What's your fancy? A rustic granite hut neatly tucked into wooded mountains, where you awake to the clatter of goat bells and the rush of a river? A posh boutique pile with spa and gourmet trimmings on the shores of Lago di Lugano? Or how about a family-run B&B with an alluring view of Bellinzona's castles? Ticino has all of these and then some.

Castles of Bellinzona

Rearing up at the convergence of several valleys amid lovely Alpine scenery, Bellinzona is Ticino's head-turning capital. Its three hulking medieval fortresses have enthralled artists and poets for centuries.

Great For...

☑ Don't Miss

The humorous 'world upside down' paintings in Castelgrande's museum.

Bellinzona's three imposing castles are the city's main draw, and a walk taking in all of them can be a full day's activity (wear comfy shoes). The city also has a clutch of museums and churches worth exploring.

Castelgrande

Rising dramatically above the Old Town, medieval stronghold **Castelgrande** (www.bellinzonese-altoticino.ch; Via Salita Castelgrande; ⊙10am-6pm Mon, 9am-10pm Tue-Sun) is Bellinzona's most visible icon. The rocky hill upon which it stands, once a Roman frontier post and later the site of a Lombard defensive tower, was eventually developed into a heavily fortified town controlled by Milan. Though now staunchly Swiss, it is nevertheless infused with a hefty dose of Italian dolce vita.

Head up Salita San Michele from Piazza Collegiata, or take the lift, buried in the rocky hill in a concrete bunker-style construction,

Castelgrande

Castelgrande 🚇

Castello di Montebello 🚇

Castello di Sasso Corbaro 🚇

❶ Need to Know

All of Bellinzona's castles are open daily throughout the year.

✕ Take a Break

Feast on food and spectacular views at Grotto Castelgrande.

★ Top Tip

Guided walking tours of Bellinzona depart from the tourist office at 11am on Saturday.

bellinzonese-altoticino.ch; Salita al Castello di Montebello; castle free, museum adult/child Sfr5/2; ⊘10am-6pm Apr-Oct, 10.30am-4pm Nov-Mar) FREE. The fortress is one of Bellinzona's most impressive with its drawbridges, ramparts and small museum catapulting you back to medieval times.

Castello di Sasso Corbaro

From central Bellinzona, it's a 3.5km hike south to the **Castello di Sasso Corbaro** (www.bellinzonese-altoticino.ch; Via Sasso Corbaro; castle free, museum & tower adult/child Sfr5/2; ⊘10am-6pm Apr-Oct, 10.30am-4pm Nov-Mar). Perched high on a wooded hillside, the castle has an austere beauty with its impenetrable walls and sturdy towers.

Dining with a Castle View

For the best view of Bellinzona's illuminated castles, dine on the vine-strewn terrace of **Grotto Castelgrande** (☏091 814 87 81; www.castelgrande.ch; Via Salita Castelgrande; mains Sfr29-39, 2-/3-course menu Sfr25/31; ⊘9.30am-midnight Tue-Sat). This atmospheric vaulted cellar restaurant specialises in dishes such as beef fillet with porcini mushrooms and Grana cheese.

from Piazza del Sole. Wander the grounds, then stroll west along the castle's snaking ramparts, with photogenic views of vine-streaked mountains and castle-studded hills.

Museo di Castelgrande

Castelgrande's **museum** (adult/child Sfr5/2; ⊘10am-6pm Apr-Oct, 10am-5pm Nov-Mar) has a modest collection of local finds dating from prehistoric times. Displayed ceiling decorations from a 15th-century noble house range from weird animals to a humorous 'world upside down' series that includes a sex-crazed woman chasing a chaste man and an ox ploughing a field with his yoked-together human assistants.

Castello di Montebello

On cloudless days, you can see Lake Maggiore from 13th-century hilltop fortification **Castello di Montebello** (www.

A Day on the Water

Extending long blue fingers towards the Alps' southern slopes, vine-terraced Lago di Lugano and palm-fringed Lago Maggiore shelter some of Switzerland's most distinctive scenery. Begin exploring from Lugano or Locarno.

Great For...

☑ Don't Miss

Taking a boat trip around Lago di Lugano – free with a Swiss Travel Pass.

Lago di Lugano

Spilling over into northern Italy, Lago di Lugano is a sparkling blue expanse at Ticino's southernmost tip, with a real holiday flavour as soon as the weather warms. Less overrun than many of the lakes over the border, it is nevertheless bewitching, whether glimpsed from one of the many trails that wriggle along its shores, from a mountain peak or from the deck of the boats that glide across it.

Boat Cruises

A relaxed way to see the lake's highlights is on a boat cruise from Lugano's waterfront, operated by **Società Navigazione del Lago di Lugano** (☎091 971 52 23; www.lakelugano.ch; Riva Vela; ☺Apr-Oct). Options include bay tours (one hour, Sfr27.40), lake and mountain tours taking in Capo Lago

Lago di Lugano

❶ Need to Know
The best time to visit is April to October, when lake cruises are operating.

✕ Take a Break
After walking to Gandria, linger over lunch and lake views at Le Bucce di Gandria (p204).

> **★ Top Tip**
> There are free guided tours (p201) of Lugano's city centre every Monday (10am to noon).

and Gandria, passing through glorious gardens where century-old olive trees and Mediterranean flowers grow. The views out across the lake and up to the slopes of Monte Brè and Monte San Salvatore are outstanding.

Museo delle Dogane Svizzere
Across the lake from Gandria is the **Museo delle Dogane Svizzere** (Swiss Customs Museum; www.zollmuseum.ch; Riva delle Cantine; adult/child Sfr3/1.50; ⏱1.30-5.30pm Apr–mid-Oct) **FREE**, accessible by boat. It tells the history of customs (and, more interestingly, smuggling) in this border area. On display are confiscated smugglers' boats that once operated on the lake.

Ceresio Peninsula
Dipping south of Lugano, this peninsula is created by the looping shoreline of Lago di Lugano. Walking trails carve up the interior, dominated by the thickly wooded peaks of Monte San Salvatore. Tiny villages cling to the slopes that rise above the lakeside, with stairways leading up to stone houses, medieval chapels and pocket-sized gardens. Morcote is the loveliest of the bunch.

and Monte Generoso (two hours, Sfr31.40) and 'magic' tours (90 minutes, Sfr41.40) via Gandria, Melide and Morcote.

For a little do-it-yourself fun on the water, hire a **pedalo** (Riva Vela; pedalo per 30 min/1 hr Sfr8/16) down by the lakefront.

Parco Ciani
Lugano's lakefront **promenade** (Viale Carlo Cattaneo; ⏱6am-11pm) necklaces the shore of glassy Lago di Lugano, set against a backdrop of rugged mountains. Notice the distinctive profiles of cone-shaped twin peaks Monte Brè and Monte San Salvatore. Linden and chestnut trees provide welcome shade in summer, while tulips, camellias and magnolias bloom in spring.

Sentiero di Gandria
The 5km, 1½-hour Gandria Trail hugs the shore of Lago di Lugano between Lugano

Monte San Salvatore

The 912m peak of **Monte San Salvatore** (www.montesansalvatore.ch; funicular one way/return Sfr23/30; ☺9am-6pm) has riveting 360-degree views over the lake and southern Ticino to the Alps beyond. A turn-of-the-century funicular hauls you up to Monte San Salvatore, operating from mid-March to early November. The panorama at the top is tremendous, reaching over lakes, rippling mountains to Italy in the south and the high Alps in the west. For more fabulous views, the walk to Paradiso or Melide is two hours well spent.

Monte Brè

Rising dramatically above the lake, the 925m-high conical peak of **Monte Brè** (www.montebre.ch; funicular one way/return Sfr16/25; ☺9.10am-6.45pm) is the trailhead for hiking and mountain-biking trails that afford wide-reaching views of the lake and stretch all the way to the Bernese and Valais Alps. Mountain bikes can be hired near the summit for Sfr24/32 for a full/half day. A funicular from Cassarate whisks you up to the mountain. If you don't fancy walking, take bus 2 from central Lugano.

Lago Maggiore

Straddling the Swiss-Italian border (it's actually Italy's second largest lake), Lago Maggiore has cinematic looks, with inky blue waters rippling against a backdrop of lush, rugged mountains where the snow lingers into spring. Necklacing the lake are Italianate villages and towns with piazzas, Renaissance churches and alfresco cafes.

Sitting at the lake's northern tip is Locarno, Switzerland's lowest-altitude town.

Locarno

It has been seducing visitors since the late 19th century with its near-Mediterranean setting and an air of chic insouciance. The sun often shines, warming gardens ripe with lemon trees, oleanders and magnolias that release their perfume as you walk along the mountain-facing lakefront promenade.

Parco Muralto

Locarno's climate is perfect for lolling about the lake. Bristling with palms and ablaze with flowers in spring and summer, **Parco Muralto** (Map p205; Viale Verbano) is a scenic spot for a picnic or swim, and tots can let off steam in the adventure playground.

☑ Don't Miss

In spring, wander among 850 varieties of fragrant camellia blooms in Parco delle Camelie (Via Respini; ⊘9am-5pm), Locarno's pretty lakefront gardens.

ELITRAVO/SHUTTERSTOCK ©

Santuario della Madonna del Sasso

Overlooking Locarno, this **sanctuary** (Map p205; www.madonnadelsasso.org; Via Santuario 2; ⊘7.30am-6pm) was built after the Virgin Mary supposedly appeared in a vision to a monk, Bartolomeo d'Ivrea, in 1480. There's a highly adorned church and several rather rough, near-life-size statue groups (including one of the Last Supper) in niches on the stairway. The church's best-known work is *Fuga in Egitto* (Flight to Egypt), painted in 1522 by Bramantino.

A **funicular** (one way/return adult Sfr4.80/7.20, child Sfr2.20/3.60; ⊘8am-10pm May, Jun & Sep, to midnight Jul & Aug, to 9pm Apr & Oct, to 7.30pm Nov-Mar) runs every 15 minutes from the town centre past the sanctuary to Orselina, but a more scenic, pilgrim-style approach is the 20-minute walk up the chapel-lined Via Crucis (take Via al Sasso off Via Cappuccini).

Cardada & Cimetta

From the Orselina funicular stop, a cable car rises every 30 minutes to 1332m **Cardada** (www.cardada.ch; adult one way/return Sfr24/28, child Sfr12/14; ⊘9.15am-6.15pm), where a chairlift soars to **Cimetta** (www.cardada.ch; return adult one way/return from Orselina Sfr30/36, child Sfr15/18; ⊘9.15am-12.30pm & 1.30-4.50pm daily Mar-Nov) at 1671m. Cardada attracts hikers, mountain bikers and families. Make for the promenade suspended above the trees here, at the end of which is a lookout point with 180-degree views over the city, Lake Maggiore and the valleys beyond. From Cimetta, a variety of marked walking trails (1½ to four hours) invite you to explore further. Cimetta is also a popular launch spot for paragliders.

★ Top Tip

Staying overnight in Lago Maggiore automatically entitles you to the free Guest Card, which gives discounts on major sights, attractions, events, transport, restaurants and more.

 Market Day in Bellinzona

Fresh produce, from Alpine cheeses to fresh bread, *salumi* (cold cuts) and fruit, is sold at the Saturday morning **market** (Piazza Nosetto; ⊙8am-1pm Sat) in the lanes of the historic centre on and around Piazza Nosetto. Take the lead of locals and turn it into an event following a shop with coffee or lunch at one of the cafe terraces.

Market stalls, Bellinzona
AGF/CONTRIBUTOR/GETTY IMAGES ©

Bellinzona

Beyond Bellinzona's medieval mystique and knockout views of oft snow-capped mountains, you'll fall for its historic centre, flower-draped alleys, Renaissance churches and cafe-rimmed piazzas, always brimming with life, laughter and chinking glasses.

EATING

Trattoria Cantinin dal Gatt   Italian $$

(☑091 825 27 71; www.cantinindalgatt.ch; Vicolo al Sasso 4; lunch menus Sfr18-28, mains Sfr25-36; ⊙11am-3pm & 6pm-midnight Tue-Fri, 9am-3pm & 6pm-midnight Sat; ☷) Slip up a side street to find this cracking little trattoria, brimming with warmth and bonhomie. The brick-vaulted interior is an inviting spot for digging into big Italian flavours courtesy of Tuscan chef Luca. Begin, say, with homemade gnocchi with lobster bisque, shrimp and black olive tapenade, followed by a main such as roasted rabbit with sweet pepper salsa.

Osteria Mistral   Italian $$

(☑091 825 60 12; www.osteriamistral.ch; Via Orico 2; 2-/3-course lunch menu Sfr33/40, 3-/4-/6-course dinner menu Sfr68/82/115; ⊙11.45am-3pm Mon-Fri & 6.45pm-midnight Mon-Sat) Luca Braghelli takes pride in local sourcing and makes the most of whatever is in season at this smart, intimate *osteria*. Be it homemade pasta or autumn venison, everything is cooked to a T and expertly matched with regional wines.

Locanda Orico   Italian $$$

(☑091 825 15 18; www.locandaorico.ch; Via Orico 13; mains Sfr40-65, lunch menu Sfr48, dinner menus Sfr110-125; ⊙11.45am-2pm & 6.45pm-midnight Tue-Sat) Seasonality is the name of the game at this Michelin-starred temple to good food, housed in a slickly converted *palazzo* in the old town. Creations such as pumpkin gnocchi in jugged chamois meat, and wild turbot with fettuccine and basil butter are served with finesse.

⊕ DRINKING & NIGHTLIFE

Il Fermento   Brewery

(www.ilfermento.ch; Via Codeborgo 12; ⊙11am-9pm Mon-Wed, to 1pm Thu-Fri, to 9pm Sat) For one of the top craft beers in town, swing across to this hip new urban microbrewery. Sip hoppy amber ales, zesty IPAs and malty bitters in the industro-cool interior, or out on the pavement terrace if the sun's out.

Peverelli   Cafe

(Piazza Collegiata; ⊙7am-7pm Mon-Fri, 7am-6pm Sat) A lively perch on picturesque Piazza Collegiata for people-watching over an ice cream or coffee – skip the food. The terrace is rammed on hot summer days.

INFORMATION

Tourist Office (☑091 825 21 31; www.bellinzona turismo.ch; Piazza Nosetto; ⊙9am-6.30pm Mon-Fri, 9am-2pm Sat, 10am-2pm Sun Apr-Oct, shorter hours rest of year) In the restored Renaissance Palazzo del Comune (town hall).

ℹ️ GETTING THERE & AWAY

Bellinzona has frequent **train connections** (Viale della Stazione) to Locarno (Sfr8.80, 27 minutes) and Lugano (Sfr10.20, 30 minutes). It is also on the Zürich–Milan route.

The A2 motorway blazes through, linking Bellinzona to Lugano in the south and running all the way north to Basel.

Lugano

The largest city in Ticino is also the country's third-most-important banking centre. Suits aside, Lugano is a vivacious city, with posh designer boutiques, bars and pavement cafes huddling in the spaghetti maze of steep cobblestone streets.

◎ SIGHTS

Museo d'Arte della Svizzera Italiana   Gallery

(MASI; Map p200; www.masilugano.ch; LAC Lugano Arte e Cultura, Piazza Bernardino Luini 6; adult/child Sfr15/free; ⊙10am-6pm Tue-Sun, to 8pm Thu) The showpiece of Lugano's striking new **LAC** (Lugano Arte e Cultura; Map p200; 📞058 866 42 22; www.luganolac.ch; Piazza Bernardino Luini 6) cultural centre, the MASI zooms in predominantly on 20th-century and contemporary art – from the abstract to the highly experimental, with exhibitions spread across three spaces. There is no permanent collection on display at present, but there is a high-calibre roster of rotating exhibitions. Recent focuses have included the work of Swiss surrealist Meret Oppenheim and the epic, thought-provoking photography of British artist Craigie Horsfield.

Piazza della Riforma   Square

(Map p200) Porticoed lanes weave around Lugano's busy main square, which is presided over by the 1844 neoclassical **Municipio** (town hall) and is even more lively when the Tuesday and Friday morning **markets** are held.

Chiesa di Santa Maria degli Angioli   Church

(St Mary of the Angel; Map p200; Piazza Luini; ⊙7am-6pm) This simple Romanesque

Lugano Arte e Cultura (LAC)

Lugano

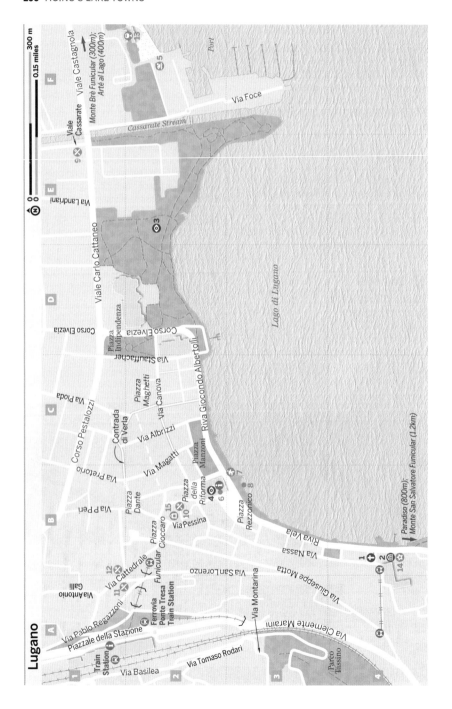

Lugano

church contains two frescos by Bernardino Luini dating from 1529. Covering the entire wall that divides the church in two is a grand didactic illustration of the crucifixion of Christ. The power and vivacity of the colours are astounding.

Parco Botanico San Grato
Gardens

(www.parcosangrato.ch; Carona; ⊘24hr) **FREE** Footpaths thread through these hilltop botanical gardens, which afford sensational lake and mountain views. In May the park is ablaze with the colour of azaleas and rhododendrons in bloom. To reach the park, take bus 434 from Lugano to Carona (Sfr6.40, 25 minutes).

Schokoland
Museum

(www.alprose.ch; Via Rompada 36, Caslano; adult/child Sfr3/1; ⊘9am-5.30pm Mon-Fri, to 4.30pm Sat & Sun; ⊡) Chomp into some cocoa culture at the Alprose chocolate museum, Schokoland – a sure-fire hit with kids. Whiz through chocolate history, watch the sugary substance being made and enjoy a free tasting. The shop, cunningly, stays open half an hour longer. Take the train to Caslano (Sfr6.60, 26 minutes).

Swissminiatur
Amusement Park

(www.swissminiatur.ch; Via Cantonale; adult/child Sfr19/12; ⊘9am-6pm mid-Mar–Oct; ⊡) At Swissminiatur you'll find 1:25 scale models of more than 120 national attractions.

It's the quick way to see Switzerland in a day. Trains run twice hourly from Lugano (Sfr6.40, six minutes).

Museo Hermann Hesse
Museum

(www.hessemontagnola.ch; Torre Camuzzi, Montagnola; adult/child Sfr8.50/free; ⊘10am-5.30pm daily Mar-Oct, 10.30am-5.30pm Sat & Sun Nov-Feb) This museum showcases German-born Swiss poet, novelist and painter Herman Hesse's personal objects, including some of the thousands of watercolours he painted in Ticino, books and other odds and ends that help re-create something of his life. From Lugano, take bus 436 to Montagnola, Bellevue (Sfr6.40, 19 minutes).

☉ ACTIVITIES

Lugano Guided Tours
Tours

(Map p200; ⊘mid-Mar–Oct) Departing from the tourist office (p203), Lugano's brilliant guided tours include a free spin of the city centre on Mondays (10am to noon). Other tours are available for a small contribution of Sfr10/5 per adult/child, including the peak of Monte San Salvatore on Wednesdays (10am to 1pm), an architectural highlights tour on Thursdays (10am to noon) and Monte Brè on Fridays (1.10pm to 5.30pm).

Lido
Swimming

(Map p200; Viale Castagnola; adult/child Sfr11/6; ⊘9am-7pm May & Sep, to 7.30pm Jun-Aug; ⊡) Right on the lake and with glorious views across to the mountains, this lido has beaches, volleyball, splash areas for kids and an Olympic-size swimming pool.

SHOPPING

Gabbani Food & Drinks

(Map p200; www.gabbani.com; Via Pessina 12; 8am-6.30pm Mon-Fri, to 5pm Sat) Look for the giant Parma hams and *salumi* dangling in the window of this irresistible delicatessen.

EATING

Pasta e Pesto Italian $

(Map p200; 091 922 66 11; Via Cattedrale 16; pasta Sfr10.50-15, menus Sfr15-19.50; 9.30am-5.30pm Mon-Sat) This cute little place near the cathedral has a pocket-size terrace for digging into fresh homemade pasta with a variety of toppings (including pesto).

Trani Italian $

(Map p200; 091 922 05 05; www.trani.ch; Via Cattedrale 12; mains Sfr29-43) Follow the cobbled steps down from Via Cattedrale

to this enticing little osteria. The candle-lit, brick-vaulted interior is a wonderfully intimate setting for antipasti, homemade pasta bursting with flavour and grilled fish and meats.

La Tinèra Swiss $$

(Map p200; 091 923 52 19; Via dei Gorini 2; mains Sfr16.50-24; 11.30am-3pm & 5.30-11pm Mon-Sat) Huddled down a backstreet near Piazza di Riforma, this convivial, rustic restaurant rolls out extremely tasty Ticinese home cooking. You might begin, say, with homemade *salumi*, moving on to polenta with porcini mushrooms or meltingly tender osso bucco. Simply pair with a good merlot from the region.

Arté al Lago Seafood $$$

(091 973 48 00; www.villacastagnola.com; Piazza Emilio Bossi 7; mains Sfr51-56, menus Sfr110-120; noon-2pm & 7-9.30pm Tue-Sat) This Michelin-starred restaurant at the exclusive lakefront Villa Castagnola is Lugano's culinary star. Chef Frank Oerthle does remarkable things with fish and seafood, with ingredient-focused, deceptively

Piazza della Riforma (p199), Lugano

WERNER DIETERICH/ALAMY ©

simple-sounding specialities such as marinated grouper with spring herbs, and veal with morels and sweet peas. Gaze out across the lake through the picture windows or up to the contemporary artworks gracing the walls.

Metamorphosis Mediterranean $$$
(☑091 994 68 68; http://metaworld.ch; Riva Paradiso 2; mains Sfr45-52, tasting menus Sfr85-120; ☺9am-3pm Mon-Tue, 9am-midnight Wed-Fri, 10.30am-midnight Sat) One for special occasions, Metamorphosis is housed in Lugano's futuristic Palazzo Mantegazza, right by the lakeshore. Chef Luca Bellanca walks the culinary high wire, bringing simple, natural Mediterranean flavours to life with imagination and flair in dishes such as red-mullet sandwich with spinach and raspberry, and glazed piglet with puffed potatoes and Greek yoghurt. Bus 431 to Paradiso stops nearby.

Al Portone Gastronomy $$$
(Map p200; ☑078 722 93 24; www.ristorante -alportone.ch; Viale Cassarate 3; mains Sfr44-57, tasting menu Sfr120; ☺6.30-9.30pm Tue-Sat) Bold artworks grace this contemporary gourmet haunt, while Francis plies you with such season-infused taste sensations as scallops and caviar on a bed of seaweed with passion vinaigrette, pumpkin ravioli with sage sauce, and freshly made *par-padelle* with wild-boar ragout.

🍷 DRINKING & NIGHTLIFE

Al Lido Lounge
(Map p200; http://allidobar.com; Viale Castag-nola 6; ☺9am-9.30pm Mar-Dec, shorter hours in winter) Partygoers flock to this cool summertime beach lounge for DJ beats, drinks, snacks and flirting by the lakefront. It's right next to Lugano's lido (p201) if you fancy a dip before or after.

ℹ️ INFORMATION

Main Tourist Office (Map p200; ☑058 866 66 00; www.lugano-tourism.ch; Piazza Riforma, Palazzo Civico; ☺9am-6pm Mon-Fri, 9am-5pm Sat,

 Out-of-Town Adventures

Several gorgeous river valleys fan out into the high Alps north and west of Locarno, including Val Verzasca, Valle Maggia, Centovalli and Valle Onsernone. Rent a car to explore these on your own, or sign up for a guided trip with **Swissraft** (☑081 911 52 50; www.swissraft. ch), which organises rafting, bungee jumping and other active adventures in Ticino and throughout Switzerland.

Val Verzasca
MATTY GENNA/SHUTTERSTOCK ©

10am-4pm Sun) Guided tours of Lugano begin at this centrally located tourist office. There is also a **tourist information** (Map p200; ☑091 923 51 20; Piazzale della Stazione; ☺9am-7pm Mon-Fri, 9am-1pm Sat) booth at the main railway station.

ℹ️ GETTING THERE & AWAY

Lugano airport (☑091 610 12 82; www.lugano -airport.ch) is served by a handful of Swiss-Italian carriers including Swiss and Etihad (p247).

Lugano has very frequent **train connections** (Piazzale della Stazione) to Bellinzona (Sfr11, 30 minutes), with onward connections to destinations further north. Getting to Locarno (Sfr15.20, one hour) involves a change at Giubiasco. Note that the train station can be reached by foot or **funicular** (Piazzale della Stazione; Sfr1.30; ☺5am-midnight).

The main artery running north–south through Ticino is the A2 motorway, which links Lugano to Bellinzona, 37km north, and Chiasso on the Italian border, 26km south.

Gandria

Looking as though it will topple off its terraced hillside with the merest puff of breath, lakeside Gandria is ludicrously pretty, with pastel-coloured houses stacked on top of one another like children's building blocks, narrow stairwells, arcades, courtyards and terraced gardens.

Climb the old-town steps and you'll be rewarded with gorgeous lake views from hillside **Ristorante le Bucce di Gandria** (Via Cantonale; mains Sfr22-32; ⊙7pm-midnight Wed-Thu, noon-3pm & 7pm-midnight Fri-Sun). The menu keeps things regional and seasonal, adding a dash of creativity in dishes such as ravioli of salt cod with onion-cardamom cream and venison fillet with fondant potatoes and cinnamon pear. It's all delicious and served with a smile.

Locarno

With its palm trees and much-hyped 2300 hours of sunshine a year, visitors have swooned over Locarno's setting since the late 19th century. As well as the lake, there's a pretty Renaissance Old Town to roam, which fans out from the Piazza Grande, host of a renowned music and film festival in summer.

 ### SIGHTS

Old Town Historic Site
(Map p205) You can feel just how close you are to Italy when exploring Locarno's hilly Città Vecchia (Old Town), an appealing jumble of piazzas, arcades, churches and tall, shuttered Lombard houses in ice-cream colours. At its centre sits the **Piazza Grande** (Map p205), with narrow lanes threading off in all directions, while the Castello Visconteo guards its southwestern fringes.

Castello Visconteo Museum, Castle
(Map p205; Piazza Castello; adult/child Sfr7/free; ⊙10am-noon & 2-5pm Tue-Sun Apr-Oct) Named after the Visconti clan that long ruled Milan, this fortified 15th-century castle's nucleus

was raised around the 10th century. It now houses a museum with Roman and Bronze Age exhibits and also hosts a small display (in Italian) on the 1925 Locarno Treaty. Locarno is believed to have been a glass-manufacturing town in Roman times, which accounts for the many glass artefacts in the museum.

 ### ACTIVITIES

Lido Locarno Swimming
(www.lidolocarno.ch; Via Respini 11; adult/child Sfr13/7, incl waterslides Sfr18/11; ⊙8.30am-9pm) ✦ Locarno's lido has several pools, including an Olympic-size one, children's splash areas and waterslides, and fabulous lake and mountain views. The huge complex uses solar and hydro power.

 ### EATING

Locanda Locarnese Italian $$
(Map p205; ☎091 756 87 56; www.locanda locarnese.ch; Via Bossi 1; mains Sfr40-45; ⊙noon-2.30pm & 7pm-midnight Mon-Sat) Elegant rusticity sums up this smart restaurant, with a beamed ceiling, crisp white tablecloths and an open fire, as well as a smattering of pavement seating. It's a romantic and intimate choice for seasonal dishes such as bresaola (cured beef) with artichokes, and wild sea bass with chanterelle sauce and peaches.

Osteria Chiara Italian $$
(Map p205; ☎091 743 32 96; www.osteriachiara. ch; Vicolo dei Chiara 1; mains Sfr34-45; ⊙10am-2.30pm & 6.30-11pm Wed-Sun) Hidden up a flight of steps, Osteria Chiara has all the cosy feel of a grotto. Sit at granite tables beneath the pergola or at timber tables by the fireplace for homemade pasta and hearty meat dishes such as veal osso bucco with saffron-infused risotto. From the lake, follow the signs uphill.

Osteria del Centenario Fusion $$$
(Map p205; ☎091 743 82 22; Viale Verbano 17; mains Sfr41-62, lunch Sfr25-45, dinner tasting menu Sfr126; ⊙11.30am-3pm & 6.30pm-midnight

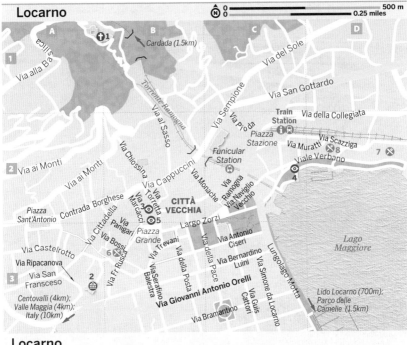

Locarno

Tue-Sat) Down by the lake, this is a top culinary address, turning out creative fusion dishes such as pigeon served two ways with green curry and lime, and panna cotta with adzuki beans, matcha-tea sauce and vanilla. Service is attentive, the ambience discreetly elegant and many ingredients hail from Ticino.

❶ INFORMATION

Tourist Office (Map p205; ☑084 809 10 91; www.ascona-locarno.com; Piazza Stazione; ⊙9am-6pm Mon-Fri, 10am-6pm Sat, 10am-1.30pm & 2.30-5pm Sun) Conveniently located at Locarno's train station, this tourist office has stacks of information about Locarno and the surrounding region. Ask about the Ticino Discovery Card and the Lago Maggiore Guest Card and its discounts.

❶ GETTING THERE & AWAY

Hourly trains from Locarno run direct to Lucerne (Sfr59, two hours). Most trains to/from Zürich (Sfr64, 2¼ hours) go via Bellinzona. There are twice-hourly train connections from Lugano (Sfr15.20, 58 minutes).

Locarno is just off the main A13 road that heads east to Bellinzona, 23km away.

Bern (p173)

In Focus

Zermatt (p69)

Switzerland Today

*They don't call it 'Fortress Switzerland' for nothing.
Seemingly immune to the troubles and travails of the
countries that surround it, Switzerland appears intent
on reinforcing its 'otherness' and its 'not in my backyard'
mentality. With a strong economy, social stability, a
trailblazing public-transport network and an emphasis
on sustainability, the country remains happy to
cultivate its independent streak and unique reputation.*

Franc Rebounds, Tourism Rises

In January 2015 the Swiss National Bank (SNB) made the highly controversial decision to
unpeg the franc and abandon the euro cap introduced in September 2011. No longer at a
fixed exchange rate with the euro, the franc soared and chaos erupted. According to *The
Economist*, 'exports of goods and services are worth over 70% of GDP' and 'an expensive
franc hurts Switzerland'. Since then, though, the Swiss economy has regained momen-
tum, as reflected in a State Secretariat for Economic Affairs (SECO) report showing that
GDP grew 0.3% in the first quarter of 2017. Despite the reverberations of the Swiss franc
shock, growth is set to continue and unemployment to fall steadily – it was 3.3% in May
2017, low compared to the European average of 9.3%.

if Switzerland were 100 people

64 would speak German

20 would speak French

7 would speak Italian

1 would speak Romansch

8 would speak another language

belief systems (% of population)

38 — Roman Catholic

27 — Protestant

21 — None

6 — Other Christian

5 — Muslim

3 — Other

population per sq km

SWITZERLAND

USA

UK

≈ 35 people

Swiss tourism has bounced back recently, too. According to the Swiss Federal Statistical Office (BFS), the number of overnight stays from November 2016 to April 2017 was 15.7 million, a year-on-year increase of 2%.

The overall economic outlook for Switzerland is rosy and this is reflected in Swiss cities once again coming top in the Mercer Quality of Living survey in 2017, with Geneva eighth and Zürich second. But all this comes at a price: Zürich earned the dubious honour of being the world's most expensive city in 2017 according to The Economist Intelligence Unit (EIU).

Green Initiatives

Switzerland's quest for more sustainable energy is powering ahead. The Swiss Energy Strategy 2050 sets goals for boosting hydropower and cost-efficient renewables while reducing per-capita consumption. In May 2017, a binding referendum saw 58.2% vote to phase out nuclear energy, which currently accounts for around a third of the country's electricity. The first of five nuclear power stations is earmarked for closure in 2019.

'Sustainability' is more than just a buzzword in Switzerland; it has become a mindset and a way of life. Take the pioneering Jungfrau region, where nearly all energy now comes from renewable sources. Even the large-scale Jungfrau Railways produces more energy than it uses: trains use electricity when they travel uphill, but on the descent the effect is reversed and the motors actually generate power.

Public Transport Sets a Precedent

The Swiss have always been pioneers when it comes to public transport. In December 2016s the environmentally friendly Gotthard Base Tunnel, the world's longest tunnel at 57km, began operation, shifting the transport load through the Alps from road to rail, and with clever measures to ensure clean air, treat waste water and protect wildlife. Then in May 2017 plans were unveiled for 29 electric high-speed 'Giruno' trains, which will travel at up to 250km/h when they take to the tracks on the Basel–Milan line through the tunnel in 2019.

Hot on the heels of such successes, the E-Grand Tour of Switzerland was kick-started in collaboration with Tesla in 2017 as the world's first-ever road trip for electric vehicles, with 300 charging stations on a new 1600km route bringing together the country's highlights. Swiss Federal Railways is piloting a new annual 'Green Class' rail pass that includes the use of an e-bike. Such eco-awareness has filtered down to tourism, with e-bikes now readily available at most stations and many regional tourist boards offering guests free public transport; an example is the Ticino Ticket, launched in 2017.

History

Switzerland is unique, and nowhere is this more explicit than in its history. An exception to the nation-state norm, this small, landlocked country is a rare and refined breed, born out of its 1874 constitution and tried and tested by two world wars (during which it remained firmly neutral). Despite the overwhelming presence of global institutions and moves towards greater international cooperation, modern-day Switzerland remains insular, idiosyncratic and staunchly singular.

58 BC	AD 1032	1273
Julius Caesar enlists Celtic tribe the Helvetii between the Alps and the Jura to watch over the Rhine frontier.	Clans in western Switzerland are swallowed up by the Holy Roman Empire but left with a large degree of autonomy.	Habsburg ruler Rudolph I becomes Holy Roman Emperor and takes control of much Swiss territory.

Château de Chillon (p56)

Clans & Castles: Swiss Roots

Modern Swiss history might start in 1291, but that's not to say that the thousands of years leading up to Switzerland's birth are not significant – this was the period that gave Switzerland the best of its châteaux and *schlösser* (castles).

The earliest inhabitants were Celtic tribes, including the Helvetii of the Jura and the Mittelland Plain, and the Rhaetians near Graubünden. Their homelands were first invaded by the Romans, who had gained a foothold under Julius Caesar by 58 BC and established Aventicum (now Avenches) as the capital of Helvetia (Roman Switzerland). Switzerland's largest Roman ruins are at Augusta Raurica, near Basel. By AD 400, Germanic Alemanni tribes had arrived to drive out the Romans.

The Alemanni groups settled in eastern Switzerland and were later joined by another Germanic tribe, the Burgundians, in the western part of the country. The latter adopted Christianity and the Latin language, sowing the seeds of division between French- and

1291	1315	1499
Modern Switzerland officially 'begins' with an independence pact at Rütli Meadow.	Swiss irregular troops win a surprise victory over Habsburg Austrian forces at the Battle of Morgarten.	The Swiss Confederation wins virtual independence from the Habsburg-led Holy Roman Empire.

German-speaking Switzerland. The Franks conquered both tribes in the 6th century, but the two areas were torn apart again when Charlemagne's empire was partitioned in 870.

When it was reunited under the pan-European Holy Roman Empire in 1032, Switzerland was initially left to its own devices. Local nobles wielded the most influence: the Zähringen family, who founded Fribourg, Bern and Murten, and built a fairy-tale castle with soaring towers and red turrets in Thun in the Bernese Oberland; and the Savoy clan, who established a ring of castles around Lake Geneva, most notably Château de Morges and the magnificent Château de Chillon, right on the water's edge near Montreux.

When the Habsburg ruler Rudolph I became Holy Roman Emperor in 1273, he sent in heavy-handed bailiffs to collect more taxes and tighten the administrative screws. Swiss resentment grew quickly.

Confoederatio Helvetica: Modern Switzerland

Rudolph I died in 1291, prompting local leaders to make an immediate grab for independence. On 1 August that year, the forest communities of Uri, Schwyz and Nidwalden – so the tale goes – gathered on Rütli Meadow in the Schwyz canton in Central Switzerland to sign an alliance vowing not to recognise any external judge or law. Historians believe this to be a slightly distorted version but, whatever the scenario, a pact does exist, preserved in the town of Schwyz. Displayed at the Bundesbriefmuseum, the pact is seen as the founding act of the Swiss Confederation, whose Latin name, Confoederatio Helvetica, survives in the 'CH' abbreviation for Switzerland (used, for example, on oval-shaped car stickers and as an internet domain extension).

In 1315 Duke Leopold I of Austria dispatched a powerful army to quash the growing Swiss nationalism. Instead, however, the Swiss inflicted an epic defeat on his troops at Morgarten, which prompted other communities to join the Swiss union. The next 200 years of Swiss history was a time of successive military wins, land grabs and new memberships. The following cantons came on board: Lucerne (1332), Zürich (1351), Glarus and Zug (1352), Bern (1353), Fribourg and Solothurn (1481), Basel and Schaffhausen (1501), and Appenzell (1513). In the middle of all this, the Swiss Confederation gained independence from Holy Roman Emperor Maximilian I after a victory at Dornach in 1499.

No More Stinging Defeats: Swiss Neutrality

Swiss neutrality was essentially born out of the stinging defeat the rampaging Swiss, having made it as far as Milan, suffered in 1515 against a combined French and Venetian force at Marignano, 16km southeast of Milan. After the bloody battle, the Swiss gave up their expansionist dream, withdrew from the international arena and declared

1515	1519	1590–1600
After Swiss forces take Milan and Pavia in Italy in 1512, the Swiss are defeated at Marignano by a French-Venetian army.	Protestant Huldrych Zwingli preaches 'pray and work' in Zürich, promoting marriage for clerics and a new common liturgy.	Some 300 women in Vaud are captured, tortured and burned alive on charges of witchcraft.

neutrality for the first time. For centuries since, the country's warrior spirit has been channelled solely into mercenary activity – a tradition that continues today in the Swiss Guard that protects the pope at the Vatican.

When the religious Thirty Years War (1618–48) broke out in Europe, Switzerland's neutrality and diversity combined to give it some protection. The Protestant Reformation led by preachers Huldrych Zwingli and Jean Calvin made some inroads in Zürich and Geneva, while Central Switzerland (Zentralschweiz) remained Catholic. Such was the internal division that the Swiss, unable to agree even among themselves as to which side to take in the Thirty Years War, stuck to neutrality.

The French invaded Switzerland in 1798 and established the brief Helvetic Republic, but they were no more welcome than the Austrians before them, and internal fighting prompted Napoleon (then in power in France) to restore the former Confederation of Cantons in 1803 – the cantons of Aargau, St Gallen, Graubünden, Ticino, Thurgau and Vaud joined the confederation at this time.

Swiss neutrality as it exists today was formally established by the Congress of

The Magic Formula: Swiss Government

Switzerland's Federal Council, the executive government, is determined not by who wins the most parliamentary seats (ie the winning party rules), but by the 'magic formula' – a cosy power-sharing agreement made between the four main parties in 1959:

○ The Federal Council consists of seven ministers, elected one by one by the parliament.

○ The four largest parties in parliament are guaranteed seats in the Federal Council according to their popular vote share.

○ The president is drawn on a rotating basis from the seven ministers, so there's a new head of state each year.

○ Each councillor takes charge of one of seven federal executive departments (finance, foreign affairs etc).

○ Many federal laws must first be approved by public referendum; several are held every year.

Vienna peace treaty in 1815 that, following Napoleon's defeat by the British and Prussians at Waterloo, formally guaranteed Switzerland's independence and neutrality for the first time. (The same treaty also added the cantons of Valais, Geneva and Neuchâtel to the Swiss bow.)

Despite some citizens' pro-German sympathies, Switzerland's only involvement in WWI lay in organising Red Cross units. After the war, Switzerland joined the League of Nations, but on a strictly financial and economic basis (which included providing its headquarters in Geneva) – it would have no military involvement.

1847
'Hare shoot' civil war between Protestants and Catholics lasts just 26 days, leaving 86 dead and 500 wounded.

1863
Businessman and pacifist Henri Dunant co-founds the International Red Cross in Geneva.

1918
With a sixth of the population living below the poverty line and 20,000 dying in a flu epidemic, workers strike.

Schweizerisches Landesmuseum

★ **Best Swiss History Museums**

Schweizerisches Landesmuseum (p165), Zürich

Historisches Museum (p183), Bern

Château de Chillon (p56), Montreux

WWII likewise saw Switzerland remain neutral, the country being unscathed bar some accidental bombings on Schaffhausen in April 1944, when Allied pilots mistook the town in northeastern Switzerland for Germany, twice dropping bombs on its outskirts. Indeed, the most momentous event of WWII for the Swiss was when Henri Guisan, general of the civilian army, invited all top military personnel to Rütli Meadow (site of the 1291 Oath of Allegiance) to show the world how determined the Swiss were to defend their own soil.

Give Cantons a Voice: The Swiss Constitution

In 1847 civil war broke out. The Protestant army, led by General Dufour, quickly crushed the Sonderbund (Special League) of Catholic cantons, including Lucerne. The war lasted a mere 26 days, prompting German Chancellor Otto von Bismarck to subsequently dismiss it as 'a hare shoot', but for the peace-loving Swiss, the disruption and disorder were sufficient to ensure they rapidly consolidated the victory by Dufour's forces with the creation of a new federal constitution. Bern was named the capital.

The 1848 constitution, largely still in place today, was a compromise between advocates of central control and conservative forces who wanted to retain cantonal authority. The cantons eventually relinquished their right to print money, run postal services and levy customs duties, ceding these to the federal government, but they retained legislative and executive control over local matters. Furthermore, the new Federal Assembly was established in a way that gave cantons a voice. The lower national chamber, the Nationalrat, has 200 members, allocated from the 26 cantons in proportion to population size. The upper states chamber, the Ständerat, comprises 46 members, two per canton.

Opposition to political corruption sparked a movement for greater democracy. The constitution was revised in 1874 so that many federal laws had to be approved by national referendum – a phenomenon for which Switzerland remains famous today. A

1940

General Guisan's army warns off WWII invaders; 430,000 troops are placed on borders but most are put in Alpine fortresses.

1979

The Jura, absorbed by Bern in 1815, withdraws to become an independent canton.

1990

The internet is 'born' at Geneva's CERN; Tim Berners-Lee develops HTML to prepare pages for the World Wide Web.

petition with 50,000 signatures can challenge a proposed law; 100,000 signatures can force a public vote on *any* new issue.

Famously Secret: Swiss Banking

Banking confidentiality, dating back to the Middle Ages, was enshrined in Swiss law in 1934 when numbered (rather than named) bank accounts were introduced. The Swiss banking industry has, for the most part, thrived ever since, thanks mainly to the enviable stability that guaranteed neutrality brings. When the Bank for International Settlements (BIS, the organisation that facilitates cooperation between central banks) chose Basel as its base in 1930 it was for one good reason: Switzerland was a neutral player.

In the late 1990s, a series of scandals erupted, forcing Switzerland to start reforming its famously secretive banking industry, born when a clutch of commercial banks was created in the mid-19th century. In 1995, after pressure from Jewish groups, Swiss banks announced that they had discovered millions of dollars lying in dormant pre-1945 accounts and belonging to Holocaust victims and survivors. Three years later, amid allegations they'd been sitting on the money without seriously trying to trace its owners, Switzerland's two largest banks, UBS and Credit Suisse, agreed to pay US$1.25 billion in compensation to Holocaust survivors and their families.

Switzerland has long been a favourite spot for the wealthy to deposit their fortunes in private banks, hence the immense pressure on Switzerland since 2009 from the US, Britain, Germany and other high-tax countries to change its 1934 banking law protecting depositors accused of tax evasion by their home countries.

The Swiss conceded, prompting critics to triumphantly ring the death knell for Swiss banking secrecy. Amid the hand-wringing, Wegelin, Switzerland's oldest bank, shut up shop in 2013, after pleading guilty in the US to aiding tax evasion. That same year, Switzerland and the US signed a joint statement allowing Swiss banks to voluntarily cooperate with US authorities on the issue of tax evasion. In 2014 Switzerland's second-largest bank, Credit Suisse, pleaded guilty to criminal wrongdoing in the form of conspiring to aid tax evasion over many years. The bank agreed to pay US$2.6 billion in penalties.

The era of secret Swiss bank accounts may soon be at an end: new rules set to come into effect by 2018 will ensure that account details are shared with the tax authorities of other nations, in line with international transparency standards.

Forever Neutral: A Nation Apart

Since the end of WWII, Switzerland has enjoyed an uninterrupted period of economic, social and political stability – thanks, in predictable Swiss fashion, to the neutrality that saw it forge ahead from an already powerful commercial, financial and industrial base while the rest of Europe was still picking up and rebuilding the pieces after the war.

2001	**2008**	**2011**
National airline Swissair collapses, a gun massacre in Zug parliament kills 14 politicians, and 11 die in St Gotthard Tunnel fire.	The world financial crisis affects Switzerland's biggest banks. The government bails out UBS, while Credit Suisse seeks funds elsewhere.	A soaring, over-valued Swiss franc prompts the Swiss National Bank to peg it to the euro.

Zürich developed as an international banking and insurance centre, and the World Health Organization and a range of other international bodies set up headquarters in Geneva. To preserve its neutrality, however, Switzerland chose to remain outside the UN (although Geneva has hosted its second-largest seat, after the main New York headquarters, from the outset) and, more recently, the European Union.

A hefty swing to the conservative right in the 2003 parliamentary elections served to further enhance Switzerland's standing as a nation staunchly apart. In 2006, the anti-EU, anti-immigration Swiss People's Party (SVP) called for the toughening of immigration and political-asylum laws; the policies were passed with an overwhelming majority at a national referendum. Then there was the rumpus over the right-wing bid to ban the building of new minarets for Muslim calls to prayer – an idea that aroused much anger internationally but was approved by the constitution after 57.7% of voters said yes to the ban in a referendum. During the campaign, the SVP published anti-immigrant posters featuring three white sheep kicking one black sheep off the striking white cross of the Swiss flag.

In spite of the SVP's tough conservative line, there have been definite signs that Switzerland is opening up to the wider world. The country became the 190th member of the UN in 2002 (a referendum on the issue had last been defeated in 1986) and three years later it voted to join Europe's passport-free travel zone, Schengen (finally completing the process at the end of 2008). In another referendum the same year, the Swiss narrowly voted in favour of legalising civil unions (but not marriage) for same-sex couples – one more defeat for the SVP.

Yet few expect Switzerland to even consider joining either the EU or the euro zone any time soon (if ever). Traditionally, the western, French-speaking cantons are more sympathetic to the idea, while the German-speaking cantons (and Ticino) have generally been opposed.

2014	2016	2017
A popular initiative to set immigration quotas is successful at the Swiss polls.	The Gotthard Base Tunnel, the world's longest at 57km, opens in December, speeding up connections between the Alps and Italy.	Swiss vote in favour of phasing out nuclear energy and switching to renewables.

Hiking with a view of the Matterhorn (p72)

GASPAR JANOS/SHUTTERSTOCK ©

Activities

In a country where a half-day hike over a 2500m mountain pass is a Sunday stroll and three-year-olds ski rings around you, to call the Swiss 'sporty' would be an understatement. They're hyperactive. Why? Just look at their phenomenal backyard, with colossal peaks, raging rivers and slopes that beg outdoor adventure. The activities on offer are virtually limitless, with options for everyone, from families with small children to seasoned Alpinists.

Planning Your Outdoor Experience

Your outdoor experiences in Switzerland are far more likely to run smoothly with a little planning. Bear in mind that you'll need to book hiking huts well in advance (particularly during the peak summer months). Or pick a central base and plan day hikes from there. Other activities in popular adventure destinations also get booked up well ahead, so arrange these before you go to avoid disappointment. You can often beat the queues and save money by purchasing ski passes and organising ski hire online.

Skiing, Mt Titlis (p112)

★ Top Slopes for...

Glacier skiing – Mt Titlis in Engelberg

Scenic skiing – Zermatt or Männlichen

Scary-as-hell descents – The Inferno from Schilthorn to Lauterbrunnen

Non-skiers – Grindelwald

When to Go

Alpine weather is notoriously fickle. Even in August you can have four seasons – sun, fog, storms, snow – in a day, so check the forecast on www.meteoschweiz.ch before you head out.

December to April The slopes buzz with skiers and boarders until Easter. Prices skyrocket during school holidays.

May and June Crowds are thin and the weather is often fine. Snow patches linger above 2000m. Many huts remain closed and mountain transport is limited.

July and August A conga line of high-altitude hikers and cyclists makes its way through the Swiss Alps. All lifts and mountain huts are open (book ahead).

September to early October Pot luck: can be delightful or drab. Accommodation prices drop, as do the crowds, but many hotels and lifts close.

Mid-October to November Days get shorter and the weather is unpredictable. Expect rain, fog and snow above 1500m. Most resorts go into hibernation.

Skiing & Snowboarding

In a land where every 10-person, 50-cow hamlet has a ski lift, the question is not *where* you can ski but *how*. Ritzy or remote, party mad or picture perfect, virgin or veteran, black run or blue – whatever your taste and ability, Switzerland has a resort to suit.

Ski-run Classifications

Ski runs are colour-coded according to difficulty:

Blue Easy, well-groomed runs that are suitable for beginners.

Red Intermediate runs that are groomed but often steeper and narrower than blue runs.

Black For expert skiers with polished technique and skills. They are mostly steep and not always groomed, and they may have moguls and vertical drops.

Safety on the Slopes

○ Avalanche warnings should be heeded and local advice sought before detouring from prepared runs.

○ Never go off-piste alone. Take an avalanche pole, a transceiver or a shovel and, most importantly, a professional guide.

○ Check the day's avalanche bulletin online at www.slf.ch or by calling 187.

○ The sun in the Alps is intensified by snow glare. Wear ski goggles and high-factor sunscreen.

○ Layers help you to adapt to the constant changes in body temperature. Your head, wrists and knees should be protected.

○ Black run look tempting? Make sure you're properly insured first; sky-high mountain-rescue and medical costs can add insult to injury.

Passes, Hire & Tuition

Yes, Switzerland is expensive; and no, skiing is not an exception. That said, costs can be cut by avoiding school-holiday times and choosing low-key villages over upscale resorts. Ski passes are a hefty chunk out of your budget and will set you back around Sfr70 per day or Sfr350 for six days. Factor in around Sfr40 to Sfr70 per day for ski hire and Sfr20 for boot hire, which can be reserved online at www.inter-sportrent.com. Equipment for kids is roughly half price.

All major resorts have ski schools, with half-day group lessons typically costing Sfr50 to Sfr80. Schweizer Skischule (www.swiss-ski-school.ch) has a clickable map of 170 ski schools across the country.

A good deal for keen skiers is the new **Magic Pass** (www.magicpass.ch; adult/child Sfr1299/799), which aims to attract more skiers to the country's lesser-known resorts. It covers 25 resorts and is valid for an entire winter season (November to April). Promotional rates are sometimes available online.

Online Ski Deals

○ For last-minute ski deals and packages, check out websites such as www.igluski.com, www.j2ski.com, www.snowfinders.co.uk and www.myswitzerland.com.

○ Speed to the slopes by prebooking discounted ski and snowboard hire at Ski Set (www.skiset.co.uk) or Snow-brainer (www.snowbrainer.com).

○ If you want to skip to the front of the queue, consider ordering your ski pass online, too. Swiss Passes (www.swisspasses.com) gives reductions of up to 30% on standard ski-pass prices.

Regions

Graubünden

Rugged Graubünden has some truly legendary slopes. Topping the list is super-chic **St Moritz**, with 350km of groomed slopes, glacier descents and freeride opportunities.

Valais

Nothing beats skiing in the shadow of the Matterhorn, soaring 4478m above **Zermatt**. Snowboarders, intermediates and off-pisters all rave about the car-free resort's 360km of scenic runs.

Bernese Oberland

At its winter-wonderland heart is the Jungfrau region, an unspoilt Alpine beauty criss-crossed with 214km of well-maintained slopes, ranging from easy-peasy to hair-raising, that grant fleeting views of the 'Big Three': Eiger, Mönch and Jungfrau. **Grindelwald**, **Wengen** and **Mürren** all offer varied skiing and have a relaxed, family-friendly vibe.

Central Switzerland

Surprisingly little-known given its snow-sure slopes and staggering mountain backdrop, **Engelberg** is dominated by glacier-capped **Mt Titlis**. The real treasures here are off-piste, including Galtiberg, a 2000m vertical descent from the glacier to the valley.

Resources

Books

Which Ski Resort – Europe (Pat Sharples and Vanessa Webb) This well-researched guide covers the top 50 resorts in Europe.

Where to Ski and Snowboard (Chris Gill and Dave Watts) Bang-up-to-date guide to the slopes, covering all aspects of skiing.

Websites

Bergfex (http://www.bergfex.com/schweiz) Comprehensive website with piste maps, snow forecasts and details of 226 ski resorts in Switzerland.

On the Snow (www.onthesnow.co.uk) Reviews of Switzerland's ski resorts, plus snow reports, webcams and lift-pass details.

If You Ski (www.ifyouski.com) Resort guides, ski deals and info on ski hire and schools.

MadDogSki (www.maddogski.com) Entertaining ski guides and insider tips on everything from accommodation to après ski.

World Snowboard Guide (www.worldsnowboardguide.com) Snowboarder central. Has the lowdown on most Swiss resorts.

Where to Ski & Snowboard (www.wheretoskiandsnowboard.com) Resort overviews and reviews, news and weather.

Walking & Hiking

It's only by slinging on a backpack and hitting the trail that you can begin to appreciate just how *big* this tiny country really is: it's criss-crossed by more than 60,000km of marked paths.

Walk Descriptions

○ Times and distances for walks are provided only as a guide.

○ Times are based on the actual walking time and do not include stops for snacks, taking photos or rests, or side trips.

○ Distances should be read in conjunction with altitudes – significant elevation can make a greater difference to your walking time than lateral distance.

Safe & Responsible Hiking

To help preserve the ecology and beauty of Switzerland, consider the following tips when hiking.

○ Pay any fees required and obtain reliable information about environmental conditions (eg from park authorities).

○ Walk only in regions, and on trails, within your realm of experience. Increase length and elevation gradually.

○ Stick to the marked route to prevent erosion and for your own safety.

○ Where possible, don't walk in the mountains alone. Two is considered the minimum number for safe walking.

○ Take all your rubbish away with you.

SOS Six

The standard Alpine distress signal is six whistles, six calls, six smoke puffs – that is, six of whatever sign or sound you can make – repeated every 10 seconds for one minute.

Walk Designations

As locals delight in telling you, Switzerland's walking trails would be enough to stretch around the globe 1.5 times. And with (stereo)typical Swiss precision, these footpaths are remarkably well signposted and maintained. That said, a decent topographical map and compass are still recommended for Alpine hikes. Like ski runs, trails are colour-coded according to difficulty:

Yellow Easy. No previous experience necessary.
White-red-white Mountain trails. You should be sure-footed, as routes may involve some exposure.
White-blue-white High Alpine routes. Only for the physically fit; some climbing and/or glacier travel may be required.
Pink Prepared winter walking trails.

Regions

Alpine hikers invariably have their sights set high on the trails in the Bernese Oberland, Valais and Graubünden, which offer challenging walking and magnificent scenery. Lowland areas such as the vine-strewn Lavaux wine region can be just as atmospheric and are accessible virtually year-round.

In summer some tourist offices, including Lugano's, run guided hikes – free with a local guest card. Other resorts give you a head start with free mountain transport when you stay overnight in summer.

Accommodation

One of the hiker's greatest pleasures in the Swiss Alps is staying in a mountain hut, and the **SAC** (SAC; www.sac-cas.ch; per person non-members Sfr20-40, members up to Sfr28) runs 152 of them. Bookings are essential. Annual membership, costing between Sfr80 and Sfr175, entitles you to discounts on SAC huts, climbing halls, tours, maps and guides.

If you are walking in the lowlands and fancy going back to nature, consider spending the night at a farmstay. Explore your options with Agrotourismus Schweiz (p242) and Swiss Holiday Farms (p243).

Resources

Books

Rother (www.rother.de) and **Cicerone** (www.cicerone.co.uk) publish regional walking guides to Switzerland.
Walking Easy in the Swiss & Austrian Alps (Chet Lipton) Gentle two- to six-hour hikes in the most popular areas.
100 Hut Walks in the Alps (Kev Reynolds) Lists 100 hut-to-hut trails in the Alps for all levels of ability.
Trekking in the Alps (Kev Reynolds) Covers 20 Alpine treks and includes maps and route profiles.

Best Hikes

High-Alpine day hike Strike out on the Faulhornweg (p138) for spellbinding views of lakes Thun and Brienz, Eiger, Mönch and Jungfrau.

Epic mountain trek Gasp at mighty Matterhorn on the Matterhorn Glacier Trail (p73), a hike taking in wild glaciers and 4000m peaks. Or get close-ups of Eiger and the other Jungfrau giants on the Eiger Trail from Kleine Scheidegg.

Glacier hike Be blown away by the Aletsch Glacier (p76) and keep an eye out for black-nosed sheep.

Family hike Please the kids on the marmot-filled Felixweg (p135) at Männlichen.

Off-the-beaten track hike Admire the pristine beauty of the Swiss National Park on the challenging Lakes of Macun hike (p88).

Pushchair hike Walking with tots is a breeze on the buggy-friendly trails in Zermatt (p79).

Websites

Get planning with the routes, maps and GPS downloads on the following websites:

Switzerland Tourism (www.myswitzerland.com) Excellent information on walking in Switzerland, from themed day hikes to guided treks and family-friendly walks. An app covering 32 walks is available for download.

Wanderland (www.wanderland.ch) The definitive Switzerland hiking website, with walks and accommodation searchable by region and theme, plus information on events, guides, maps and packages.

Maps

A great overview map of Switzerland is Michelin's 1:400,000 national map No 729 *Switzerland*. For an interactive walking map, see http://map.wanderland.ch. Or visit www.myswitzerland.com/map for a zoomable country map.

To purchase high-quality walking maps online, try:

Kümmerly + Frey (www.swisstravelcenter.com) Has the entire country mapped. Most are scaled at 1:60,000 and are accurate enough for serious navigation.

Swiss Alpine Club (www.sac-cas.ch) Highly detailed and reliable walking maps at a scale of 1:25,000.

Cycling & Mountain-Biking

Switzerland is an efficiently run paradise for the ardent cyclist, laced with 9000km of cycling trails and 4500km of mountain-biking routes.

Bike Hire

Reliable wheels are available in all major towns, and many cities now offer free bike hire from April to October as part of the ecofriendly initiative Schweiz Rollt (p249), including Bern, Zürich and Geneva.

Available at all major train stations, SBB Rent a Bike (p248) has city bikes, mountain bikes, e-bikes and tandems. For an additional cost, you can pick your bike up at one station and drop it off at another. Bikes can be reserved online. A one-day bike pass for SBB trains costs Sfr20.

If you're planning on a longer stay, it's worth registering for public bike-sharing scheme PubliBike (p249).Use the website to order and check sales and station locations.

Resources

Veloland (www.veloland.ch) Info on cycling in Switzerland – from national routes to bike rental, events and family tours.

Mountainbikeland (www.mountainbikeland.ch) The lowdown on national, regional and local routes.

GPS Tour (www.gps-tour.info) Hundreds of GPS cycling and mountain-bike tours in Switzerland available for download.

Adventure & Water Sports

Rock Climbing

Switzerland has long been a rock climber's mecca, with an inexhaustible supply of climbs ranging from the straightforward to the spine-tinglingly hard-core. Serious Alpinists will find some of Europe's most gruelling climbs: Monte Rosa (4634m), the Matterhorn (4478m), Mont Blanc (4807m) and Eiger (3970m).

If you're eager to tackle the biggies, Zermatt's Alpin Center arranges some first-class climbs to surrounding 4000ers.

The climbing halls in places such as Interlaken are perfect for limbering up.

Some resources:

SAC (www.sac-cas.ch) Browse for information on countrywide climbing halls, tours and courses.

Schweizer Bergführerverband (www.4000plus.ch) The official site of the Swiss Mountain Guide Association.

Rock Climbing (www.rockclimbing.com) Gives details of hundreds of climbing tours in Switzerland, many with climbing grades and photos.

Verband Bergsportschulen Schweiz (www.bergsportschulen.ch) The leading mountain-sports schools in Switzerland.

Vie Ferrate

For the buzz of mountaineering but with the security of being attached to the rock face, clip onto a *via ferrata* (*Klettersteig* in German). These head-spinning fixed-rope routes are all the rage in Switzerland.

Via Ferrata (www.viaferrata.org) provides maps and routes graded according to difficulty.

Paragliding & Hang-gliding

Where there's a beautiful breeze and a mountain, there's tandem paragliding and hang-gliding in Switzerland.

In the glacial realms of the Unesco–listed Aletsch Glacier, Fiescheralp is a prime spot to catch thermals, as is First for spirit-soaring vistas to mighty Jungfrau. If lake scenery is more your style, glide like a bird over glittering Lake Lucerne and Lago di Lugano.

Bungee Jumping

Regional tourist offices have details of bungee-jumping specialists. Great leaps include Grindelwald's glacier-gouged Gletscherschlucht and the 134m jump from Stockhorn near Interlaken. If you fancy yourself a bit of a Bond, head to Ticino's Verzasca Dam, the world's second-highest bungee jump at 220m, which starred in the opening scene of the film *GoldenEye*.

Skydiving & BASE Jumping

Extreme-sports hub Interlaken is the place for heart-stopping skydiving moments. Free fall past the vertical face of Eiger, then drink in the scenery in glorious slow motion.

Even more nerve-racking is BASE jumping, the decidedly risky pursuit of leaping off fixed objects and opening the parachute just before you splat. While it is exhilarating to watch in Lauterbrunnen, this is one sport best left to the experts.

Rafting & Hydrospeeding

In summer, the raging Saane, Rhine, Inn and Rhône rivers create a dramatic backdrop for rafting and hydrospeeding. **Swissraft** (www.swissraft.ch) has bases all over the country. Expect to pay around Sfr115 for a half-day rafting/hydrospeeding tour, including transport and equipment.

Kayaking & Canoeing

Lazy summer afternoons are best spent absorbing the slow, natural rhythm of Switzerland's crystal-clear lakes and rivers. Consult **Kanuland** (http://kanuland. myswitzerland.com) for routes and paddle-friendly accommodation tips. A half-day canoeing tour costs between Sfr85 and Sfr120.

Windsurfing & Kitesurfing

See www.windsurf.ch for windsurfing clubs and schools across Switzerland and www. wannakitesurf.com for an interactive map of kitesurfing hot spots.

Zürich (p149)

Swiss Way of Life

*Chocolate, cheese, cuckoo clocks, precision watches, banking
secrecy, bircher muesli, Heidi, William Tell, yodelling
and the Alps: a swath of stereotypes envelops Switzerland
and the Swiss. This perfectly well-behaved country is
hard-working, super organised, efficient, orderly, obedient
(have you ever seen a Swiss pedestrian cross the road
when the little man is red?), overly cautious and ruthlessly
efficient – a mother-in-law's dream. Or maybe not...*

Special-Case Switzerland

The Swiss see themselves as different, and they are. Take their country's overwhelming cultural diversity, eloquently expressed in four languages and attitudes; German-, French- and Italian-speaking Swiss all display similar characteristics to German, French and Italian people respectively, creating an instant line-up of reassuringly varied, diverse and often surprising psyches. Then, of course, there are those in Graubünden who speak Romansch. There is definitely not one cookie-cutter shape to fit *Sonderfall Schweiz* (literally 'special-case Switzerland') and its dramatically different inhabitants.

Quite the contrary: from centuries-old Alpine traditions, positively wild in nature, such as wrestling and stone throwing, to new-millennium Googlers in Zürich who shimmy into work down a fire pole, to Geneva jewellers who make exclusive watches from moon dust or ash from Iceland's Eyjafjallajökull volcano, to fashionable 30-somethings sporting bags made of recycled truck tarps, the Swiss like to innovate.

They also have the determination to complement their creativity – keenly demonstrated by their restless quest to test their limits in the sporting arena, and the extraordinarily tough, independent spirit with which Swiss farmers resolutely work the land to create a sustainable lifestyle. That *Sonderfall Schweiz* halo might not shine quite as brightly as it did a few decades back, but Switzerland definitely still glows.

A Quality Lifestyle

To be born Swiss is to be born lucky, thanks to a combination of universal healthcare, quality education and a strong economy (not to mention one hell of a backyard in the form of all those lakes and mountains). No less an authority than the Economist Intelligence Unit declared Switzerland the best place in the world to be born in 2013, based on 11 indicators (including geography, job security and political stability). In addition to this, Swiss cities – such as Zürich and Geneva – regularly appear on 'world's best cities' lists. In the Mercer Consulting 2017 quality-of-life report, these cities were ranked second and eighth respectively.

Yet the Swiss don't necessarily enjoy a particularly different lifestyle from other Westerners; they just enjoy it more. They can rely on their little nation, one of the world's 10 richest in terms of GDP per capita, to deliver excellent health services, efficient public transport and all-round security. Spend a little time among them and you realise their sportiness and concern for the environment is symptomatic of another condition: they simply want to extract as much as possible from life.

The Swiss lifestyle is not all hobnobbing on the ski slopes during weekend visits to the chalet. Rural regions – particularly Appenzellerland, Valais and the Jura – are not about money-driven glam but traditional culture that lives and breathes. The people mark the seasons with time-honoured local traditions and rituals, such as the autumnal grape harvest, celebrated with ancient feasts, or spring shepherds decorating their cattle with flowers and bells to herd them in procession to mountain pastures for the summer.

Alpine Tourism

The geography of Switzerland is what gives the country its sporting backbone and makes its people so outrageously outdoor-orientated. It's also how little Switzerland put itself on the map as a big tourist destination. In the 19th century, during the golden age of Alpinism, it was the Swiss Alpine peaks that proved particularly alluring to British climbers. Alfred Wills made the first ascent of the Wetterhorn (3692m) above Grindelwald in 1854, which was followed by a rash of ascents up other Swiss peaks, including Edward Whymper's famous Matterhorn expedition in 1865. This flurry of pioneering activity in the Swiss Alps prompted the world's first mountaineering club, the Alpine Club, to be founded in London in 1857, followed by the Swiss Alpine Club in 1863.

With the construction of the first mountain hut on Tödi (3614m) the same year and the emergence of St Moritz and its intoxicating 'champagne climate' a year later as *the* place to winter among British aristocracy, winter Alpine tourism was born. Hotels, railways and cable cars followed and, by the time St Moritz hosted the second Winter Olympics in 1928, Switzerland was the winter-wonderland-action buzzword on everyone's lips. Not surprisingly, one year on, the first ski school in Switzerland opened its doors in St Moritz.

Fast forward almost a century and the Swiss Olympic Committee is backing Sion in its bid for the 2026 Winter Olympics.

The Scientific Swiss

The Swiss have more registered patents and Nobel Prize winners (mostly in scientific disciplines) per capita than any other nationality.

It was while he was working in Bern (between 1903 and 1905) that Albert Einstein developed his special theory of relativity. German-born Einstein studied in Aarau and later in Zürich, where he trained to be a physics and maths teacher. He was granted Swiss citizenship in 1901 and, unable to find a suitable teaching post, wound up working as a low-paid clerk in the Bern patent office. He gained his doctorate in 1905 and subsequently became a professor in Zürich, remaining in Switzerland until 1914, when he moved to Berlin. Bern's Einstein-Haus museum (p177) tells the full story.

The internet, meanwhile, was born in Geneva at the European Organization for Nuclear Research, better known as CERN, on Christmas Day 1990. The genius behind the global information-sharing tool was Oxford graduate Tim Berners-Lee, a software consultant for CERN who started out creating a program for the research centre to help its hundreds of scientists share their experiments, data and discoveries. Two years on it had become a dramatically larger and more powerful beast than anyone could imagine.

Equally dramatic, large and powerful is CERN's Large Hadron Collider (p42), where Geneva scientists play God with Big Bang experiments. A guided tour of the world's biggest physics experiment, quietly conducted in a Geneva suburb, is phenomenal.

Other great Swiss science forays include the ground-breaking glacial research carried out by courageous 19th-century scientists on the extraordinary 23km-long Aletsch Glacier in the Upper Valais, and a chemist in Basel called Albert Hofmann inadvertently embarking on the world's first acid trip – ingesting lysergic acid diethylamide (LSD) – in 1943.

The Swiss Flag, Repurposed

No national flag better lends itself to design than Switzerland's:

Swiss Army Recycling Collection (www.swissbags.de) Created by a Valais shoemaker and saddler, this hip line makes bags from old Swiss Army blankets. Handles are recycled gun straps or soldiers' belts and the icing on the cake is the bold white cross emblazoned across the front.

Sigg (www.sigg.ch) Switzerland's signature water bottle, adorned with a white cross and stopped with a black hockey-puck-shaped lid, is the essential companion on any mountain hike.

Victorinox (www.victorinox.com) Take the Swiss flag, remodel it as a pocket knife and you have the original Swiss Army Knife, aka Victorinox. Recent models, complete with USB key, metal saw and hard-wire cutter, quite put those made in the 1880s to shame.

On Guard

'The Swiss are most armed and most free', wrote Machiavelli. Yet more than 400 years after their last major military excursion, even the Swiss are losing enthusiasm for 'armed neutrality'.

While Switzerland is one of only a few Western nations to retain conscription, the country's armed defences are diminishing. At the height of the Cold War, the country had more than 600,000 soldiers and 'universal militia' of reservists with a gun at home, comprising almost the entire adult male population. Today, every able-bodied Swiss man must still undergo military training and serve 260 days' military service between the ages of 20 and 36. But community service is now an alternative option and the

Wacky Sports

Swiss specialist sports include *Hornussen*, a game of medieval origin played between two 16- to 18-strong teams. One launches a 78g *Hornuss* (ball) over a field, whipping the ball around with a flexible rod in a motion halfway between shot-putting and fly-fishing. The other team tries to stop the 85m-per-second ball with a *Schindel*, a 4kg implement resembling a road sign, used as a bat or simply tossed into the air at the *Hornuss*.

Schwingen is a Swiss version of sumo wrestling. Two people, each wearing short Hessian shorts, face off across a circle of sawdust. Through a complicated combination of pre-scribed grips (including crotch grips), jerks, feints and other manoeuvres, each tries to wrestle their opponent onto his or her back. See it at Alpine festivals, most notably Interlaken's phenomenal **Unspunnenfest** (www. unspunnenfest.ch; late Aug-early Sep), held every 12 years.

number of soldiers that can be mobilised within 72 hours has been reduced to 220,000.

For many years, Switzerland maintained bunkers with food stockpiles to house just about the entire population underground in the event of attack. As a result of army cost-cutting measures, thousands have been decommissioned – and, in true Swiss spirit, recycled in various ways (as digital-data storage facilities and temporary asylum-seeker centres, to name a couple). Once-top-secret bunkers disguised as farmhouses (at Faulensee in the Bernese Oberland, for example) are a Swiss speciality. A great place to see such a thing is **Fort de Pre-Giroud** (021 843 25 83; www.pre-giroud.ch; Le Rosay, Vallorbe; adult/ child Sfr15/7; 11.15am-5.30pm Wed-Sun Jul & Aug, 11.45am-5pm Sat & Sun mid-May–Jun & Sep–mid-Oct), in Vallorbe.

Solar Mobility

In typical green-thinking Swiss fashion, the Swiss are playing around with solar power – and setting new ground-breaking records in sustainable technology along the way. In 2016, *Solar Impulse 2* (www.solarimpulse.com), an ultra-light solar-powered aeroplane, made history by becoming the first plane to journey 40,000km around the world without a single drop of fuel. For pioneering Lausanne adventurers, explorers and scientists André Borschberg and Bertrand Piccard, it was a dream come true. A remarkable achievement that involved overcoming many logistical challenges, it marked firsts in the history of aviation and in renewable energy.

The Swiss don't restrict their solar-transport innovations to the air. On water, *Planet-Solar*, the world's largest solar-powered boat, set sail in 2010 from Monaco on a world tour covering 50,000km. The catamaran, flying the Swiss flag, is energised by 536 sq metres of photovoltaic panels on deck and is headed by Swiss expedition leader and project founder Raphaël Domjan. Since 2015 it has been operated by the Swiss-based Race for Water Foundation as a scientific platform in the fight against plastic pollution in the oceans. Follow the boat at www.planetsolar.org.

Chiesa di San Giovanni Battista (p230), by architect Mario Botta

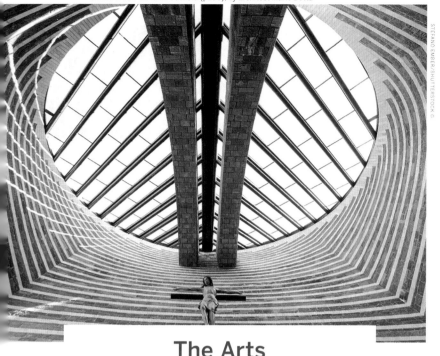

STEFANO EMBER/SHUTTERSTOCK ©

The Arts

Switzerland's arts are mind-bogglingly diverse. Take literature, for example, which skips from the light-hearted tales of Heidi to the deep works of Nobel Prize–winning Hermann Hesse. Or the music scene, which encompasses yodelling and hip-hop. Dada, the bold abstract works of Paul Klee and a string of architects from Le Corbusier to Mario Botta are emblematic of the country's ever-progressive nature.

Forever Innovating: Architecture

Switzerland's contribution to modern architecture has been pivotal thanks to Le Corbusier (1887–1965), born in the small Jura town of La Chaux-de-Fonds. Known for his radical economy of design, formalism and functionalism, Le Corbusier spent most of his working life in France but graced his country of birth with his first and last creations.

Swiss architects continue to innovate. Basel-based partners Jacques Herzog and Pierre de Meuron are the best known. Strings in their bow include London's Tate Modern gallery and the main stadium for the 2008 Beijing Olympics. In Switzerland you can admire their work at an art gallery in Basel and – hopefully in the next decade – in Davos, in the shape of a 105m-tall pencil twisting above the famous Schatzalp hotel, should the debate over whether to start construction or not ever end.

Zentrum Paul Klee (p183), Bern

★ **Best Art Museums**

Sammlung Rosengart (p107), Lucerne

Kunsthaus (p165), Zürich

Kunstmuseum Basel (p179), Basel

Zentrum Paul Klee (p183), Bern

Musée d'Art et d'Histoire (p43), Geneva

The other big home-grown architect is Ticino-born Mario Botta, who basks in the international limelight as creator of San Francisco's Museum of Modern Art. Closer to home, his Chiesa di San Giovanni Battista in Mogno (www.chiesadimogno.ch) in Ticino's Valle Maggia and his cathedral-style Tschuggen Bergoase spa hotel in Arosa, Graubünden, are soul-soothing creations, while his futuristic remake of Leuk's Romanesque *schloss* (castle) in Upper Valais is nothing short of wacky. His latest Swiss creation is Fiore di Pietra (Stone Flower), which opened in spring 2017, with astonishing views of Lago di Lugano and the Alps from its fabulous Monte Generoso perch in Ticino.

Then there's the award-winning 7132 Therme in Vals by Basel-born Peter Zumthor, Davos' Kirchner Museum by Zürich's Annette Gigon and Mike Guyer, and a clutch of design hotels in Zermatt by resident avant-garde architect Heinz Julen.

In true Swiss fashion, contemporary Swiss architects don't confine their work to urban Switzerland. Increasingly their focus is on the mountain hut and how it can be modernised in keeping with nature, ecology and the environment. Stunning examples are the Tschierva Hütte (2753m) in the Engadine Valley; Chetzeron, a concrete 1960s cable-car station turned hip piste hangout on the slopes in Crans-Montana; and, most significantly, the visionary Monte Rosa Hütte (2883m) on Monte Rosa.

Heidi & Co: Literature

Thanks to a 1930s Shirley Temple film, Johanna Spyri's *Heidi* is Switzerland's most famous novel. The story of an orphan living with her grandfather in the Swiss Alps who is ripped away to the city is unashamedly sentimental and utterly atypical of Swiss literature, which is otherwise generally quite serious and gloomy.

Take German-born, naturalised Swiss Hermann Hesse (1877–1962). A Nobel Prize winner, he fused Eastern mysticism and Jungian psychology to advance the theory that Western civilisation is doomed unless humankind gets in touch with its own essential humanity – as in *Siddharta* (1922) and *Steppenwolf* (1927). Later novels such as the cult *The Glass Bead Game* (1943) explore the tension between individual freedom and social controls.

Ich bin nicht Stiller (I'm Not Stiller/I'm Not Relaxed; 1954), by Zürich-born Max Frisch (1911–91), is a dark, Kafkaesque tale of mistaken identity. More accessible is the work of Friedrich Dürrenmatt (1921–90), who created a wealth of detective fiction.

Green Henry (1854), by Gottfried Keller (1819–1900), is a massive tome revolving around a Zürich student's reminiscences and is considered one of the masterpieces of Germanic literature.

Pastoral to Pop: Music

Yodelling and alpenhorns are the traditional forms of Swiss music. Yodelling began in the Alps as a means of communication between peaks, but it became separated into two disciplines: *Juchzin* consists of short yells with different meanings, such as 'it's dinner time' or 'we're coming', while *Naturjodel* involves one or more voices singing a melody without lyrics. Yodelling is fast becoming the trendy thing to do in urban circles, thanks in part to Swiss folk singers such as Nadja Räss who yodel with great success.

'Dr Schacher Seppli' is a traditional song reyodelled by Switzerland's best-known yodeller, farmer and cheesemaker Rudolf Rymann (1933–2008). The other big sound is Sonalp, a nine-person band from the Gruyères/Château d'Œx region, whose vibrant ethno-folk mix of yodelling, cow bells, musical saw, classical violin and didgeridoo is contagious.

The alpenhorn, a pastoral instrument used to herd cattle in the mountains, is 2m to 4m long with a curved base and a cup-shaped mouthpiece; the shorter the horn the harder it is to play. Catch a symphony of a hundred-odd alpenhorn players blowing in unison on the 'stage' – usually alfresco and invariably lakeside between mountain peaks – if you can. Key dates include September's Alphorn in Concert festival (www.alphorninconcert.ch) in Oesingen near Solothurn and July's International Alphorn Festival (www.nendaz.ch), held on the Alpine shores of Lac de Tracouet in Nendaz, 13km south of Sion in Valais; hike or ride the cable car up for a complete Alpine experience.

If jazzy-folky pop's more your cup of tea, the fragile voice of Bern-born singer Sophie Hunger, who flips between English, German and Swiss German, will win you over. Her recent albums, *1983* (2010), *The Danger of Light* (2012) and *Supermoon* (2015), were huge successes. For some (much) harder beats, Stress, Switzerland's hottest hip-hop artist, is known for his at times controversial and political lyrics.

House of the fictional character Heidi

Painting, Sculpture & Design

Dada aside, Switzerland has produced little in the way of 'movements'. In terms of Swiss 'themes', the painter Ferdinand Hodler (1853–1918) depicted William Tell and other folk heroes and events from history, such as the first grassroots Swiss vote. Unlike many of his fellow Swiss artists, Bern-born Hodler remained resident in Switzerland. His colourful landscapes of Lake Geneva and the Alps are worth seeking out in Swiss museums.

The country's best-known artist, abstract painter and colour specialist, Paul Klee (1879–1940), spent most of his life in Germany, including with the Bauhaus school, but the largest showcase of his work is at the striking and fascinating Zentrum Paul Klee (p183) in Bern. Sculptor Alberto Giacometti (1901–66) was born in Graubünden and worked in Paris, but many of his trademark wiry sculpted figures (often walking or standing) can be seen in Zürich's Kunsthaus (p165). Quirky meta-mechanic sculptures by Paris-based Jean Tinguely (1925–91) are clustered around Basel (where there's a museum dedicated to his work) and Fribourg.

Completely Dada

Antibourgeois, rebellious, nihilistic and deliberately nonsensical, the Dada movement grew out of revulsion to WWI and the mechanisation of modern life. Its proponents paved the way for nearly every form of contemporary art by using collage, extracting influences from indigenous art, applying abstract notions to writing, film and performance, and taking manufactured objects and redefining them as art.

Zürich was the movement's birthplace. Hugo Ball, Tristan Tzara and Emmy Jennings' creation of the Cabaret Voltaire in February 1916 kicked off a series of raucous cabaret and performance-art events in a bar at Spiegelgasse 1 (still in place today). The name Dada was allegedly randomly chosen by stabbing a knife through a French-German dictionary.

By 1923 the movement was dead, but its spirit lives on. See Dadaist works in Zürich's Kunsthaus (p165).

The Swiss excel in graphic design. The 'new graphics' of Josef Müller-Brockmann (1914–96) and Max Bill (1908–94) are still extremely well regarded, as is the branding work by Karl Gerstner (1930–2017) for IBM and the Búro Destruct studio's typefaces, a feature of many album covers.

Product design and installation art are Switzerland's other fortes. It gave the world Europe's largest urban lounge in St Gallen in Northeastern Switzerland, courtesy of Pipilotti Rist (b 1962), and Cow Parade, processions of life-size, painted fibreglass cows trotting around the globe. The first 800-head herd had its outing in Zürich in 1998 and stray animals in different garb continue to lurk around the country.

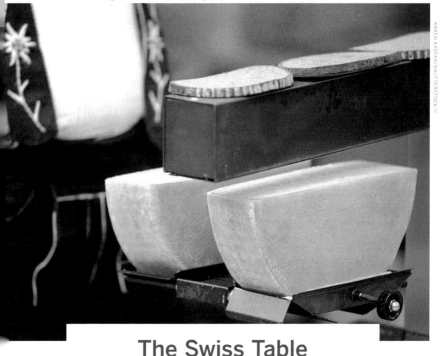
Melting raclette on a 'rack oven' (p234)

KAREN KASPAR/SHUTTERSTOCK ©

The Swiss Table

There's more to Swiss cuisine than cheese and chocolate.
The food in this largely rural country is driven by
season and setting. If Alpine tradition gives Swiss food
its soul, geography gives it an unexpected edge. Cooks in
French-speaking cantons take cues from France, Ticino
kitchens turn to Italy and a fair chunk of the country
looks to Germany and Austria for culinary clues.

Not Only Holes: Cheese

First things first: not all Swiss cheese has holes. Emmental, the hard cheese from the
Emme Valley east of Bern, does – as does the not dissimilar Tilsiter from the same
valley. But, contrary to common perception, most of Switzerland's 450 types of cheese
(*käse* in German, *fromage* in French, *formaggio* in Italian) are hole-less: take the well-
known hard cheese Gruyère, made in the town of Gruyères near Fribourg; the over-
whelmingly stinky Appenzeller used in a rash of tasty, equally strong-smelling dishes in
the same-name town in Northeastern Switzerland; or Sbrinz, Switzerland's oldest hard
cheese and the transalpine ancestor to Italian Parmesan, ripened for 24 months to
create its distinctive taste – eat it straight and thinly sliced like carpaccio or grated on
top of springtime asparagus.

Fondue

DREAM79/SHUTTERSTOCK ©

★ Best Fondues

Whymper Stube (p81), Zermatt

Café Tivoli (p66), Châtel-St-Denis

Bains des Pâquis (p39), Geneva

Memory (p144), Grindelwald

Another distinctive Swiss cheese with not a hole in sight is hard, nutty-flavoured Tête de Moine (literally 'monk's head') from the Jura, which comes in a small round and is cut with a flourish in a flowery curl using a special handled cutting device known as a *girolle* (a great present to take back home – look for them in supermarkets).

Just as unique is L'Etivaz, which, in the finest of timeless Alpine traditions, is only made up high on lush summer pastures in the Alpes Vaudoises (Vaud Alps). As cows graze outside, shepherds inside their century-old *chalets d'alpage* (mountain huts) heat up the morning's milk in a traditional copper cauldron over a wood fire. Strictly seasonal, the Appellation d'Origine Contrôlée (AOC) cheese can only be made from May to early October, using milk from cows that have grazed on mountains between 1000m and 2000m high.

This is by no means the only cheese to be made at altitude using traditional methods; when travelling around the Valais, Bernese Alps, Ticino and other predominantly rural mountain areas in summer, look for signs pointing to isolated farmsteads where *fromage d'alpage* (mountain cheese, *hobelkäse* in German, *fromaggio d'Alpe* in Italian) is made and sold.

On the Swiss–Italian border, Zincarlìn is a raw-milk, cup-shaped cheese that, unusually, is made from unbroken curds.

Fondue & Raclette

It is hard to leave Switzerland without dipping into a fondue (from the French verb *fondre*, meaning 'to melt'). The main French contribution to the Swiss table, fondue entails a pot of gooey melted cheese being placed in the centre of the table and kept on a slow burn while diners dip in cubes of crusty bread using slender two-pronged fondue forks. If you lose your chunk in the cheese, you buy the next round of drinks or, should you be in Geneva, get thrown in the lake. It's traditionally a winter dish, and the Swiss tend to eat it mostly if there's snow around or they're at a suitable altitude.

The classic fondue mix in Switzerland is equal amounts of Emmental and Gruyère cheese, grated and melted with white wine and a shot of kirsch (cherry-flavoured liquor), then thickened slightly with potato or cornflour. It is served with a basket of bread slices (which are soon torn into small morsels), and most people order a side platter of cold meats and tiny gherkins to accompany it. *Fondue moitié moitié* (literally 'half-half fondue') mixes Gruyère with Vacherin Fribourgeois, and *fondue savoyarde* sees equal proportions of Comté, Beaufort and Emmental thrown into the pot. Common variants involve adding ingredients such as mushrooms or tomato.

Switzerland's other signature Alpine cheese dish, another fabulous feast of a meal in itself, is raclette. Unlike fondue, raclette – both the name of the dish and the cheese at its gooey heart – is eaten year-round. A half-crescent slab of the cheese is screwed onto a specially designed 'rack oven' that melts the top flat side. As it melts, cheese is scraped onto plates for immediate consumption with boiled potatoes, cold meats and pickled onions or gherkins.

When buying your own tangy wheel of raclette (or, indeed, discussing the topic with a born-and-bred Valaisian), be aware of the difference between *raclette Suisse* (Swiss raclette), made industrially with pasteurised milk anywhere in Switzerland, and Raclette du Valais, produced in the Valais using *lait cru* (raw milk) since the 16th century. In 2007 Raclette du Valais – never other than 29cm to 31cm in diameter and 4.8kg to 5.2kg in weight – gained its own AOC, much to the horror of cheesemakers in other cantons, who vehemently argued, to no avail, that raclette (from the French verb *racler,* meaning 'to scrape') refers to the dish, not the cheese, and thus shouldn't be restricted to one region.

Rösti, Spätzli, Meat & Wild Game

For a quintessential Swiss lunch, nothing beats an alfresco platter of air-dried beef, a truly sweet and exquisitely tender delicacy from Graubünden that is smoked, thinly sliced and served as *Bündnerfleisch.* Eat it neat or in *Capuns*, a rich mix of *Spätzli* (egg noodle) dough, air-dried beef, ham and herbs cooked, cut into tiny morsels, wrapped with spinach and mixed with yet more *Spätzli* (a Germanic cross between pasta and dumplings). The same wafer-thin slices of *viande séchée* (air-dried beef) are a staple in the Val d'Hérens, a delightfully remote valley in the Valais where fertile pastures are mowed by silky black Hérens cattle and local gourmets feast on butter-soft Hérens beef served in every imaginable way. **Au Vieux Mazot** (027 283 11 25; Rue Centrale, Evolène; mains from Sfr20; 10am-midnight Tue-Sat) in Evolène and **Au Cheval Blanc** (027 322 18 67; www.au-cheval-blanc.ch; Rue du Grand-Pont 23; mains from Sfr30; 10am-midnight Tue-Fri, 11am-midnight Sat) in Sion are two Swiss-simple but superb insider addresses to sample this succulent local beef any way you like it.

Travel east and *Würste* (sausages) become the local lunch feast, typically served with German-speaking Switzerland's star dish: rösti (a shredded, oven-crisped potato bake), perhaps topped with a fried egg. (If only to prove they're different, Swiss French cook it in oil, while Swiss Germans throw a lump of butter or lard into the frying pan.) As common and cheap as chips it might be these days, but be aware that the vacuum-sealed packs of rösti sold in supermarkets cannot be compared to the real McCoy dish cooked up in authentic mountain restaurants. Baked to a perfect crisp, often in a wood-fuelled oven, the shredded potato is mixed with seasonal mushrooms and bacon bits to create a perfect lunch, paired with nothing more than a simple green salad. This is Swiss Alpine heaven.

Veal is highly rated and is usually thinly sliced and smothered in a cream sauce as *geschnetzeltes Kalbsfleisch* in Zürich. Horse meat is also eaten. Two unusual Swiss salami to look out for, and sufficiently rare to be on Slow Food's list of endangered world food products (see www.slowfoodfoundation.com), are *sac* (made from pork, liver, lard and spices aged for 12 months) and *fidighèla* (packed in veal intestine when straight, pork intestine if curved, and aged for two to three weeks).

For true blue-blooded meat-lovers there's no better season to let taste buds rip in this heavily forested country than autumn, when restaurants everywhere cook up fresh game (*Wildspezialitäten, chasse* or *cacciagione*). Venison and wild boar are deservedly popular.

Time to Pig Out

Autumn, with its fresh game, abundance of wild mushrooms, chestnuts and grape harvests, is exquisitely gourmet in Switzerland, and as the days shorten this season only gets better. Fattened over summer, the family pig – traditionally slaughtered on the feast of St Martin (11 November) marking the end of agricultural work in the fields and the start of winter – is ready for the butcher. On farms and in villages for centuries, the slaughter would be followed by the salting of meat and sausage-making. Their work done, people would then pass over to feasting to celebrate the day's toil. The main dish for the feast? Pork, of course.

In the French-speaking Jura, in particular, the feasting tradition around Fête de la St-Martin lives on with particular energy and enthusiasm in Porrentruy. Local bars and restaurants organise feasts for several weekends on the trot in October and November. A typical pork feast consists of seven copious courses, kicking off perhaps with *gelée de ménage*, a pork-gelatine dish. *Boudin, purée de pommes et racines rouges* (black pudding, apple compote and red vegetables) and piles of sausages accompanied by rösti and *atriaux* (a dish based on pork fat, sausage and liver, all roasted in sizzling fat) follows. Next up is the main course, with *rôti, côtines et doucette* (roast pork, ribs and a green salad). A liquor-soaked sorbet might follow to aid digestion, followed by a serving of *choucroute* (boiled cabbage enlivened by bacon bits). Finally, a traditional dessert, such as *striflate en sauce de vanille* (strings of deep-fried pastries in vanilla sauce), is served.

Pork dishes to look out for year-round include *Rippli* (a bubbling pot of pork-rib meat cooked up with bacon, potatoes and beans) in and around Bern, and in the canton of Vaud, *papet vaudois* (a potato, leek, cabbage and sausage stew) and *taillé aux greubons* (a crispy savoury pastry, studded with pork-lard cubes). In the Engadine, sausage is baked with onions and potato to make *pian di pigna*.

Around the Lake: Fish

Fish is the speciality in lakeside towns. Perch (*perche* in French) and whitefish *(féra)* fillets are common, but don't be fooled into thinking the *filets de perche* chalked on the blackboard in practically every Lake Geneva restaurant are from the lake; the vast majority cooked around its shores, in Geneva too, come frozen from Eastern Europe.

Ever-Fabulous Fruit & Sweets

Sensible Swiss: they don't simply eat the plump Valais apricots, plums, pears and sweet black cherries that fill their orchards with a profusion of pretty white blossoms in April and May. As their 19th-century cookbook spells out, the Swiss also dry, preserve and distil their abundance of fruit to create fiery liqueurs, winter compotes and thick-as-honey syrups for baking or spreading on bread.

Berudge eau de vie is made from Berudge plums grown on the slopes of Mont Vully in the Fribourg canton, and cherries from around Basel go into thick *Chriesimues* syrup and sweet cherry kirsch – the ingredient that gives Zug's to-die-for *Zuger Kirschtorte* (cherry cake made from pastry, biscuit, almond paste and butter cream, all infused with cherry liqueur) its extra-special kick. (There are fears for genuine Swiss kirsch as fruit farmers replace ancient cherry varieties with less aromatic modern equivalents.) Apple or pear juice is simmered for 24 hours to make Fribourgois *vin cuit* (a dense, semihard concentrate used in tarts and other fruity desserts) and Vaudois *raisinée*; *Buttemoscht* is a less common rose-hip equivalent.

The Botzi pear cultivated around Gruyères is deemed precious enough to have its own AOC. Bite into it as nature intended or try it with local *crème de Gruyères*, the thickest cream ever, traditionally eaten by the spoonful with sugary-sweet meringues. *Cuisses de dame* (lady's thighs) are sugary, deep-fried, thigh-shaped pastries, found in French-speaking cantons next to *amandines* (almond tarts). Apart from the ubiquitous *Apfelstrudel* (apple pie), typically served with runny vanilla sauce, German cantons cook up *Vermicelles*, a chestnut-cream creation resembling spaghetti.

Swiss Chocolate

In the early centuries after Christ's death, as the Roman Empire headed towards slow collapse on a diet of rough wine and olives, the Mayans in Central America were pounding cocoa beans, consuming the result and even using the beans as a system of payment.

Harvest Feasts

Every Swiss village and region has its own way of celebrating the harvest season.

In the Valais, as grapes are harvested and *châtaignes* (chestnuts) tumble from the trees, family and friends gather for La Brisolée, a copious feast unchanged for centuries. It comprises hot roasted chestnuts and five local cheeses – *d'alpage* (high pasture), *de laiterie* (dairy), *tomme* (semihard and made from raw milk), *sérac* (whey) and Tête de Moine – along with ham, air-dried beef, buttered rye bread, grapes and apples. All this is washed down with *vin nouveau* (the year's first wine) and *moût* (must; wine that is still fermenting).

Around Fribourg, centuries-old harvest festival Le Bénichon features *cuchaule*, a saffron-scented bread served with *moutarde de Bénichon* (a thick condiment made from cooked wine must, spices, sugar and flour).

A millennium later, Spanish conquistador Hernán Cortés brought the first load of cocoa to Europe, in 1528. He could not have anticipated the subsequent demand for his cargo. The Spaniards, and soon other Europeans, developed an insatiable thirst for the sweetened beverage produced from it. The solid stuff came later.

Swiss chocolate (www.chocolat.ch) built its reputation in the 19th century, thanks to pioneering spirits such as François-Louis Cailler (1796–1852), Philippe Suchard (1797–1884), Henri Nestlé (1814–90), Jean Tobler (1830–1905), Daniel Peter (1836–1919) and Rodolphe Lindt (1855–1909). Cailler established the first Swiss chocolate factory in 1819 near Vevey. Daniel Peter added milk in 1875 and Lindt invented conching, a rotary aeration process that gives chocolate its melt-in-the-mouth quality.

Swiss Wine

Savouring local wine in Switzerland is a rare joy in this globalised world: Switzerland exports just a tiny percentage of its wine (around 1.5%), meaning that most of its quality reds, whites and rosé vintages can only be tasted in situ. Most wines hail from the French-speaking cantons, with vineyards on the shore of Lake Geneva rising sharply up hillsides in tightly packed terraces knitted together by ancient drystone walls.

Wine Regions

Lake Geneva & Vaud

Some small family producers on the fringes of Geneva open their doors for *dégustation* (tasting) – the canton's annual Caves Ouvertes (Open Cellars) day, held on one weekend in late May, is a fabulous opportunity to discover the wines of cellars and *domaines viticoles* (estates) otherwise closed to visitors. However, most of Lake Geneva's winemaking estates are further east, lying either side of Lausanne in the canton of Vaud. Whites from the pea-green terraced vineyards of the Lavaux wine region between Lausanne and Montreux are outstanding, and the area is a Unesco World Heritage Site. Lavaux' two *grands crus* are Calamin and Dézaley.

Vineyards, Lavaux region (p60)

The generic Vaud red is the Salvagnin, divided into several labels and generally combining Pinot noir and Gamay grapes. A home-grown offshoot is the Gamaret or Garanoir, a throaty red created in the 1970s that ages particularly well. Straddling Vaud is the small Chablais winemaking area, best known for its Yvorne whites.

Winemakers around Lausanne party hard in late September and October, when the grapes are harvested and the *vin nouveau* (new wine) is tasted.

Valais

Drenched in extra sunshine and light from above the southern Alps, much of the land north of the Rhône River in western Valais is planted with vines – this is where some of Switzerland's best wines are produced. Unique to the Valais are the *bisses* (narrow irrigation channels) that traverse the vineyards.

Dryish white Fendant, the perfect accompaniment to fondue and raclette, and best served crisply cold, is the region's best-known wine, accounting for two-thirds of Valais' wine production. Johannisberg is another excellent white and comes from the Sylvaner grape, while Petite Arvine and Amigne are sweet whites.

Dôle, made from Pinot noir and Gamay grapes, is the principal red blend and is full-bodied, with a firm fruit flavour. Reds from Salgesch are generally excellent and the region increasingly uses innovative blends to create exciting wines such as Maîtresse de Salquenen, an assemblage of 13 grape varieties.

Tasting and exploring opportunities abound. Year-round, the region's many gentle walking trails through the vines make a perfect introduction: top trails include the Chemin du Vignoble (www.cheminduvignoble.ch) from Martigny (Lower Valais) to Leuk (Upper

Ordering Wine

When ordering wine in a wine bar or restaurant, use the uniquely Swiss approach of *déci* (*décilitre* – ie a tenth of a litre) multiples. Or just order a bottle...

Valais), which passes the world's highest drystone walls, ensnaring green vines near Sion; the Sierre-Salgesch Sentier Viticole (6km), linking a twinset of wine museums and host to September's fabulous Marché des Cépages; and the 2½-hour trail from Visp up to Europe's highest vineyards (1150m) in Visperterminen.

The Vinea wine fair (www.vinea.ch), held for three days in early September in Sierre, Valais, is a brilliant opportunity to meet winegrowers from around Switzerland and taste their wines.

Lacs de Neuchâtel & Bienne

The lake-dotted landscape west of Bern is another prime wine-growing region. The fruity rosé Œil-de-Perdrix (literally 'Partidge's Eye') comes from the scenic shores of Lac de Neuchâtel: taste and drink it along the Route du Vignoble, a wine itinerary that trails the 30km of steeply terraced water-facing vineyards between Lac de Neuchâtel and the western shore of Lac de Bienne (Bieler See) in Mittelland.

For stunning scenery sufficiently delightful to rival Lavaux and sublime vineyard trails and tasting, the enchanting hamlet of Ligerz on Lake Biel's northern shore is a magnificent winegrowing area.

Ticino

Switzerland's Italianate climes produce wonderful merlot, which accounts for almost 90% of Ticino's wine production. Some white merlots are also produced, as well as wines made from a handful of other grape varieties. The main winemaking areas are between Bellinzona and Ascona, around Biasca and between Lugano and Mendrisio (with its lovely September wine festival).

Swiss-German Wines

Less known than their Swiss-French counterparts and produced in substantially smaller quantities, Swiss-German vintages are nonetheless worth tasting. About 75% are reds, predominantly Pinot noir (Blauburgunder) – taste and enjoy in wine taverns and tasting rooms in Bündner Herrschaft, Graubünden's premier wine region north of Chur.

Gewürztraminer is a dry white variety. The main white is Müller-Thurgau (a crisp mix of riesling and Sylvaner), produced in the town of Spiez on Lake Thun in Bernese Oberland. The best time to taste is at the nearby Läset-Sunntig wine festival (late September).

Spirits & Liqueurs

Locally produced fruit brandies are often served with or in coffee. Kirsch is made from distilled cherry juice. Appenzeller Alpenbitter (Alpine Bitters) is a liqueur made from the essence of 67 flowers and roots. Damassine (most likely found in the French cantons) is made from small prunes and is a good digestive. A pear-based drop is the popular Williamine, and Pflümli is a typical plum-based schnapps in the German cantons.

After a century on the index of banned beverages, absinthe – aka the green fairy – is legal again. Try it in Neuchâtel canton, where the wormwood drink was first distilled in the 18th century.

PRASIT RODPHAN/SHUTTERSTOCK ©

Survival Guide

Directory A–Z

Accommodation

Switzerland offers accommodation in every price range. Tourist offices have listings and make reservations.

Hotels Hotels range from chains to luxury retreats in the Alps and city hotels with all the five-star trappings.

B&Bs Small and usually family run, B&Bs reach from simple country places to boutique-style pads with first-class facilities.

Farmstays Family-friendly *Bauernhöfe* in country or mountain locations often offer home produce and animals to pet.

Campgrounds Campgrounds are generally well maintained and often have beautiful lake or mountain settings.

Mountain huts Bare-bones *Hütten* are dotted throughout the Alps. Most have basic dorms or *Matratzenlager* (bunkhouses with mattresses on the floor).

B&Bs

Some of Switzerland's most charming accommodation comes in the form of a B&B: a room in a private home (anything from castle to farm), which includes breakfast, often consisting of homemade produce. Some hosts will also, if you order in advance, cook up an evening meal, served for an additional Sfr30 to Sfr40 per person including wine.

Tourist offices have lists of B&Bs in their area – they're rare in cities but plentiful in the countryside – and hundreds can be tracked through **BnB** (www.bnb.ch). In rural areas, private houses frequently offer inexpensive 'room(s) vacant' (*Zimmer frei* in German, *chambres libres* in French, *camere libere* in Italian).

Camping

Campsites have one to five stars depending on amenities and location. They are often scenically situated out of the way by a river or lake. Charges per night are from around Sfr10 per person plus Sfr8 to Sfr15 for a tent, and from an additional Sfr5 for a car.

Wild camping (*wildes camping* in German, *camping sauvage* in French) is not strictly allowed, but it's viable in the wide-open mountain spaces.

Useful resources:

www.camping.ch Directory with 350 detailed listings, plus practical info, tips and news on camping and caravanning in Switzerland.

www.sccv.ch Search online for the perfect pitch for you with the Swiss Camping and Caravanning Federation (SCCV).

www.tcs.ch Road and traffic conditions in real time, insurance, campsite listings and everything else you could possibly require to organise camping trips in Switzerland.

Dorms

Dormitory accommodation (*Touristenlager* or *Massenlager* in German, *dortoir* in French) has been well established for years in ski and other resorts. Mattresses are often crammed side by side in massive bunks, but there are usually no curfews and the doors aren't usually locked during the day. Take care when studying accommodation lists, as dormitories may only take groups.

Farmstays

A unique way to experience life on a Swiss farm is Switzerland's **Agrotourismus Schweiz** (☑031 359 50 30; www.agrotourismus.ch) – the ultimate adventure in the straw. When the cows are out to pasture in summer, Swiss farmers charge travellers Sfr20 to Sfr30 per adult and Sfr10 to Sfr20 per child under 15, to sleep on straw in their hay barns or lofts (listen to the jangle of cow bells!). Farmers provide cotton undersheets (to avoid straw pricks) and woolly blankets for extra warmth, but guests need their own sleeping bags and – strongly advisable – pocket torch. Nightly rates include a farmhouse breakfast, and a morning shower and evening meal are usually available for an extra Sfr2 and Sfr20 to Sfr30, respectively. Reservations are necessary in summer. A list of the 170-odd farms across Switzerland offering this accommodation is available on the website.

Should you prefer a room in the farmhouse rather than above the cows, try **Swiss Holiday Farms** (☑031 329 66 99; www.bauernhof-ferien.ch), an association of 200-odd farms countrywide that open their doors to both overnight B&B guests and self-caterers keen to rent a renovated barn or farmhouse cottage for a week or longer.

Hostels

Swiss youth hostels (*Jugendherberge* in German, *auberge de jeunesse* in French, *alloggio per giovanni* in Italian) range from older institutional affairs to modern establishments bordering on designer accommodation – Saas Fee's dazzling new **Wellness-Hostel** (☑027 958 50 50; www.wellnesshostel4000.ch; Panoramastrasse 1; dm/s/d incl breakfast from Sfr43/106/127; ⊙reception 7am-10pm Jun-Apr; ☺❄☎⚐) with pool and spa is a striking example.

○ Most are run by Switzerland's national hostelling organisation **Swiss Youth Hostels** (www.youthhostel.ch), affiliated with Hostelling International (HI). Non-HI members must take out an annual membership (Sfr22/33 for those under/over 18, Sfr44 per family) or pay Sfr6 a night extra to stay in an HI hostel.

○ Hostels charge Sfr30 to Sfr45 for a dorm bed with breakfast and sheets (sleeping bags are forbidden in HI-affiliated hostels for fear of bedbugs).

○ Hostels with a **Swiss Hostels** (www.swisshostels.com) tag tend to be more flexible in their regulations (some allow sleeping bags, for example), reception times and opening hours; membership is not required.

○ Hostels take bookings via their websites; few accept telephone reservations. During busy times a three-day maximum stay may apply.

Hotels & Pensions

○ The cheapest hotel rooms have a basin but share a toilet and shower; these rooms cost around Sfr70 for a single and Sfr100 for a double in a small town, and around Sfr90 for a single and Sfr140 for a double in cities or mountain resorts. Add a private shower and the nightly rate rises by at least Sfr20. Rates usually include breakfast.

○ A *Frühstückspension* or *Hotel-Garni* serves only breakfast. Small pensions with a restaurant often have a 'rest day' when check-in may not be possible except by prior arrangement (telephone ahead).

○ Hotels with the 'Green Living' label are eco-hotels with sustainable credentials.

Book Your Stay Online

For more accommodation reviews by Lonely Planet authors, check out hotels.lonelyplanet.com/switzerland. You'll find independent reviews, as well as recommendations on the best places to stay. Best of all, you can book online.

Rental Accommodation

Self-caterers can opt for a chalet or apartment, both of which need booking in advance; for peak periods, reserve six to 12 months ahead. A minimum stay of one week in season is common.

Useful resources include **REKA** (www.reka.ch), **Interhome** (www.interhome.ch) and **Switzerland Tourism** (www.myswitzerland.com). For self-catering chalets and apartments in ski resorts – summer and winter – surf **Ski Suisse** (http://en.ski-suisse.com).

Electricity

The electrical current in Switzerland is 230V, 50Hz. Swiss sockets are recessed, three-holed, hexagonally shaped and incompatible with many plugs from abroad. They usually, however, take the standard European two-pronged plug.

230V/50Hz

230V/50Hz

Food

Switzerland has a range of eating options. Booking a day or two ahead is wise, especially in high season. For top-end places, book at least a couple of weeks in advance.

Restaurants Switzerland's restaurants swing from simple taverns to Michelin-starred temples.

Cafes These range from bakery-cafes to organic delis and round-the-clock cafes offering full meals.

Hotels Many of Switzerland's top restaurants are found in hotels; you don't need to be a guest to dine.

Stübli Cosy, timber-clad taverns serve fondue, raclette, rösti and other traditional Swiss treats.

Confiserie/Konditoreien Traditional cake shop–cafes often do a sideline in chocolate and confectionery.

Eating Price Ranges

The following price ranges refer to a main course.

$	under Sfr25
$$	Sfr25-45
$$$	over Sfr45

Health

Health care in Switzerland is of very high quality, but it's expensive. An embassy, consulate or hotel can usually recommend a local doctor or clinic.

A European Health Insurance Card (EHIC) enables European citizens to access state-provided health care in Switzerland at a reduced cost. Otherwise, expect to pay around Sfr150 for a straightforward, non-urgent consultation with a doctor. Over-the-counter medications are available at a local *Apotheke* (pharmacy), where staff usually speak English and are well informed.

Altitude Sickness

Can occur above 3000m, but very few treks or ski runs in the Swiss Alps reach such heights. Headache, vomiting, dizziness, extreme faintness, and difficulty in breathing and sleeping are signs to heed. Treat mild symptoms with rest and simple painkillers. If symptoms persist or get worse, descend to a lower altitude and seek medical advice.

Hypothermia

Hypothermia occurs when the body loses heat faster than it can produce it and the core temperature of the body falls. It is surprisingly easy to progress from very cold to dangerously cold due to a combination of wind, wet clothing, fatigue and hunger, even if the air temperature is above freezing. It is best to dress in layers of good insulating materials and to wear a hat and a strong, waterproof outer layer when hiking or skiing. A 'space' blanket for emergencies is essential. Carry basic supplies, including food containing simple sugars and fluid to drink.

Symptoms include exhaustion, numb skin (particularly toes and fingers), shivering, slurred speech, irrational or violent behaviour, lethargy, stumbling, dizzy spells, muscle cramps and violent bursts of energy.

To treat mild hypothermia, get the person out of the wind and/or rain, remove their clothing if wet and replace it with dry, warm clothing. Give them hot liquids – not alcohol – and high-kilojoule, easily digestible food. Do not rub victims; allow them to slowly warm themselves. The early recognition and treatment of mild hypothermia is the only way to prevent severe hypothermia (a critical condition).

Insurance

If you're skiing, snowboarding or trekking, ensure your policy covers helicopter rescue and emergency repatriation. Most standard policies don't cover many outdoor activities; you'll need to pay a premium for winter-sports cover and further premiums for adventure sports like bungee jumping and skydiving.

LGBT+ Travellers

Attitudes to homosexuality are progressive. Same-sex partnerships are recognised (although gay couples are not permitted to adopt children or have fertility treatment). Major cities have gay and lesbian bars, and pride marches are held in Geneva (early July) and Zürich (mid-July). Useful websites include:

❍ www.gay.ch (in German)

❍ www.pinkcross.ch (in German and French)

Practicalities

Newspapers German readers can gen up with Zürich's *Neue Zürcher Zeitung* (www.nzz.ch) and *Tages Anzeiger* (www.tagesanzeiger.ch); Geneva's *Le Temps* (www.letemps.ch) and *La Tribune de Genève* (www.tdg.ch) are sold in Suisse Romande; Lugano-based *Corriere del Ticino* (www.cdt.ch) is in Italian.

Radio WRS (World Radio Switzerland; FM 101.7; www.worldradio.ch) is a Geneva-based English-language station broadcasting music and news countrywide.

Smoking Illegal in all enclosed indoor public spaces, including restaurants, pubs, offices and public transport, smoking is allowed in separate smoking rooms and outside on pavement terraces.

Twitter For a dose of daily news and insights into Swiss cultural affairs and happenings, follow @Switzerland, @TheLocalSwitzer, @swissinfo_en, @MySwitzerland_e.

Websites Swissinfo (www.swissinfo.org) is the national news website.

Weights & Measures The metric system is used. Like other continental Europeans, the Swiss indicate decimals with commas and thousands with full points.

❍ http://360.ch (in French) A Swiss LGBT magazine, with guides to Geneva, Lausanne, Bern and more.

Money

ATMs

ATMs – called *Bancomats* in banks and *Postomats* in post offices – are widespread and accessible 24 hours. They accept most international bank or credit cards and have multilingual instructions. Your bank or credit-card company will often charge a 1% to 2.5% fee, and there may also be a small charge at the ATM end.

Cash

Swiss francs are divided into 100 centimes (*Rappen* in German-speaking Switzerland). There are notes for 10, 20, 50, 100, 200 and 1000 francs, and coins for five, 10, 20 and 50 centimes, as well as one, two and five francs.

Businesses, including most hotels and some restaurants and souvenir shops, will accept payment in euros. Change will be given in Swiss francs at the rate of exchange calculated on the day.

Credit Cards

Credit cards are widely accepted at hotels, shops and restaurants. EuroCard/MasterCard and Visa are the most popular.

Money Changers

Change money at banks, airports and nearly every train station until late into the evening. Banks tend to charge about 5% commission; some money-exchange bureaus don't charge commission at all.

Tipping

Tipping is not necessary, given that hotels, restaurants, bars and even some taxis are legally required to include a 15% service charge in bills.

Restaurants Locals round up the bill after a meal for good service.

Hotels Hotel and railway porters expect a franc or two per bag.

Telephone

Search for phone numbers at http://tel.local.ch/en.

National telecom provider **Swisscom** (www.swisscom. ch) provides public phone booths that accept coins and major credit cards.

Area codes do not exist in Switzerland. Although the numbers for a particular city or town share the same three-digit prefix (for example Bern ✆031, Geneva ✆022), numbers must always be dialled in full, even when calling from next door.

Mobile Phones

Prepaid local SIM cards are available from network operators **Salt** (www.salt. ch), **Sunrise** (www.sunrise. ch) and **Swisscom Mobile**

(www.swisscom.ch/mobile) for as little as Sfr10. You can also purchase (and recharge) SIM cards at newsagents throughout Switzerland. Prepaid cards must be officially registered, so bring your passport.

Phone Codes

○ The country code for Switzerland is ✆41. When calling Switzerland from abroad, drop the initial zero from the number; hence to call Bern, dial ✆41 31 (preceded by the international access code of the country you're dialling from).

○ The international access code is ✆00.

○ Telephone numbers with the code ✆0800 are toll free; those with ✆0848 are charged at the local rate. Numbers beginning with ✆0900, 156 or 157 are premium rate.

○ Mobile-phone numbers start with ✆076, 078 or 079.

Important Phone Numbers

Police	✆117
Ambulance	✆144
Swiss Mountain Rescue	✆1414

Travellers with Disabilities

Switzerland ranks among the world's most easily navigable countries for travellers with physical disabilities. Most train stations have a mobile

lift for boarding trains, city buses are equipped with ramps, and many hotels have disabled access (although budget pensions tend not to have lifts).

Switzerland Tourism (www.myswitzerland.com) has excellent travel tips for people with physical disabilities. Or get in touch with Mobility International Switzerland.

Download Lonely Planet's free Accessible Travel guide from http://lptravel.to/AccessibleTravel.

Visas

For up-to-date details of visa requirements, go to the **Swiss State Secretariat for Migration** (www.sem. admin.ch).

Visas are not required if you hold a passport from the UK, Ireland, the USA, Canada, Australia or New Zealand, whether visiting as a tourist or on business. Citizens of the EU, Norwegians and Icelanders may also enter Switzerland without a visa. A maximum 90-day stay in a 180-day period applies, but passports are rarely stamped.

Other non-European citizens wishing to come to Switzerland have to apply for a Schengen Visa, named after the agreement that has abolished passport controls between 26 European countries. It allows unlimited travel throughout the entire Schengen zone for a 90-day period. Apply to the consulate of the country you are entering first, or your main destination.

In Switzerland, carry your passport at all times. Swiss citizens are required to always carry ID, so you will also need to be able to identify yourself at any time.

Transport

Getting There & Away

Landlocked between France, Germany, Austria, Liechtenstein and Italy, Switzerland is well linked, especially by train. Formalities are minimal when entering the country by air, rail or road, thanks to the Schengen Agreement.

Flights, tours and rail tickets can be booked online at www.lonelyplanet.com/bookings.

Air

Switzerland's national carrier is **Swiss** (www.swiss.com), commonly known as Swissair. In addition to many national carriers, the following budget and/or smaller airlines connect Switzerland with the rest of Europe.

Air Berlin (www.airberlin.com) Flights from Geneva, Zürich and EuroAirport (Basel) to scores of destinations across Europe.

EasyJet (www.easyjet.com) Low-cost flights to Geneva, Zürich and EuroAirport (Basel) from destinations across Europe and the UK.

Etihad Regional (www.etihadregional.com) Connections from Geneva, Lugano and Zürich to Spain, France, Italy, Germany, Asia and the United Arab Emirates.

Eurowings (www.eurowings.com) German low-cost carrier

flying from Zürich and Geneva to Europe and the UK.

Flybe (www.flybe.com) Flights from Geneva and Zürich to Manchester, Birmingham and other UK cities.

Helvetic Airways (www.helvetic.com) Budget Swiss airline, with flights from Zürich to Shannon (Ireland) and Bordeaux (France), and from Bern to Olbia (Sardinia) and Palma de Mallorca (Spain).

Hop (www.hop.com) Low-cost carrier of Air France, with flights from Geneva to/from Biarritz and Calvi (Corsica).

Jet2.com (www.jet2.com) Connections between Geneva and UK destinations London Stansted, Birmingham, East Midlands, Edinburgh, Leeds Bradford and Manchester.

SkyWork Airlines (www.flyskywork.com) Airline based in Bern (BRN; ☎031 960 21 11; www.flughafenbern.ch) with flights to European cities including London, Amsterdam, Berlin, Munich and Vienna.

Land
Bus

Eurolines (www.eurolines.com), a group of 29 long-haul coach operators, runs buses all over Europe from most large towns and cities in Switzerland, including Basel, Bellinzona, Bern, Bulle, Fribourg, Geneva, Lausanne, Lucerne, Lugano, Martigny, Sion, St Gallen and Zürich. Discounts are available to people under 26 and over 60. Make reservations, especially in July and August.

Car & Motorcycle

Fast, well-maintained roads run from Switzerland

Climate Change & Travel

Every form of transport that relies on carbon-based fuel generates CO_2, the main cause of human-induced climate change. Modern travel is dependent on aeroplanes, which might use less fuel per kilometre per person than most cars but travel much greater distances. The altitude at which aircraft emit gases (including CO_2) and particles also contributes to their climate change impact. Many websites offer 'carbon calculators' that allow people to estimate the carbon emissions generated by their journey and, for those who wish to do so, to offset the impact of the greenhouse gases emitted with contributions to portfolios of climate-friendly initiatives throughout the world. Lonely Planet offsets the carbon footprint of all staff and author travel.

through to all bordering countries; the Alps present a natural barrier, meaning that main roads generally head through tunnels to enter Switzerland. A foreign motor vehicle entering the country must display a sticker or licence plate identifying its country of registration.

○ An EU driving licence is acceptable throughout Europe.

○ Third-party motor insurance is a minimum requirement; get proof of this in the form of a Green Card issued by your insurers. Also ask for a 'European Accident Statement' form. Taking out a European breakdown-assistance policy is a good investment.

○ If using Switzerland's motorways, drivers must purchase and display a special sticker (*vignette* in French and German, *contrassegno* in Italian), available for Sfr40 at major border crossings.

○ A warning triangle, to be displayed in the event of a breakdown, is compulsory.

○ Recommended accessories include first-aid kit, spare-bulb kit and fire extinguisher.

Train

Ecofriendly Switzerland makes rail travel a joy.

○ Book tickets and get train information from **Rail Europe** (www.raileurope.com). In the UK contact **Railteam** (www.railteam.eu), an alliance of several high-speed-train operators in Europe, including Swit-

zerland's very own **Swiss Federal Railways** (www.sbb.ch), commonly abbreviated to SBB in German, CFF in French and FFS in Italian. The latter accepts internet bookings but does not post tickets outside Switzerland.

○ A very useful train-travel resource is the information-packed website **The Man in Seat 61** (www.seat61.com).

○ From the UK, hourly **Eurostar** (www.eurostar.com) trains scoot from London (St Pancras International) to Paris (Gare du Nord) in 2¼ hours, then onward by French TGV from Paris (Gare de Lyon) to Basel, Bern, Geneva, Lausanne, Zürich and more; passengers aged under 26 and over 60 get slight discounts.

○ Zürich is Switzerland's busiest international terminus, with trains to Munich and Vienna, from where there are extensive onward connections to cities in Eastern Europe.

○ Most connections from Germany pass through Zürich or Basel.

○ Nearly all connections from Italy pass through Milan before branching off to Zürich, Lucerne, Bern or Lausanne.

River & Lake

Switzerland can be reached by steamer from several lakes, but it's a slightly more unusual option. From Germany, arrive via Lake Constance; from France, via Lake Geneva. You can also cruise down the Rhine to Basel.

CGN (✆0848 811 848; www.cgn.ch) has ferry connections on Lake Geneva.

Getting Around

Switzerland's fully integrated public-transport system is among the world's most efficient. However, travel is expensive and visitors planning to use inter-city routes should consider investing in a Swiss Travel Pass. Timetables often refer to *Werktags* (work days), which means Monday to Saturday, unless there is the qualification '*ausser Samstag*' (except Saturday). For timetables and tickets, head to www.sbb.ch.

Bicycle Switzerland is well equipped for cyclists. Many cities have free-bike-hire schemes. Bicycle and e-bike rental is usually available at stations.

Bus Filling the gaps in more remote areas, Switzerland's PostBus service is synchronised with train arrivals.

Car Handy for hard-to-reach regions where public transport is minimal.

Train Swiss trains run like a dream. Numerous discount-giving travel cards and tickets are available.

Bicycle

Bicycle Hire

The super-efficient bike-rental service run by Swiss railways, **SBB Rent a Bike** (✆041 925 11 70; www.rentabike.ch; half/full day from Sfr27/35), offers bike hire at 100-odd train stations. Wheels can be reserved online or by phone and – for a Sfr10 surcharge – can be collected at one station and returned to another. In addition to regular adult/child bikes, most train stations have e-bikes and tandems, trailer bikes for kids unable to pedal alone, and trailers to tow little kids in. Rates include helmets.

If you're sticking around awhile, it's worth registering for public bike-sharing scheme **PubliBike** (www.publibike.ch/en), with almost 100 'pick-up and return' stations dotted around Switzerland and a low yearly membership fee. You can also purchase a 'DayBike' card from most tourist-information centres located near the stations. Use the website to order and check sales and station locations.

From May to October, the ecofriendly initiative **Schweiz Rollt** (Suisse Roule; www.schweizrollt.ch) offers free bike hire in Bern, Geneva, Zürich and the cantons of Valais and Neuchâtel.

Transport
Bikes can be taken on slower trains, and sometimes even on InterCity (IC) or EuroCity (EC) trains, when there's room in the luggage carriage. A one-day bike ticket costs Sfr20 (Sfr13 with Swiss Travel Pass). Between 21 March and 31 October, you must book (Sfr5) to take your bike on ICN (intercity tilting) trains.

Scenic Drive: Grand Tour of Switzerland
Imagine if you could see all of Switzerland's highlights in one unforgettable road trip. Well, the Swiss have done just that with the new 1600km **Grand Tour of Switzerland** (http://grandtour.myswitzerland.com) ✐, which links 12 Unesco World Heritage Sites while taking in glaciers, mountain passes, cities, medieval villages, lakes, castles, abbeys – you name it. As of 2017, it's also doable by electric vehicle, with charging points en route.

Consult the website for an interactive map of the Grand Tour and details on its highlights. The recommended travel period is April to October.

Trains that don't permit accompanied bikes are marked with a crossed-out pictogram in the timetable. Sending a standard bike unaccompanied costs Sfr20. Taking your bike as hand luggage in a transport bag is free.

Boat
All the larger lakes are serviced by steamers operated by **Swiss Federal Railways** (www.sbb.ch), or allied private companies for which national travel passes are valid. These include Lakes Geneva, Constance, Lucerne, Lugano, Neuchâtel, Biel, Murten, Thun, Brienz and Zug, but not Lago Maggiore.

Rail passes are not valid for cruises offered by smaller boat companies.

Bus
Canary-yellow PostBuses supplement the rail network, following postal routes and linking towns to the less accessible mountain regions. Departures are synchronised with train arrivals, with bus stops conveniently located next to train stations. Travel is one class only and fares are comparable to train fares.

❍ Swiss national travel passes are valid on postal buses, but a few tourist-oriented Alpine routes levy a surcharge.

❍ Tickets are purchased from the driver, though on some scenic routes over the Alps (eg the Lugano–St Moritz run) reservations are necessary. See www.postauto.ch for details.

Car & Motorcycle
Public transport is excellent in city centres – unlike parking cars, which is usually hard work.

Automobile Associations
The **Swiss Touring Club** (www.tcs.ch) provides information and services for motorists, including a national 24-hour emergency breakdown service, free for members of TCS and its affiliates. The **Swiss Automobile Club** (www.acs.ch) offers a similar Europe-wide service.

Child-Seat Rules

Car-seat rules for children in Switzerland are among the most stringent in Europe:

o Children aged under 12 years old and measuring less than 150cm tall must use a size-appropriate type of front-facing child seat or booster car seat.

o Providing they are strapped into the appropriate seat or booster for their weight, children of any age are permitted to ride in the front seat.

o Many taxis carry booster seats appropriate for children weighing 15kg or more; taxis that don't have a booster and/or the appropriate car seat for your child are highly likely to refuse to take you.

Car Hire

o Major car-rental companies have offices at airports and in major cities and towns.

o Reserve cars online. If you're flying into Geneva Airport, note that it's cheaper to rent a car on the French side.

o The minimum rental age is usually 25 but falls to 20 at some local firms; you always need a credit card.

o In winter, rental cars are usually equipped with winter tyres.

Car Sharing

Mobility (☑0848 824 812; www.mobility.ch) has some 2950 cars at 1500 points throughout Switzerland and you can use the cars from one hour to up to 16 days, although one-way travel is not permitted. Reserve a car online or by phone, collect it at the reserved time, and drive off. If you don't want to take out an annual subscription (Sfr290), you can

pay a single-use subscription (Sfr25) plus Sfr1 per hour on top of the standard hourly rates (from Sfr2.80 per hour, plus Sfr0.50 per kilometre).

Fuel

Unleaded (*bleifrei, sans plomb, senza piombo*) petrol is standard, found at green pumps, and diesel is also widely available. Expect to pay around Sfr1.41 per litre for unleaded and Sfr1.43 for diesel.

Road Conditions

o Swiss roads are well built, well signposted and well maintained.

o Phone 163 for up-to-the-hour traffic conditions (recorded information in French, German, Italian and English).

o Most major Alpine passes are negotiable year-round, depending on the weather. However, you will often have to use a tunnel instead at the Great St Bernard, St Gotthard and San Bernardino passes.

o Passes that are open only from June to October: Albula, Furka, Grimsel, Klausen, Oberalp, Susten and Umbrail. Other passes are Lukmanier (open May to November), Nufenen (June to September) and Splügen (May to October).

Road Rules

o Headlights must be turned on at all times, day and night; the fine for not doing so is Sfr40.

o The minimum driving age for cars and motorcycles is 18 and for mopeds it's 14.

o The Swiss drive on the right-hand side of the road.

o Give priority to traffic approaching from the right. On mountain roads, the ascending vehicle has priority, unless a postal bus is involved, as it always has right of way.

o The speed limit is 50km/h in towns, 80km/h on main roads outside towns, 100km/h on single-lane freeways and 120km/h on dual-lane freeways.

o Car occupants must wear a seatbelt at all times and vehicles must carry a break-down-warning triangle.

o Headlights must be dipped (set to low beam) in all tunnels.

o Motorcyclists and their passengers must wear crash helmets.

o The blood alcohol content (BAC) limit is 0.05%.

o If you're involved in a car accident, the police must be called if anyone receives more than superficial injuries.

o Proof of ownership of a private vehicle should always be carried.

Road Signs

There are road signs in Switzerland that you may not have seen before.

o A criss-crossed white tyre on a blue circular background means that snow chains are compulsory.

o A yellow bugle on a square blue background means that you should obey instructions given by postal-bus drivers.

Tolls

Drivers of cars and motorcycles must pay an annual one-off charge of Sfr40 to use Swiss freeways and semi-freeways, identified by green signs. The charge is payable at the border (in cash, including euros), at Swiss petrol stations and post offices, and at Swiss tourist offices abroad. Upon paying the tax, you'll receive a sticker (*vignette* in French and German, *contrassegno* in Italian) that must be displayed on the windscreen and is valid for 14 months, from 1 December to 31 January. If you're caught without it, you'll be fined Sfr200. A separate *vignette* is required for trailers and caravans. For more details, see www. vignette.ch.

On the Swiss–Italian border you'll need to pay an additional toll if using the Great St Bernard Tunnel between Aosta, Italy, and Valais

(car and passengers single/ return Sfr29.30/46.90).

Tunnels

Take your car on trains through these tunnels, open year-round:

Furka Tunnel (📞0848 642 442; www.mgbahn.ch; car & up to 9 passengers Sfr33) From Oberwald to Realp in just 15 minutes through this 15.4km-long tunnel.

Lötschberg Tunnel (📞0900 553 333; www.bls.ch; car & up to 9 passengers Kandersteg-Iselle Sfr98, Kandersteg-Goppenstein Mon-Thu Sfr27, Fri-Sun Sfr29.50) From Kandersteg to Goppenstein (15 minutes, year-round), or Iselle (Italy; one hour, April to mid-October), which must be booked in advance.

Vereina Tunnel (📞081 288 37 37; www.rhb.ch; car & up to 9 passengers low/mid/ high season Sfr34/39/44) Alternative to the Flüela Pass, which is closed in winter; from Selfranga outside Klosters to Sagliains in the Engadine. Trains run half-hourly and the journey time is 18 minutes.

Mountain Transport

The Swiss have many words to describe mountain transport: funicular (*Standseilbahn* in German, *funiculaire* in French, *funicolare* in Italian), cable car (*Luftseilbahn*, *téléphérique*, *funivia*), gondola (*Gondelbahn*, *télécabine, telecabinoia*) and chairlift (*Sesselbahn*, *télésiège, seggiovia*). All are subject to regular safety inspections.

Always check what time the last cable car goes down

the mountain – in winter it's as early as 4pm in mountain resorts.

Train

The Swiss rail network combines state-run and private operations. **Swiss Federal Railways** (www.sbb. ch) is abbreviated to SBB in German, CFF in French and FFS in Italian.

o Second-class compartments are perfectly acceptable but are often close to full; 1st-class carriages are more spacious and have fewer passengers. Power points for laptops let you work aboard and some seats are in wi-fi hot spots.

o Standard 2nd-class fares cost about Sfr40 per 100km; 1st-class fares average 75% more. Return fares are only cheaper than two singles for longer trips.

o Train schedules, revised every December, are available online and at train stations. For information, see www.sbb.ch or call **Rail Service** (📞0900 300 300; calls per min Sfr1.19).

o Larger train stations have 24-hour left-luggage lockers (per day Sfr3 to Sfr6), usually accessible from 6am to midnight.

o Seat reservations (Sfr5) are advisable for longer journeys, particularly in high season.

o European rail passes such as Eurail and Interrail passes are valid on Swiss national railways. However, you cannot use them on postal buses, city transport, cable cars or private train lines (eg the Zermatt route and the Jungfraubahn routes at the heart of the Bernese Oberland), which makes Swiss Travel Passes better for those exploring scenic Switzerland.

Fly-Rail Baggage Service

Travellers bound for Geneva or Zürich airports can send their luggage directly to any one of 50-odd Swiss train stations, without waiting for their bags at the airport. Upon departure, they can also check their luggage in at any of these train stations up to 24 hours before their flight and collect it upon arrival at their destination airport. The cost is Sfr22 per item of luggage; maximum weight per item is 32kg and bulky items such as bicycles and surfboards are a no go. Similar luggage forwarding is possible within Switzerland; see www.sbb.ch.

Scenic Journeys

Swiss trains, buses and boats are more than a means of getting from A to B. Stunning views invariably make the journey itself the destination. No matter how you travel, you'll never look at public transport in the same way again. Switzerland has it down to a fine art, with even bog-standard buses taking you up to remote mountain passes for eye-to-eye wildlife encounters.

The **Swiss Travel System** (www.swisstravelsystem.co.uk) is an interconnected web of trains, boats, cable cars and postal buses that puts

almost the entire country within easy car-free reach – and, naturally, with its famous precision you can set your watch by it.

Panorama Trains

Switzerland boasts the following routes among its classic sightseeing journeys; for each you're able to choose just one leg of the trip. Note that scheduled services often ply the same routes for standard fares, which are cheaper than those for the named trains. However, the first three named trains below offer the unique advantage of panoramic coaches with extra-large windows; reserve ahead.

Bernina Express (www.bernina express.ch; one way Chur–Tirano Sfr64; ⊘mid-May–early Dec) Travels 156km through the Engadine from Chur to Tirano in four hours. Between May and October, you can continue from Tirano to Lugano by bus.

Centovalli Railway (www.centovalli.ch; one way adult/child Sfr45/22.50) An under-appreciated gem of a line (two hours) that snakes along fantastic river gorges from Locarno to Domodossola, Italy.

Chocolate Train (www.mob.ch) Return trip in a belle époque Pullman car from Montreux to the chocolate factory at Broc.

Glacier Express (www.glacier express.ch; one way adult/child Sfr153/76.50; ⊘mid-May–late Oct & mid-Dec–early May) Legendary train journey between Zermatt and St Moritz. The Brig–Zermatt Alpine leg makes for pretty powerful view-

ing, as does the area between Disentis/Mustér and Brig.

Golden Pass Route (www.goldenpass.ch) Travels between Lucerne and Montreux. The journey is in three legs, and you must change trains twice. Regular trains, without panoramic windows, work the whole route hourly.

Mont Blanc/St Bernard Expresses (www.tmrsa.ch) From Martigny to Chamonix, France, or over the St Bernard Pass.

Voralpen Express (www.voralpen-express.ch) Lake Constance to Lake Lucerne, through St Gallen, Rapperswil and Romanshorn.

Postal Buses

Beginning in St Moritz, the four-hour **Palm Express** (www.palmexpress.ch) takes travellers from the glacier-capped peaks of the Engadine via the Maloja Pass, through the Val Bregaglia valley to Chiavenna, Italy, then further along Lakes Como and Lugano.

Another half a dozen scenic Alpine routes can be found at **PostBus** (www.postauto.ch).

Rail & Boat: The Gotthard Panorama Express

The newly launched **Gotthard Panorama Express** (www.sbb.ch; ⊘Sat & Sun mid-Apr–May, daily Jun-Oct) starts with a wonderful 2½-hour cruise across Lake Lucerne to Flüelen, from where a train winds its way through ravines and past mountains to Bellinzona or Lugano.

Language

Switzerland has three official federal languages: French, German and Italian. A fourth language, Romansch (semi-official since 1996), is spoken by less than 1% of the population, mainly in the canton of Graubünden.

Read our pronunciation guides as if they were English, and you'll be understood just fine. The stressed syllables are in italics.

To enhance your trip with a phrasebook, visit **lonelyplanet.com**. Lonely Planet iPhone phrasebooks are available through the Apple App store.

French

Hello.	Bonjour.	bon·zhoor
Goodbye.	Au revoir.	o·rer·vwa
Yes.	Oui.	wee
No.	Non.	non
Please.	S'il vous plaît.	seel voo play
Thank you.	Merci.	mair·see
Excuse me.	Excusez-moi.	ek·skew·zay·mwa
Sorry.	Pardon.	par·don
Help!	Au secours!	o skoor
Cheers!	Santé!	son·tay

Do you speak English?
Parlez-vous anglais? — par·lay·voo ong·glay
I don't understand.
Je ne comprends pas. — zher ner kom·pron pa
How much is this?
C'est combien? — say kom·byun
I'd like ... please.
Je voudrais ... — zher voo·dray ...
s'il vous plaît. — seel voo play
Where are (the toilets)?
Où sont (les toilettes)? — oo son (lay twa·let)
I'm lost.
Je suis perdu(e). (m/f) — zhe swee·pair·dew

German

Hello.	Guten Tag.	goo·ten taak
Goodbye.	Auf Wiedersehen.	owf vee·der·zey·en
Yes.	Ja.	yaa
No.	Nein.	nain
Please.	Bitte.	bi·te
Thank you.	Danke.	dang·ke
Excuse me.	Entschuldigung.	ent·shul·di·gung
Sorry.	Entschuldigung.	ent·shul·di·gung
Help!	Hilfe!	hil·fe
Cheers!	Prost!	prawst

Do you speak English?
Sprechen Sie Englisch? — shpre·khen zee eng·lish
I don't understand.
Ich verstehe nicht. — ikh fer·shtey·e nikht
How much is this?
Was kostet das? — vas kos·tet das
I'd like ... please.
Ich hätte gern ... bitte. — ikh he·te gern ... bi·te
Where are (the toilets)?
Wo sind — vaw zind
(die Toilette)? — (dee to·a·le·te)
I'm lost.
Ich habe mich verirrt. — ikh haa·be mikh fer·irt

Italian

Hello.	Buongiorno.	bwon·jor·no
Goodbye.	Arrivederci.	a·ree·ve·der·chee
Yes.	Sì.	see
No.	No.	no
Please.	Per favore.	per fa·vo·re
Thank you.	Grazie.	gra·tsye
Excuse me.	Mi scusi.	mee skoo·zee
Sorry.	Mi dispiace.	mee dees·pya·che
Help!	Aiuto!	a·yoo·to
Cheers!	Salute!	sa·loo·te

Do you speak English?
Parla inglese? — par·la een·gle·ze
I don't understand.
Non capisco. — non ka·pee·sko
How much is this?
Quanto costa? — kwan·to ko·sta
I'd like ... please.
Vorrei ... per favore. — vo·ray ... per fa·vo·re
Where are (the toilets)?
Dove sono — do·ve so·no
(i gabinetti)? — (ee ga·bee·ne·ti)
I'm lost.
Mi sono perso/a. (m/f) — mee so·no per·so/a

Behind the Scenes

Acknowledgements

Climate map data adapted from Peel MC, Finlayson BL & McMahon TA (2007) 'Updated World Map of the Köppen-Geiger Climate Classification', *Hydrology and Earth System Sciences*, 11, 1633–44.

This Book

This first edition of Lonely Planet's *Best of Switzerland* guidebook was curated by Gregor Clark and researched and written by Kerry Christiani, Craig McLachlan and Benedict Walker. This guidebook was produced by the following:

Destination Editor Daniel Fahey

Product Editors Hannah Cartmel, Grace Dobell

Senior Cartographer Mark Griffiths

Book Designer Clara Monitto

Assisting Editors Sarah Bailey, Andrew Bain, Janice Bird, Lucy Cowie, Victoria Harrison, Jodie Martire, Kate Mathews, Kristin Odijk

Assisting Cartographer Valentina Kremenchutskaya

Assisting Book Designer Fergal Condon

Cover Researcher Naomi Parker

Thanks to Imogen Bannister, Shona Gray, Andi Jones, Jenna Myers, Jessica Rose, Kathryn Rowan, Lyahna Spencer

Send Us Your Feedback

We love to hear from travellers – your comments keep us on our toes and help make our books better. Our well-travelled team reads every word on what you loved or loathed about this book. Although we cannot reply individually to postal submissions, we always guarantee that your feedback goes straight to the appropriate authors, in time for the next edition. Each person who sends us information is thanked in the next edition, the most useful submissions are rewarded with a selection of digital PDF chapters.

Visit lonelyplanet.com/contact to submit your updates and suggestions or to ask for help. Our award-winning website also features inspirational travel stories, news and discussions.

A – Z